Classic Teddy Bear
Heirlooms To Make & Dress

by Estelle Ansley Worrell

Photography by Norman Worrell and Bill Lafevor

**24 Teddy Bear Patterns
With Numerous Costumes**

Front Cover: *Basic Bear looks every inch the gourmet chef in his apron and cap as he cooks on his 1934 stove — which still cooks! Huggy stops in for a taste wearing his little jog shorts and shirt.*

Front Cover Inset: *The Tiny Teddy Family enjoys a picnic in the country. Shown, from left, in the back row are Tiny Papa, Tiny Mama and Uncle Theodore; in front are Bubba, Baby and Sissy.*

Back Cover: *Two Old Timeys a sittin' and a rockin' are dressed in their Sunday best. Rosie, left, has on a pastel sweater and long stocking cap made from a pair of knee socks. Sweetie Pie wears a little tweed coat made from Cubby's Rough Rider jacket pattern and an off-white corduroy hat made from Ginger's pattern. Their chairs were hand-crafted in Tennessee; a 1935 telephone sits between them.*

Hobby House Press

Published by Cumberland, Maryland 21502

Dedicated to

Viola Henson Ansley

The kindest, most loving, forgiving and generous mother of them all.

ACKNOWLEDGEMENTS

It is impossible to create so many Teddy Bears, do so many illustrations and set up for so many photographs without needing other people. It is always such a wonderful feeling to complete another book and then look back and realize how many friends offered help and encouragement in some way.

I offer my thanks to my sister-in-law, Merrill Everett Ansley, for sharing her own childhood toys with me and those of her mother, Elizabeth Merrill Everett; and to Martha Jean Johnson and Roberta Lochte for sharing their old toys, too. I am grateful, as well, to son, Sterling; daughter, Anne; and Warren Kirbo who made things especially for me such as miniature bicycles, harnesses and furniture.

I would like to give a thank you also to Judy Smith, Allison Smith, Frances Bayer and my daughters, Clare, Elizabeth and Anne for loaning me Teddy Bears I had previously made for them as well as their own interpretations of my patterns. A special thanks to Judy Martin who rounded up the bears for the "Bunch-o-bears" photograph.

To my pattern testers, daughters Anne Rogers and Elizabeth Worrell, I couldn't have done it without you!

To old friend Bill Colsher of the Nashville Public Library, my gratitude for always being ready to assist me. My gratitude also to Kathy Griswold and Pam Francis for all the typing they did for me.

To author-historian Patricia N. Schoonmaker, a thank you for contributions to the accumulated knowledge of the history of Teddy Bears and their clothes. To Jeanne Miller for designing my exhibit of 65 Teddy Bears at Cheekwood Fine Arts Center and selecting "Basic" to be the angel to reign over all from his perch atop the Teddy Bear Tree. To Betty Caldwell and Gloria Ballard of the *Tennessean* and Leila Phillips of the *Nashville Banner* newspapers and Gary R. Ruddell and Virginia Ann Heyerdahl of Hobby House Press, Inc., thanks for telling the world about the Worrell Teddy Bears.

To my husband, Norman, the most special thanks of all for the countless things he has done to help and encourage me. I love you all!

Estelle Ansley Worrell

TABLE OF CONTENTS

Ginger, a bear made from patterns on pages 61-64, can become either a female hostess or a sportsman. See suggestions for these and other outfits on pages 65 and 66.

INTRODUCTION

Probably no other toy in history ever made as tremendous an imprint upon the world as the Teddy Bear. There are few facets of our lives that have not been touched by him. Everything from stationery to china and from silverware to throw pillows have been decorated with images of these lovable creatures. The best music publishing houses have published records and sheet music with titles such as "The Teddy Bear's Picnic" and "Teddy Bear Blues." Songs about Teddy have been, through the years, sung by big name stars such as Anna Held in 1907, when she sang, "Will you Be My Teddy Bear?" and more recently by Elvis Presley in the 1960s when he sang, "I Wish I Were a Teddy Bear."

Teddy has even had a long involvement with newspapers and politics. It was, in fact, a newspaper cartoonist who was credited with the idea of *Teddy's bear* and it was newspapers that kept the idea alive. And what newspaper even today can resist a good Teddy Bear story?

More than one politician has used the Teddy Bear symbol in his election campaign and Teddy has even been used as table decorations for White House dinners.

It can truly be said that everybody loves a Teddy Bear — in fact, he has come to symbolize love and security for us. Child psychologists today are actually recommending that children be allowed to take their Teddies to bed with them.

The Teddy Bear was "born" in 1902 and took the entire nation by storm in 1906. Teddy has remained a favorite toy throughout the century and shows no signs of losing favor. Instead, interest is continuing to grow. Today almost any store selling stuffed animals has as much display space for Teddy Bears as for all other soft toys combined.

Not only does virtually every child in America (and England) have a Teddy, but it is estimated that adult owners number in the millions, too. Few young women leave home and head for college or career without at least one Teddy Bear to accompany them. Year after year new variations of a theme are introduced, adding to their lore and traditions. Of all the millions of people who have loved Teddies for the past 83 years, a surprising number still have them — and a surprising number are male.

More than once during the life of this soft toy he has been responsible for a virtual stampede. In California in 1976, the Crocker National Bank offered a "Sunny the Bear" with each new checking account of $100. or more. Well, not only new customers came in to open accounts but customers already having accounts began to withdraw money and open new accounts! Some even opened new accounts for each child in the family. People became so irate when the bank began to run out of bears that bank officials ordered a strict accounting of bears. The tellers had to "balance their bears as well as their drawers." In all, 100,000 Sunnies went to bank customers and still weeks later a lot of people were upset that they did not get one before they ran out. The whole bear affair has been called the "Great Teddy Bear Caper." The moral of the story: Do not underestimate the appeal of a Teddy Bear!

As antique bears become scarcer, prices keep going higher. Fine quality bears manufactured today are expensive. But, the very term "manufactured" is misleading because Teddy Bears have always been basically handmade — that is why each one is unique and why they are expensive.

The designs presented in this book will enable you to make your own beautiful Teddy Bears of as fine a quality as you desire. The wide variety of designs makes it possible for you to match the bears to your own sewing skills and taste. The variety also enables any sewer to fashion a Teddy Bear that is properly suited to the age and needs of a particular child.

Included in the chapters are clothing patterns for both modern and "old fashioned" designs because clothing has always been an important part of a Teddy Bear's personality. You can create an entire wardrobe for your favorite bear.

Chapter 1
ATTITUDES AND HISTORY

The Teddy Bear recently reached an acceptance undreamed of a few decades ago when pro football star, John Matuszak of the Los Angeles Raiders, posed with one for a center-fold photograph in *Playgirl* magazine. And that is not all — Greg Louganis, 1988 Olympic diving superstar admits that he "Listens to music and talks to his Teddy Bear, 'Gar,' between dives."

In the long-running television show, M*A*S*H, one of the most beloved fictional characters was a young corporal who had brought his childhood Teddy Bear off to war with him.

Up until the Teddy Bear came along at the beginning of this century, a little boy dared not cuddle a doll for fear of being called a "sissy" and causing concern for his parents. At that time toys were strictly labeled as for boys or girls. The Teddy Bear broke the ice and opened the way for a whole new set of attitudes. Nursery schools and kindergartens now *encourage* little boys to cuddle dolls and Teddy Bears as part of their learning to express paternal instincts — for, after all — most will become fathers someday.

One of the most intriguing facts concerning little boys and Teddy Bears appeared in an article in *Playthings* magazine way back in 1906. The story, relating the then short history of Teddy Bears, stated that the first bear sold was at a summer resort on the Jersey shore. It further stated that it was sold to a *little boy* and soon every other *little boy* on the boardwalk had to have one, too! It went on to explain that little sisters soon wanted bears, too, and it was a little sister who first dressed her bear in doll clothes, making an instantaneous hit!

Young boys of school age today are not self-conscious about enjoying bears. They have no hesitation at picking up a Teddy Bear and cuddling it, proclaiming that they have several of their own at home, or that they would like to have a new one. It is no secret among college students, too, that a lot of guys today have a Teddy Bear or two sitting in their dorm rooms.

Our attitudes toward children have changed drastically since the turn of the century and as a result, young peoples' attitudes towards themselves have changed. Boys have been freed from the old stereotypes as much as girls and who knows how big a part the winsome Teddy Bear and his male namesake played in those changes?

The Teddy Bear was an idea whose time had come. It is almost as if the world had been waiting for him. By mid 19th century, the old puritan attitudes toward play as being a waste of time and even sinful had begun to slowly change, particularly among the well-to-do.

Christmas, as we know it, with a decorated tree, gifts and children's toys was begun in the middle of the 19th century. By the beginning of the 20th century, not only was play no longer considered sinful, but it actually was realized to be educational, as well. Eventually children's books, games and educational toys were used to both enlighten and amuse a child. In just half a century play went from being a sin, to being wholesome fun and, finally, to being encouraged as educational.

Grown-ups were openly having fun at the beginning of the century, too. The brownie camera was invented and whole families or groups of adults, in their new electric automobiles, drove out in the country or to local parks and recorded themselves for posterity — having fun! And what a change those snapshots were from the old grim portraits of earlier days. Yes, the times were right for a nation to have fun, for a fun-loving President and a lovable, totally engaging toy — so along came the Teddy Bear.

The Teddy Bear's appeal is universal. Not only is he loved by both boys and girls, but by women and even men as well. Like the circus, which reached a peak in popularity at the same time he did, Teddy appeals to "children of all ages."

But where did the Teddy Bear come from and who conceived the idea of this beloved toy? English actor, Teddy Bear author and designer, Peter Bull, told of his shock and dismay at discovering that the Teddy Bear was not an English invention! The Germans claim to have originated the Teddy Bear as do we Americans.

There are several versions of the origin of the world's favorite toy; the following seems to be the most generally accepted: When President Teddy Roosevelt, (a popular former Colonel of a dismounted cavalry regiment) went to Mississippi on November 10, 1902, to settle a boundary dispute between Mississippi and Louisiana, he went hunting during his stay. He did not shoot a bear while hunting so later a bear cub was dragged to outside his tent by two of his staff (or two of the newsmen accompanying him). Hearing shouts of "Bear! Bear!," he ran out with his gun, only to see a poor frightened little cub tied with a rope. Roosevelt turned away and said, "I draw the line. If I shot that little fellow, I couldn't look my own boys in the face again." A cartoonist for the *Washington Post*, Clifford Berryman, was along on the trip and sketched the famous cartoon showing Roosevelt refusing to shoot the little bear. (He did several more Teddy Roosevelt-and-the-bear cartoons during the next few years.) The rest, they say, is history.

After the famous cartoon appeared, a Mr. Morris Michtom had his wife make up some sample toy bears which he marketed under the name of The Ideal Novelty &

Toy Co. Later the name was shortened to Ideal Toy Corporation. About this same time Teddy Bears began pouring into America from the Steiff Company of Germany and the great Teddy Bear craze was in full swing. The demand for Teddy Bears was so great that by 1906 other toy firms began making bears, some even putting aside all other manufacture in order to fill the orders.

Teddy Roosevelt served as President of the United States from 1901 to 1909. The Teddy Bear craze had its beginnings in 1902 and peaked in 1908, with millions being sold. The President Teddy and the toy Teddy are inseparable in history.

It is a fact, according to the editors of *Time-Life Books*, that Teddy Roosevelt's six children's menagerie kept at the White House included several dogs, rabbits, flying squirrels, a badger — *and a small black bear!* Yes, Virginia, there really was a bear in the White House with Teddy Roosevelt. Also, a story in *National Magazine* in March 1907 states that President Roosevelt purchased not one, but *two orphaned bear cubs* from a man in New York who was exhibiting them. Later, when they grew too large for pets, Roosevelt gave them to a zoo in New York where they became a favorite attraction and were referred to as "Teddy's Bears" until the end of their days.

The President was such an authority on North American animal life that one time the Smithsonian Institution asked him to help them identify a mystifying specimen of mammal in their collection. He also managed to save 148 million acres of forest land to set aside our first national parks. How many bears, one wonders, have since then enjoyed a safe refuge in which to live and grow old in our national parks! Teddy Roosevelt was, indeed, a friend of the bear.

Why A Bear?

Back in Roosevelt's day a lot of people thought the Teddy Bear was just a fad but now, eight decades later, Teddy is still alive and well and living in millions of hearts. What are the reasons for this incredible popularity down through the generations?

The Teddy Bear is, first of all, associated with a tremendously popular namesake, who symbolized patriotism and fair play. The Teddy Bear was the first toy made of fur cloth and the first soft toy animal to have movable joints. The real bear is an animal native to the United States — but can these reasons really account for such continued popularity? There has to be something else, perhaps something deeper in us, that the Teddy Bear touches. There has to be

something about him that enables him to stand on his own all these years. The answer becomes clearer when we ask ourselves a simple question, "Why a toy bear?" Why not the favorite of all pets, the dog? Or, perhaps a cat? If one observes real bears with this question in mind, the answer becomes apparent. When a bear stands on his hind legs, he "looks so human." But *why* is he more human-like than the other creatures of the forest or household?

Well, a bear's limbs are so different from other creatures' limbs that you soon realize how unique he is. Dogs, cats, tigers, lions, pigs and horses all have hind legs which are quite crooked. Not only that, but their lower legs are skinny in proportion to their upper leg or thigh. The bear is chubby and cuddly right down to his paws. And, his front legs are held down like arms when he stands upright, not stiffly out or up like those of other animals. One more thing makes a bear unique in the animal world — no other animal stands as straight, as upright as he does. Add to that the fact that when he walks upright, he looks like a fat, human toddler in slow motion.

So, it is the bear's proportions and the human-like way he stands and walks. It also is those big feet and his face, his friendly face.

Once, circus tradition says, a famous animal trainer was asked which of all the animals in the circus was the most dangerous. Surprisingly he answered, "The bear!" The reason was, he explained, that you can tell by a cat's or other animal's face and body language when it is about to attack. The bear, not so; he always looks so lovable and pleasant that you can never be sure of what mood he is in. *You are swayed by the bear's looks to trust him too much.*

If adult bears are this lovable, then it stands to reason that a *baby bear* — the cub — is even more lovable. And indeed he is.

The wonderful, early Steiff Teddy Bears were designed in Germany by Margarete Steiff's nephew, Richard, who spent many hours sketching and studying the playful bear cubs at Stuttgart's zoo. He used the cub's proportions of a shorter snout, rounder eyes, rounder and fatter ears and a larger head in proportion to the body than the adult bear.

Yes, the Teddy Bear "stands on his own two feet" and is based on one of the most appealing of all animals, the bear cub. When he took his name from one of the most popular American heroes of all times, he became a combination of the symbols of something good in both the animal and human worlds — an unbeatable combination, to say the least.

Chapter 2
CONSTRUCTING YOUR TEDDY BEAR

When discussing the merits of handmade bears in relation to manufactured ones, it is well to remember that there really is no great difference. Cutting out cloth has been, in recent years, sometimes done with a machine similar to a band saw and stuffing is done now by a blowing machine, but even so, there still is really no machine that can make a Teddy Bear. Seams have to be sewn on a sewing machine by a real, live person; stuffing has to be put into each individual limb, body or head, and a joining mechanism of some type must be put into place by hand. There is machinery to help speed up the work but it is still basically done by human hands. Factories in many parts of the world still farm out piecework to be done by employees at home. Faces on the finest bears are still hand-embroidered and hand-trimmed.

Remember that when you sew your own bear from good quality materials and keep it accurate and neat, you are making a toy comparable to the best commercially-made product that would cost you many times as much to buy. Plus that, you will experience the satisfaction and joy of creating something — of having a small creature "come alive" in your very hands.

An author-designer can create the designs and patterns for you and give you directions but each reader selects his/her own materials and puts them together with his/her own personal touch, with the result that each bear is different from all others. Not only will each bear be unique, but for the cost of this book and a few dollars worth of materials, you can make yourself hundreds of dollars worth of fine quality Teddy Bears.

Fur Cloth

There is such a variety of fur cloth pile length, pile density and color, there are a few facts a beginning Teddy Bear maker needs to know. Although there are many weights and qualities of pile fabrics, there will not necessarily be much choice in any one particular store. Most stores will have only one or two fur fabrics suitable for Teddy Bears but different stores usually have different cloth to choose from.

The length of the pile or fur should be kept in proportion to your bear, so you might want to measure it on any you are considering. For some reason many fur fabric's pile lengths are really longer than they appear to be. Many beginners have a tendency to want to use longer fur than is really appropriate for the bear size they want. For your first attempt you might use no more than 1/2in (1.3cm) pile for large bears, 1/4in (0.65cm) for medium sizes and 1/8in (0.31cm) length pile or fleece for those under 12in (30.5cm) in height. After that, experiment with longer furs if you want fatter bears.

Some fur fabrics are quite dense with many fibers standing up like on a carpet while others have more thinly spaced pile that leans down somewhat. The thinner pile is easier to work with, especially for your first bear.

It is important to purchase a fur cloth with a *soft backing*. Occasionally you will find a beautiful fur cloth with a backside stiffened with a plastic-like coating, making it a bit hard to sew. *If the back is soft and pliable, even a very thick fur will be easy to sew.* Recently, there was a fabric available in two shades of beige and several pastel colors with a nice soft

Illustration 1. *Three Classic Cubby bears, all made from the same pattern, appear to be different sizes because they were constructed from three different fabrics. On the left, a fat Cubby was made of thick fur cloth with 1/2in (1.3cm) pile, and the center Cubby, with 1/4in (0.65cm) pile. On the right he is made of a thick velour with 1/8in (0.31cm) pile.*

fur that was absolutely terrible to sew! It had a gummy coating on the backside that got your needle and thread all sticky during sewing. The main rule to follow is: Check the fur fabric on *both sides*, feeling it, bending it, even crumpling it in your hand to make sure it is supple enough to be handled easily during sewing.

For your first bear it will be advisable to use a tan, white, beige, light brown or pastel color cloth because *dark fur* is difficult to see properly during sewing. If you have ever sewn black cloth of any kind, you know that it requires plenty of light and extra concentration and effort.

All pile fabrics, as well as real fur, have a nap because the pile tends to lean slightly to one side. You can find the direction by rubbing your hand across the cloth in several directions. When you rub *with* the pile, it will feel smooth; when you rub against it, you will rough it up.

When laying out your patterns, place them on the cloth so that the fur goes back *away from the nose*, down on the torso pieces and down on the legs. It should go down or sideways on the arms and up or sideways on the ears.

The finest quality Teddy Bears usually are made with all fur going *down* with *the face fur going back*, although you will find both modern and antique bears with fur "growing" in all directions. Some even have the two front torso pieces going in different directions! If you run short of material and find it necessary to lay your patterns in all directions, try to at least make the head fur go towards the back and the two front torso pieces go in the same direction.

Paw Pad Fabric

Although felt has been recommended by authors and toy makers for many years for bear paws — the truth is that it wears out much too soon. Some felts available today will only hold up for a few months before wearing out and even the best quality wool felt breaks down after a disappointingly short time.

The best and most beautiful paw and foot pads are made from the new suede-like fabrics, cotton velveteen, velour and wool flannel. You, of course, can splurge and even make them of suede or kid. Sometimes gloves can be found at rummage sales but be sure the leather is not so old that it is rotten. Soft vinyl, with a knit fabric backing, is a little difficult to work with but makes interesting and life-like paw pads. Satin gives a realistic look, too, but if you use it, first strengthen it with iron-on innerfacing.

If in an emergency you cannot find anything else suitable, you can always just make the pads out of your fur cloth scraps and use the *back side* or just use another color fur cloth.

A small piece of beautiful fabric will make paw pads for a number of Teddy Bears.

Your Bear's Face

Did you know that one of the most famous Teddy Bear factories in the world has workers who spend their days "shaving" the bear's noses with barber clippers? Real live bears have very short hair on their snouts or muzzles with the hairs gradually becoming longer toward the eyes, cheeks and forehead. Only expensive Teddy Bears, as a rule, have trimmed snouts because the trimming has to be done by hand.

There are two main ways to trim or "shave" your Teddy Bear before embroidering his features. First, you can cut the fur pile short on the tip of the nose and then graduate the length toward the sides and top of the head. This takes a bit more skill than the second method.

Illustration 2. *Two Cubby bears show their clipped snouts, cut so that a definite line is formed at its base.*

Illustration 3. *A Basic Bear with his snout unclipped for a more furry look. Paula Smartt Collection.*

The other way is to clip the fur on the snout, ending the cutting in a definite line around its base where the head begins to round out as in *Illustration 2*. Either way is charming but the second method gives a bit more modern appearance.

(If you use a pattern without separate paw pads on the hands such as Buddy and Huggy, paw pads can be formed by simply shaving or clipping off the fur on the inside or palm of the paw.)

The Eyes

A Teddy Bear can look you straight in the eyes sometimes and absolutely pull at your heart strings, just as surely as if he were alive. Sometimes when a bear or bears are nearby, you can suddenly become aware that one of them is "staring at me." It is absolutely unbelievable how two mere buttons can take on such depth of character — but they do, somehow!

Traditionally, Teddy Bear eyes have been made of black shoe buttons. Originally, these were half spheres on a metal wire shank. Today there are a variety of buttons available which are quite similar to the old shoe buttons. Many are one-piece with the shank being a molded or carved part of the button. Some buttons are almost complete spheres while others come in varying degrees of roundness. One rule to follow when selecting eye buttons is: the roundest eyes should go with the deepest fur cloth pile. If your fur cloth is short, a flatter button will look best. As long as your buttons have a slight roundness to them, they will look right on your bear.

Shiney black buttons are usually the most expressive eyes but dark blue or brown ones will work, too. You can find faceted buttons which will cause the eyes to twinkle when the bear is moved and, occasionally, buttons with a ring or dot in the center, like eyes, can be found.

There are a number of animal eyes that you sew on, snap on or put on with various clips. Be sure to purchase eyes that will not come apart or fall out if you are making your bear for a young child. Remember though, for very young children there is *only one really safe eye* and that is the embroidered one.

Eyes can be made from brown or beige buttons with a painted black pupil. Use airplane dope or India ink for the pupil; then coat the whole thing with clear dope or nail polish. Both Sitting Bear in *Color Illustration 14* and Ginger in *Illustration 55* (left) have painted button eyes.

For embroidering eyes, use a satin stitch in several different directions, over and over, making the eyes round out like buttons. You can go one step more and embroider a speck of white to resemble the reflection on a shiney button. Autograph Bear in *Color Illustration 14* has brown eyes with a black pupil embroidered on top.

Felt, cut out in various eye shapes, can become modern eyes. Felt can also be used in combination with button eyes in a number of different designs.

Finally, you can experiment with cutting away the fur pile in different shapes around the eyes to create an individual look, or add other fur cloth of a different shade as with a panda's or raccoon's eyes. Experiment first on a scrap of cloth.

When placing the eyes, pin them on with large-headed silk pins until you have done the nose and mouth. The final touch to the bear's expression comes from shifting the level of the eyes or the distance between them till you and your bear agree on where they should go. You will discover some funny expressions, some unhappy or cock-eyed ones and you are sure to find one that seems to look up at you and say,

"Hi there; Its me!" Its spooky, sometimes, how a personality just suddenly emerges and your bear becomes more than mere cloth and stuffing — he is suddenly "born."

When ready to sew on the eyes, just pull one of the pins out part of the way and take a stitch with your needle and thread where the pin goes into the head. Remove the pin and finish sewing. Use four strands of thread and sew it on firmly. Do the same with the other eye. One interesting thing about the eyes: they always look even better when sewn on than when pinned on because they are nestled snugly down in the fur. You can even push on them a bit after sewing to make them take on an even more natural look.

Large eyes give a bear a wide-eyed innocent look, like a baby bear. Smaller eyes give a more adult and serious look, just as lovable, only more serious. As a general rule, large eyes have a more modern look to them, too, than small eyes. There are no real rules, however, covering eyes. It is just a matter of what appeals to you personally. You might cut out varying sizes of circles from any black fabric scraps and pin them on your bear to determine what size buttons you like. File the circles away to try on future bears.

The Nose

Brown crewel yarn makes beautiful noses and mouths on bears. It is small but strong and works better than knitting yarn. Cotton embroidery floss can be used also.

Use a satin stitch horizontally, beginning with the middle stitch and working toward the top, then the bottom. Some people prefer to embroider the nose with vertical stitches. For a rounded nose you can embroider it with a padded satin stitch going first horizontally, then vertically, then horizontally again. This nose gives your bear a nice profile.

One of the most fun-to-do noses is the felt one. First, cut several different sizes of ovals, circles and even rounded triangles in different shades of brown felt and pin them on, along with pinned-on eyes, in different positions and combinations. You will see how the bear's personality changes as you switch from a circle to an oval or a light brown to a dark one, for instance. Dark or polar bears need black noses and mouths.

When you have the nose you want, use a matching sewing thread or embroidery floss and attach the nose with a buttonhole stitch going all the way around it. (Keep all the felt noses you made to try on other bears.)

You can, of course, use a black button for a nose and there are some commercially manufactured plastic snouts available in many large discount stores, either at the needlework or craft counters.

The Mouth

The mouth, of course, will determine your bear's disposition more than any other feature. It can make him happy, pensive, cross or sad, depending on its width and angle.

Too, many bear makers today are careless with the mouth or have a formula by which they make all mouths the same but a Teddy Bear should have rights, too! He should be able to reflect his owner's personality in his own face and he should have the right to "find himself" — and most of all he should have the right to be *happy* if he wants to be!

Real live bears in the forest (or zoo) have a tiny upward curve at the corners of the mouth — yes, they really do —that is partly what makes them so lovable looking.

The most fun way to embroider a mouth is to make two large, but slightly loose horizontal stitches with a large needle and crewel yarn. On the second one go in at the corner of the mouth and bring the point of the needle out at the bottom of the nose in the center. Then take your needle and go down to the mouth, *under the yarn only* (not into the cloth), then back up toward the nose. You can pull the yarn firmly so that it pulls the mouth up at the center, making the corners point down. By pulling or loosening it you can vary the bear's look. Try pushing the mouth way down so that your bear appears to smile or laugh, then up into a straight line so that he looks thoughtful, then up more so he looks sad or even angry. When you find your look, push the needle in where it earlier had come out at the edge of the nose. If you have a yarn nose, just make a couple more stitches over the others to anchor the thread. If you have a felt nose, bring the needle out behind an eye or on the cheek or neck. Tie a tiny knot, clip it close and, using the blunt end of your needle, push the knot into the cloth where the yarn came out.

With the addition of tiny couching stitches across the yarn you can make a mouth curve in any expression you desire. First of all, make the mouth stitches a bit loose or relaxed as described earlier; then try some *curved* positions by holding it in shape with straight pins. When your bear's personality emerges, you are ready to anchor the mouth in place. Couching means simply that you use a perfectly matching thread and go over the yarn in several places where you want it to stay. The couching thread should exit directly *under* the mouth yarns, go over them and then enter underneath them near where it exited. These stitches should be as inconspicuous as possible.

Another way to make curved or smiling mouths or upturned corners is to just use a chain stitch. You can make it go anywhere you like. Take a little scrap of yarn first and pin it on at different angles and curves to find your bear's character; then embroider the mouth in its place.

Add a little pink tongue if you like as on the Hanimals in *Color Illustrations 20, 21* and *22*.

The Ears

As with all other features, the placement and curve of ears can also have a great deal to do with your bear's personality. There are several ways to make a bear's ears cup in a realistic and expressive way. The first, by use of a dart sewn in the front half of the ear, as on 18in (45.7cm) Classic Cinnamon. This automatically forces the back part of the ear to curve around to the front slightly, cupping it.

Another way is to stitch around the seam by hand and pull just slightly on the threads to make the whole ear cup as on Classic Cubby in *Illustration 58*, right. It may need to be tacked at the center to keep the front part of the ear back "inside."

The most important thing you can do to ears is clip the fur pile down low inside the front piece where it joins the head. This gives it marvelous depth and makes it look like it really grew there. All the bears have this done but Basic Bear's ears are an especially good example in *Illustrations 35 and 60*.

By the way, ears do not need to be stuffed when the bear is made of fur cloth. If you use a flannel or light weight cloth, they may need the *tiniest bit of stuffing* to keep them from being floppy.

The way you sew them on can give character to a bear's ears. They should be sewn in a slightly curved half-moon position. Several firm stitches made over the corners of the ear toward the face will help to give them a "grown" look.

A row of stitching through the outside of the ear about 1/2in (1.3cm) from the edge in a "quilting" fashion will hold the inside back and give the edge a nice roll as on Benjamin in *Illustration 59*.

On bears with ears cut as a part of the head, like Buddy and Hanimal, clipping is very important for depth.

When you sew across the ear base, as indicated on the pattern, take a couple of light stitches over each corner, pulling the ear ever so slightly toward the front. This will give them a "grown-in" look.

Remember that children (and adults, too) will pick a bear up by an ear from time to time so sew your Teddy Bear's ears on *securely*!

Chapter 3
TEDDY BEAR CLOTHES

The earliest known description of Teddy Bear clothes seems to be the one in an article in *Playthings* magazine in 1906 concerning the origin of a then very new toy bear. That first dressed Teddy Bear was described as wearing a "blue and white sweater with a skating cap to match." The article related that two stores were stocking Teddy Bear sweaters in pink and white or blue and white, Tam O'Shanters, skating caps, blue overalls with either "Teddy G" or "Teddy B" embroidered on the bib, little white shirts with turn-down collars and red cravats, and hunting outfits with toy guns. The "Teddy G" and "Teddy B" monograms stood for the two bears in Seymour Eaton's popular stories of the *Roosevelt Bears* just published the year before, in 1905. A whole series of *Roosevelt Bears* books were eventually published, beginning in 1906. In these books the rather realistic bears, upright like humans, were always dressed. They wore everything from frock coats and top hats to band uniforms to clown suits.

One set of beautiful paper dolls published about 1907, judging from the doll's clothing, includes three Teddy Bears. The largest of these bears wears a little blue and white

sweater and matching cap with a suspended tassel — the exact outfit in the description of that first Teddy Bear outfit. He can be seen in *Illustration 4*.

By 1906, several firms like Kahn and Mossbacher, manufacturers of doll clothing, advertised they had enlarged their firms due to the demand for Teddy Bear clothes! Ladies magazines like *Woman's Home Companion* and *The Delineator* published either advertisements for Teddy Bear clothes patterns or directions for making clothes. By 1908, the rage for the little clothes was in full force. Bears were not enough — it seems everyone wanted *dressed* bears! And today — things have not changed that much because dressed bears often outsell undressed ones.

Although always referred to as a "he" in the beginning, the Teddy Bear traditionally has not been considered to be of one particular gender. Each bear owner dresses his/her bear in clothes he/she likes, regardless of sex. People, and young children in particular, apparently have few qualms about dressing him in boy clothes one moment and girl clothes the next. A few bears look so masculine or feminine they take on the characteristics of one or the other — but only to one person — for another person may see that bear in a totally different light.

The patterns in this book are primarily for clothes associated with both genders such as sweaters, raincoats, coats, pajamas, sleepers, sailor middies, bathrobes, night-shirts, aprons, kilts, overalls, vests, jackets, clown suits and scarves and caps. Only the dresses, frilly nightgowns, Santa suit and Rough Rider suit are associated with only one sex or the other.

In spite of the fact that Germany has produced some of the most elegant toy bears ever made, Teddy is, and always will be, American as apple pie. He will always be associated with President Teddy Roosevelt, for whom he was named, with the first decade of the 20th century, and with several items of apparel that sprang into American fashion at the same time that he did.

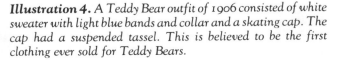

Illustration 4. A Teddy Bear outfit of 1906 consisted of white sweater with light blue bands and collar and a skating cap. The cap had a suspended tassel. This is believed to be the first clothing ever sold for Teddy Bears.

Illustration 5. A set of paper dolls of about 1907 included a Teddy Bear dressed in a pink and white sweater and cap like that of Illustration 4. The dressed bear is cuddled by a young girl.

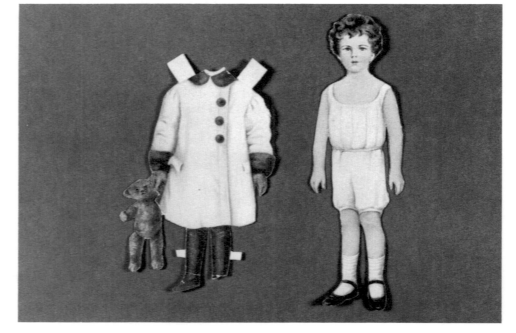

Illustration 6. The same paper doll set has a young boy holding an undressed Teddy Bear which seems to substantiate a 1906 article in Playthings magazine that gave credit for the first dressed Teddy Bears to little girls. The first Teddy Bears were said to have been for little boys but little girls soon demanded bears of their own and in no time began putting clothes on them.

Sweaters

Sweaters suit a bear's nature. They are soft like a bear, warm like a bear and snugly like a bear. They are informal but can be quite elegant. Their history began only a few years before Teddy was "born" and it all started with — the bicycle!

Ten million Americans were riding bicycles by the 1890s, because the new bikes had brakes, rubber tires, pedals and two wheels the same size. The turtleneck sweater was designed in England for cyclists but soon was taken up by football players, golfers, college and school boys and ice skaters. Teddy Roosevelt wore the turtleneck while playing ball and is also known to have worn it under his military jacket when the weather was cool. Advertisements continued

to call all pullover sweaters "bike sweaters" for a number of years, in spite of their popularity for all kinds of sports.

Sweaters were usually wine, black, navy or tan. One of the first "fancy" sweaters had white bands knit in at the wrists and hips. At the turn of the century they had open collars or V-necks as well as turtlenecks and some were striped with bold horizontal stripes. Cable stitching, ribbing and other novelty knits soon became popular, too. Even babies and children were being dressed in sweaters, usually either pink or blue with white bands as on the 1907 paper doll bear. The sweater had ushered in our modern age of comfortable knit clothing.

Sweaters reached a peak in popularity at the same time Teddy Bears did so the two became quickly identified with

12

each other. Teddy Bear sweaters were offered for sale by 1906. They were hand knit, sometimes with crochet edging as on the old Teddy sweaters in *Illustration 7*. By 1907, Teddy Bears wearing the football sweaters of Columbia, Yale or Princeton and carrying footballs could be purchased in large department stores.

Rough Rider Suits

During the Spanish American War in 1898 our army officers wore the new khaki uniforms for the very first time. "Khaki" comes from the Hindu word meaning dust. Bright blue had been the official U.S. Army color from the American Revolution to the Civil War when a darker blue took its place. Although the new khaki became regulation in 1898, there were not enough new uniforms for enlisted men so they had to swelter in the Cuban heat in the old blue ones.

Officers sported the new khaki jackets with a blue collar and epaulettes and two pleated breast pockets when the Rough Rider Regiment stormed Kettle Hill near San Juan in the battle that brought fame to Colonel Teddy Roosevelt.

The regiment was dismounted cavalry and not infantry but they wore light blue kerchiefs instead of yellow. (Cavalry traditionally has used yellow trim, infantry used light blue, and artillery, red trim.) The blue scarf or bandanna was sometimes worn tucked inside the collar, probably to absorb perspiration.

Under the khaki jackets they wore traditional army blue shirts as they had for decades. Of course, it was very hot in Cuba so enlisted men removed their jackets but not all the officers did.

Wide-brimmed, tan floppy hats were rolled or pressed into individual shapes for each man with the brims turned up in front, on one side or on both sides. Officers wore crossed sword insignia on the turned up brim.

Teddy Bear clothes advertisements of 1906 to 1908 offered little khaki Rough Rider jackets, sometimes with trousers and a toy gun! Besides Rough Rider suits, they were sometimes referred to as hunting suits or just labeled "The Hunter." Cloth hats with the crown in four sections usually came with these popular toy suits.

It would seem, judging from photographs of the real Teddy Roosevelt, that there was justification for Teddy Bear clothes manufacturers calling the same toy outfit a Rough Rider suit one time and a hunting suit the next.

There is a famous photographic portrait of Colonel Teddy Roosevelt with a bandanna tucked inside his khaki uniform collar and a most battered hat with crossed-sword insignia on the up-turned brim perched on his head shown in *Color Illustration 7*.

The famous Clifford Berryman cartoon of November 1902 depicts the President wearing a hunting outfit identical to his khaki Rough Rider uniform of a few years earlier.

On another hunting trip to Yosemite National Park in 1903, President Teddy had been photographed wearing a hunting outfit almost identical to his earlier military uniform. His jacket is open, showing a sweater underneath and he wears the ever-present bandanna around his neck (not tucked in this time), the ever-present eye glasses and the wide-brimmed hat.

Red trim (which stands for artillery) was suggested for a Teddy Bear Rough Rider suit to be made from a pattern advertised in a 1907 *Ladies' Home Journal*. It is not known whether the pattern designer was unaware of the color symbolism in the military or just thought red would be attractive.

There has been some confusion through the years about the Regimental colors since dismounted cavalry are really infantry instead of cavalry but watercolor paintings done on

Illustration 7. Two old Teddy Bear sweaters from the 1920s. Left, a white cotton crocheted sweater with red crochet edging; and right, a pale green and white knit sweater of silk and wool. It has crocheted edging at the neck and side openings. Underneath is an old toy pillow with tiny tucks and bobbin lace from about 1907.

13

the spot in Cuba by a young newspaper artist, Charles Johnson Post, are historic evidence that blue trim and blue kerchiefs were worn.

Frederic Remington was an artist at San Juan Hill, also, and one of his paintings shows Colonel Roosevelt with his khaki jacket removed, revealing a dark blue shirt. The most interesting thing, though, is that he has his blue kerchief tied around his hat with the ends streaming out behind as he gallops up the hill on the only horse present!

On later hunting trips, after Roosevelt was no longer President, he was photographed wearing the pith helmet while in Brazil and Africa.

With all this information on Colonel Teddy's actual clothes as well as toy Rough Rider and hunting suits in the 1900s, there is no end to the authentic interpretations you can create for your own "Colonel Teddy Bear."

Sailor Suits

It was in the Spanish American War in 1898 that our navy's middy was for the first time in history officially worn on the *outside* of the trousers. Middies were either navy blue or white with two rows of braid trim on the collar and cuffs. (Only a few dark middies were worn during the fight in Manilla Bay because of the heat.) A whistle hung on a cord around the neck and there was a special breast pocket provided for it. The new canvas sailor hat was somewhat like sailor hats of today except the stitched brim was more flared.

Little boys everywhere in the United States took up the sailor middy, worn on the outside, and made it almost a uniform for them, too. They wore stitched brim canvas hats and every middy had a whistle and whistle pocket, just like official ones.

As if the sailor suit was not already popular enough, it became even more so in 1907 when President Roosevelt dispatched 16 American battleships on a world cruise lasting 14 months. It was planned to show our potential enemies our Great White Fleet, but the effect at home was to further stimulate the already tremendous interest in nautical clothing for both boys and girls — and for adults, too. It was only natural that it would also cause an interest in sailor suits for, you guessed it, Teddy Bears. Virtually every bear clothing advertisement in 1907 and 1908 offered sailor suits with little whistles on a cord.

Teddy Roosevelt was Assistant Secretary of the Navy until he resigned to become a Lieutenant Colonel in the Rough Rider Regiment. He was later advanced to Colonel. Although he did not wear a navy uniform as Assistant Navy Secretary, he did dress his two youngest sons, Archie and Quentin, in the newly fashionable sailor middies, worn on the outside of the trousers. The boys appear in a number of photographs in their sailor suits in pictures on file in both the Library of Congress and the Theodore Roosevelt Birthplace.

Raincoats and Car Coats

Something new came along near the turn-of-the-century

that made raincoats tremendously popular for all ages — the commercialization of rubber. Raincoats had been around since mid-century when Mr. Macintosh had invented water-repellant coats but they were oiled or waxed and not entirely reliable. Rubber was so successful that soon almost every school child had a rubber or rubber-coated raincoat to wear as he walked to the new public school nearest him.

Early raincoats were blue, black or red, usually continuing the tradition of having a macintosh tartan lining. It is interesting that although cowboys wore yellow oilcloth "slickers," the thought of making children's raincoats in yellow had not occurred to manufacturers. It was not till later, after the automobile became a common danger, that the safety value of the yellow slicker would be perceived.

Rainhats, floppy tams and stocking caps were worn with the new raincoats as were black rubber boots, and galoshes with the name of the rubber company usually molded or printed on the sides.

If kids needed waterproof coats, then their new Teddy Bears would "need" them, too. Some of the old waterproof Teddy Bear coats were probably car coats according to one shown in *Playthings* in 1907. The checked coat had a belt and velvet collar and the bear modeling it was outfitted in leather goggles — very dapper!

Pajamas

Did you know it was the new pullman sleeping car that brought about a startling and novel sleeping fashion for men called the pajama? The name came from India, from the loose trousers of cotton or silk called a *paejamah*. Climbing into the train berth in a long nightshirt was a bit undignified so the sleeping suit or pajama solved the problem for fashionable gentlemen.

By the time the Teddy Bear came along after the turn-of-the-century, the pajama was being worn at home as well as for travel although the nightshirt would continue to be preferred by older and less fashion-conscious gentlemen. It should be pointed out here that the front cover of one of Seymour Eaton's famous books about Teddy G and Teddy B, *The Adventures of the Traveling Bears*, in 1905, has both bears wearing old style nightshirts while traveling in a pullman car.

Pajamas were one of the most popular outfits of the new Teddy Bear clothes being manufactured by several doll clothes companies by 1906. And, what could be more natural than pajamas for such a soft, cuddly sleeping mate?

Illustration 8 shows a pair of 55-year-old Teddy Bear pajamas which have been on the same bear all these years!

Women began sleeping in pajamas after 1910, although some people thought them shocking. They were usually of a peach-colored silk.

Overalls

"Brownie suits" or "apron overalls" were invented just before the turn-of-the-century for young boys. By the time the Teddy Bear came along, after 1903, they were being advertised not only for little girls but for very little boys,

Illustration 8. A much-loved 12in (30.5cm) Teddy Bear owned by Merrill Everett Ansley for 55 years. "Teddy" has worn these same pink and white striped cotton flannel pajamas and silk socks for all those years! He may be even older as Merrill is not sure that he was not her mother's bear before he became hers. The pajamas have little soutach braid frog fasteners with tiny pearl buttons on the jacket and a silk cord drawstring in the trousers.

too, because the new rubber-coated diaper covers meant that now toddlers could wear trousers for the first time in history. Before this time, little boys had always had to wear skirts until they were trained.

Either plain or frilly blouses with large collars were worn under overalls as in *Illustration 48* and soon the practical new sweaters were, too. Overalls became a classic item of play clothes for children, continuing in popularity today.

Almost every Teddy Bear clothes advertisement at mid-decade pictured Teddy Bears in overalls. Sometimes labeled "little farmer suits," they were one of the most popular garments for Teddy Bears as well as for children. Early Teddy overalls were of chambray or denim in plain blue or red, or they were of gray or blue striped cloth. They were sometimes one-piece from hem to the top of the bib, or trousers joined to a bib by a waistline seam.

Overalls are so versatile that blouses of all kinds, sweaters of all styles, modern T-shirts or no top at all can be worn under them. They can be made in a wide variety of fabrics to suit any bear's personality.

Sleepers

A direct result of the new rubber or rubber-coated diaper covers was the introduction of children's "night suits" or sleepers. Infants and toddlers had, for centuries, been wrapped in long flannel skirt-blankets in cold weather in an attempt to keep them warm and dry. The new waterproof diaper covers enabled them to wear trousers at night as well as day — and parents did not have to worry as much about their little ones kicking off the covers.

Advertisements offered Canton flannel sleeper suits constructed with drop seats, moccasin feet gathered around the ankles and even fold-down cuffs to cover small hands on cold nights. They were remarkably like modern sleepers in appearance, changing little during the decades — right up to today.

Although there is little evidence to show that the Teddy Bear was ever dressed in sleepers during the first decade of the 20th century, the Teddy Bear and the sleeper were none-the-less conceived at the same time in history. And they certainly have, in recent years, taken to each other as though they were made for each other. Not only is a Teddy Bear a most charming sight in his little sleepers, he also is absolutely the softest, most huggable and yummiest thing to hold you can imagine! Now that he is so acceptable to child psychologists that they actually *recommend* him as a bedtime toy, Teddy needs to be properly dressed when he retires.

Clown Suits

The extremely popular Barnum and Bailey Circus played their entire season of 1902 in France, receiving much publicity about it at home. In 1907, Ringling Brothers Shows purchased the Barnum and Bailey Circus to give us the "Greatest Show on Earth."

They promoted their clowns with slogans advertising, "100 clowns — count 'em — 100," or "an army of clowns." It was truly the great age of the circus and one can only speculate on how many Teddy Bears attended a circus or at least looked longingly with their owners at one of the 5000 to 8000 posters the circus put up in each town announcing its visit. Is it any wonder that virtually every Teddy Bear clothes advertisement for decades included a clown suit?

Polka dotted Teddy Bear clown suits like that in *Color Illustration 18*, were obviously the most popular, with half and half designs as in *Color Illustration 20*, the second most advertised from 1906 on up until World War II. Ladies' magazines offered clown suit patterns for ten to fifteen cents a piece from 1906 to the end of the decade. Red and white was definitely the preferred color scheme for Teddy clown suits with red and blue or pink and blue combinations also popular.

From 1907 up until World War II there was a clown-teddy available which was not actually a dressed bear. Fur cloth in bright red, pink and blue was used for a half-and-half body design. Buttons were sewn directly onto the bear's center front seam and a ruff was sewn to his neck. The only part that could be considered a costume was his little clown hat.

One of the reasons for this bear-costume combination was to promote the bright colored plush cloth which followed the earlier neutral colors. The bears must have been popular because toy companies produced them over a period of several decades.

Stocking Caps

Stocking caps suit a Teddy Bear because they are soft like he is and because they will fit his head snugly and stay in place so nicely while other caps and hats fall off. They are right for Teddy, also, because they were the fashion for children when he came along.

There was nothing new about the stocking cap; it had been around as long as knitted stockings. Originally it was simply a worn out wool stocking with the foot cut off and a knot tied in the end. Sometimes instead of a knot, a string was tied around it, forming a ruffled pouf at the end.

At the turn-of-the-century when the old-fashioned stocking cap became a fashionable knitted toque for children (and grown-ups, too), it was topped with a tassel or a pompon suspended from the end of a string. Through the years this long tasseled toque has become shorter and the tassel or pompon is attached directly to its end now but it has never gone out of style for children or for adult winter sports clothing.

Boots and Shoes

There was a fad for Teddy Bear boots in 1907. They were quite tall and could be purchased in black, red or tan with contrasting color turn-down tops.

Although there are not many pictures of Teddy Bears actually wearing them, they were shown in *Playthings* magazine in 1907. One political postcard of 1908 shows a Teddy Bear sitting in front of the White House dressed in boots, eyeglasses and Rough Rider hat with a "big stick" beside him.

It was on the popular Teddy Bear paper dolls where boots were commonly seen. Virtually every set of these paper dolls had at least one pair of boots with costumes such as pirate suits, Rough Rider outfits and police or soldier uniforms.

Teddy Bear paper dolls were sold as toys, given as premiums or published regularly in some large newspapers showing Teddy in every imaginable kind of outfit.

Color Illustration 1. *Classic Cinnamon sports a beautiful sweater with Teddy Bears across the body and sleeves made from a new adult-size sweater. Of a luscious light beige fur cloth, Cinnamon has suede cloth paws and black shoe-button eyes. Allison Smith Collection.*

Color Illustration 2. *A very feminine Cinnamon primps in her best party outfit beside her 1934 dresser. The polka-dot dress is cotton, the ruffled pinafore, eyelet batiste. Anne Rogers Collection.*

Color Illustration 3. *Elegant enough for such an elegant bear, Cinnamon's cotton flannel pajamas have pink bias tape frog closures. Cubby, on the 1959 four-poster bed, is snug and warm in yellow sleepers. Both the quilt and rug are handmade; the miniature engraving is antique.*

Color Illustration 4. *Ginger, of a very pale beige fur, has glass animal eyes and suede cloth paws. His sweater with heart designs and cap were fashioned from a pair of new knee socks. His toy cards are antique.*

TOP LEFT: Color Illustration 5. *April showers bring May flowers as Classic Ginger models a raincoat with Teddy Bear buttons, a sou'wester hat and little brown boots. He carries a satchel of crayons and a miniature notebook for school.*

TOP RIGHT: Color Illustration 6. *A very feminine version of Classic Cubby, Cuddles models her best party dress as she stands by an old toy swing of uncertain age. Her flower-bedecked felt hat has ribbon streamers in back. She wears brown suede slippers with white socks and a koala bear pin on her dress. She carries a toy folding fan. Becky, the feminine interpretation of the Benjamin pattern tops off her green dotted swiss skirt and blouse with a red checked sunbonnet. Trimmed with tatting, it has slits for her ears.*

BOTTOM: Color Illustration 7. *Colonel Cubby stands among books about his hero. The open book shows Colonel Teddy below, and the charge up Kettle Hill, above, by newspaper artist Charles Johnson Post.*

Color Illustration 8. *Becky, the feminine version of Benjamin's pattern, and Benjamin are ready for a long winter's hibernation in green silk bathrobe and cotton pajamas. Benjamin's pajamas have printed Teddy Bears between miniature sprigs of holly and fasten with red heart buttons. Benjamin, Frances Bayer Collection.*

Color Illustration 9. *Buddy, left, has on his favorite T-shirt and red trousers while next to him a feminine Buddy wears a simple print dress. Third from left, Huggy is charming in a green print dress nice enough for a birthday party. Basic Bear could be the life of any party in his red clown suit and red button nose. Their party table is set with antique toy china.*

Color Illustration 10. *Two Buddys, all ready for a winter's nap, look warm and cuddly in their sleepers. The red ones, left, are one-piece buttoned in front; the pink ones, center, fasten onto the shirt. Basic Bear wears his favorite Teddy Bear patterned nightshirt of soft knit. Both Buddy and Basic like stocking night caps with suspended pompons. Elizabeth Worrell Collection.*

LEFT: Color Illustration 11. Old Timey Rosie loves to wear Ginger's Teddy Bear printed cotton nightgown with pink heart buttons. Her mob cap ties with a pink satin ribbon drawstring. Her bed is outfitted with antique mattress and pillows, crochet-edged blanket and a handmade Teddy Bear quilt.

Color Illustration 12. Old Timey Rosie models a pale green Teddy Bear sweater played with for three generations in the Duncan Everett family! Her iron was a Christmas gift in 1933; her hat box is from the 1920s. Very special indeed!

Color Illustration 13. *A basket o'Bea Bears. A pink rattle Bea, left, has a rattle embedded in her torso; two furry Bean Bag Beas stand in the rear waiting for a game to begin and two washable Bath Beas of terry cloth wait in front for bath time. All are overtime bears ready for extra work.*

Color Illustration 14. *A fur Sitting Bear, right, likes to sit among the throw pillows while Autograph Bear, of a smooth cloth, wears his school colors and collects autographs from his friends. They, too, are Overtime Bears. Clare Worrell Collection.*

Color Illustration 15. *Sitting Bear can just wear clothes and play all the time and be a plain lovable polar bear when not working overtime. He loves his set of warm cap, muffler and mittens on wintry days.*

TOP: Color Illustration 16. *Ma Petite Famille of the jointed miniature bears is dressed for dinner on a Barbie-sized doll house dining room table and chairs. Petite Babette, left, chose a pink dress made from Tiny Sissy's robe pattern while Philippe chose his favorite red sweater. Bebé, in front, is sweet in a delicate pink jacket with satin ties. Petite Mère loves her pink and white sweater with rose pleated skirt; Père likes his brown checked suit and tiny pocket watch (a baby button).*

BOTTOM: Color Illustration 17. *"To Grandmother's house we go," sing a group of miniature bears from both the Tiny Teddy family and Ma Petite Famille. All are wearing vests, sweaters, scarves or hats to keep them warm. The sleigh and horse are second generation, the leather harness and rigging hand-crafted. Anne Rogers and Elizabeth Worrell Collections.*

LEFT: Color Illustration 18. A quartet of Barnum bears perform in their ruffs, caps and clown suits in front of an old circus poster. Barnum, at top right, wears miniature running shoes which came from two key rings. The two red neck ruffs were made from antique gold-edged ribbon.

Color Illustration 19. Daniel, the "wild bruin" who stands on all-fours, becomes a circus bear too when he dons his satin and iridescent neck ruff.

Color Illustration 20. *A hand-puppet toy-animal or Hanimal Bear can wear Barnum's clown suit. Hanimal can be both a puppet and a soft Teddy Bear.*

Color Illustration 21. *Baby Hanimal, a most innocent baby bear, just loves to be held and cuddled. His little blue knit sleepers make him the softest, most lovable bedtime companion ever. He has his own security blanket with circus designs and an antique doll pillow.*

Color Illustration 22. *Baby Hanimal is dressed for her christening in a long dress made with Cubby's dress pattern. She sleeps in her second-generation doll bassinet when she is not being a hand-puppet-animal.*

Chapter 4
CONSTRUCTING THE CLOTHES

A young mother of two recently wrote to tell me how much her family was enjoying the fashionably dressed Teddy Bear I had made for her. "You have no idea how much that bear changed my children's attitudes toward toy animals," she wrote. The letter went on to explain that soon after the 15in (38.1cm) Teddy entered their home, all the children's Teddy Bears began appearing dressed in doll or old baby clothes; then, eventually, all the stuffed dogs, cats, bunnies and whatever needed clothes, too. Before long there was not a "critter" in the house that did not wear clothes and she said, now even two years later, the children cannot imagine having a toy animal that does not wear clothes.

She was not unusual; she was just one of millions of Teddy Bear fans who have realized what fun dressing Teddy Bears can be. You can even make a political statement with a dressed bear such as a "Ronnie Bear" wearing his little Reaganhood suit or a "Ronnie Riding Bear" wearing jodphurs, sweater and riding boots. A "Jimmy Who Bear" can wear his green plaid shirt or perhaps his fireside cardigan. "Lyndon Bear Johnson" in a ten-gallon hat or "Dickie Bear" in a green polka-dot tie (like the one Nixon wore at one of his last White House parties) can be funny and political at the same time. Movie stars and famous sports heroes can be represented by bears, too.

Few gifts will thrill a person more than a bear dressed to represent him or her in a sports outfit, school sweater, company or club blazer or a work uniform. Such a personalized gift is sure to be treasured for years.

The following section on fabrics and accessories is intended merely to inspire you to browse the fabric and variety stores and keep an eye out for some of the charming and unexpected Teddy Bear items to be discovered.

Fabrics

Even years ago you could sometimes find cloth in the cotton flannel and batiste sections that had Teddy Bear designs. Now, with the explosion in interest in Teddy Bears, you can find Teddy Bear designs at the knit and cotton counters, as well. *Illustration 9* shows a charming Americana-type fabric (background) with seated bears wearing overalls. Between the bears are tiny navy blue hearts and still smaller polka dots. The quilt in *Color Illustration 11* was made from this fabric. On the left is a Christmas design cloth with very authentic antique looking Teddies in several positions. They appear to have been inspired by an old advertisement of 1909. Benjamin's pajamas in *Color Illustration 8* are made of this. There are tiny sprigs of holly between the bears.

In the foreground is a batiste showing Teddy Bears carrying balloons. They are definitely bears but the fabric

designer, for some reason, put little cotton tails on some of them! Rosie wears a nightgown of this interesting design in *Color Illustration 11*. Another cloth, a knit (not included in this photograph) also has authentic bears with balloons. Basic Bear wears a nightshirt of this very soft cloth in *Color Illustration 10*.

To find these Teddy fabrics you must browse the fabric stores when you are nearby and keep a sharp eye out for Teddy Bears who may be lurking in the folds of cottons, knits and cotton flannels, especially at holiday and children's fabrics counters.

Buttons and Decals

Illustration 10 shows 9in (22.9cm) Benjamin with a small collection of buttons and decals from local fabric and discount stores. Some of the most charming buttons you will ever find for Teddy are in the baby buttons section of the buttons' department. You can find buttons that look like pocket watches, alphabet blocks or flowers. There are Teddy Bears and Teddy Bear heads in several shapes and colors as well as pandas and koalas. You will find bunnies, all sizes of hearts, ABC's, "Love" buttons, fire engines, cars and so many other clever things, you will think of all kinds of ways to use them on your own bear's wardrobe.

Benjamin wears his heart button on his chest. On each

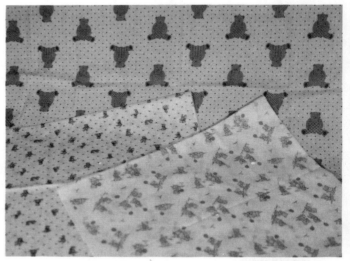

Illustration 9. Just three of the many Teddy Bear design fabrics available in many stores today. The large bears and tiny hearts on cotton in the background were used for the quilt in Color Illustration 11, *the pastel batiste with modern bears and balloons in the foreground was used for Rosie's nightgown for the same photograph, and a cotton with brown antique style Teddy Bears, left, was used for Benjamin's pajamas in* Color Illustration 8.

Illustration 10. *Classic Benjamin sits among a collection of several sizes and colors of heart buttons, four different bear shaped buttons and one style shaped like tiny pocket watches. Baby button counters in fabric and department stores always have clever finds for Teddy Bears. In the back are two embroidered Teddy Bear decals. Benjamin's heart is a button.*

side of him are just two of several of the embroidered sew-on decals available in fabric stores around the country. It is interesting to know that the 1908 *Sears Roebuck Catalog* carried Teddy Bear decals to be sewn on children's clothes and one coat in the children's section had a Teddy waving an American flag decal on the sleeve. Basic Bear, 18in (45.7cm) wears an apron with an especially charming Teddy decal in *Color Illustration on cover.*

In the same photograph with Benjamin, the four cards of buttons to the left are all bears. The two in front are Teddy heads while the two in back are koalas, left, and brown very raised Teddies on the right. Cuddles wears the koala on her dress in *Color Illustration 6* and Ginger wears the brown Teddy buttons on his raincoat in *Color Illustration 5.*

The six cards directly in front of Benjamin are all heart buttons. Some are on quite tall shanks for thick fabrics; some are flatter. The hearts are pink and several shades of red, manufactured by several different companies. The most unusual are the ones at the back right by Benjamin's foot — unusual because they are flat hearts with holes rather than shanks. They were used on Huggy's dress in *Color Illustration 9.*

In the front, right, are buttons that look like little pocket watches and a card of tiny green alligators for the status-conscious bear. Petite Père of the jointed miniature bear family has one of the tiny pocket watches hanging from his suit pocket in *Color Illustration 16.*

These buttons and decals were not purchased on one shopping expedition, of course, but instead were gathered over a period of months.

I always browse the baby buttons section for a few minutes when I'm in a fabric store and purchase at least one card of any I feel are special. Store inventories are constantly changing and some buttons may not be there the next time I shop. I have some buttons that I wish I had bought several cards of because I cannot find them any more, but there are always clever new ones to take their place.

GENERAL DIRECTIONS FOR CLOTHES

Sweaters

Teddy Bears wear sweaters so well and are so incredibly cuddly in them that every bear should have one or more — perhaps a whole wardrobe of them for different occasions. But everyone knows beautiful, well-made toy sweaters are expensive and hard to come by — or are they?

Cinnamon models a very special sweater of white with lavender Teddy Bears across the front and sleeves in *Color Illustration 1.* Ginger models a ski sweater and cap in *Color Illustration 4* and two Basics show off their pullover and cardigan in *Illustration 62.* These and all the other precious Teddy Bear sweaters shown in this volume were created from "people" sweaters, knee socks, leg warmers, ski caps and even long wool gloves!

You can create tennis sweaters, ski sweaters, school sweaters, dressy ones, sporty ones, cardigans with buttons or zippers, and even one with your or your bear's name on it. Although most of the items used here were purchased especially for making these sweaters, most people have a few old sweaters around the house which can be used. You can buy sweaters for just a few cents apiece at garage and rummage sales or ask friends to save you old ones. The most elegant items may be purchased at the finest stores if you are a spare-no expense collector or you can buy them at your nearest discount or bargain store, making your bear's sweaters cost only a fraction of the cost of a ready-made toy sweater.

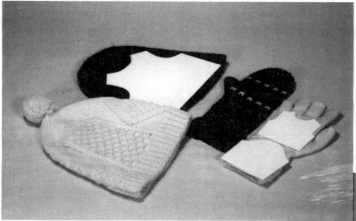

Illustration 11. Charming little Teddy Bear sweaters can be made from ski caps, mittens or gloves. Caps can be used for larger sizes while gloves and mittens are the right scale for Benjamin and the miniature bears.

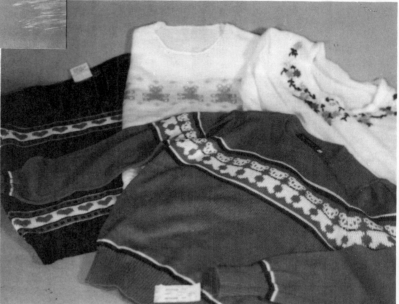

Illustration 12. These are some interesting adult-size sweaters that will make marvelous Teddy Bear sweaters. On the left is a navy sweater with white bands and red hearts; rear center, a white one with lavender Teddy Bears used for Cinnamon's sweater in Color Illustration 1; right rear, an embroidered white sweater found at a garage sale for only a few cents, and a brand new red sweater with white Teddy Bears purchased especially for bear sweaters.

Illustration 13. Sweaters often have knit belts that make nice warm scarves for all sizes of Teddy Bears. Sweetie Pie sits among a collection of belts saved from old sweaters.

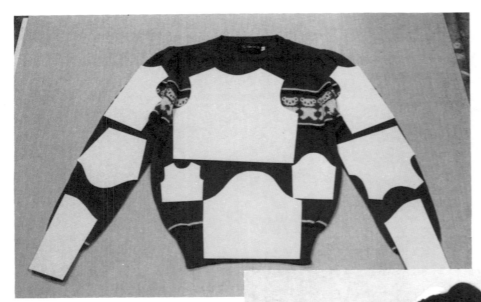

Illustration 14. You can get from four to seven Teddy Bear sweaters from one adult sweater depending on the sizes you want. Shown here is a new sweater with an 18in (45.7cm) and a 12in (30.5cm) Teddy pattern on the body, and two 15in (38.1cm) patterns on the sleeves. At least two 9in (22.9cm) or miniature size sweaters can be made from the smaller pieces remaining.

Illustration 15. Benjamin models a wonderful sweater and cap made from a hand-embroidered Austrian sock purchased on a trip to Europe a few years ago. Such a sweater makes a very special keepsake for years to come. Clare Worrell Collection.

It is possible to get four to six Teddy Bear sweaters of varying sizes from one adult sweater as shown in *Illustration 14.* Some of the smaller items such as knee socks or leg warmers often have stripes or designs on them that are perfectly scaled to Teddy Bears.

When I was in Europe several years ago, I purchased some hand-embroidered knee socks in Austria for my daughter, Clare. She wore them for two seasons and then I kept them, out of sentiment, even though there were holes worn at the heels. Later, when I began making bears' sweaters, I remembered those socks and spent an afternoon in the attic searching for them. I made Clare a 9in (22.9cm) bear with a sweater from her own Austrian

socks for a keepsake.

If you make these little sweaters, you will find that your friends are amazed to discover you did not actually knit them!

Cutting the Sweater

You can utilize the ribbing at the bottom of a sweater or slide your pattern higher in order to make use of the designs on a patterned sweater. Hemmed sweaters can be as charming on bears as those with ribbing. Of course, ribbing can be cut off and sewn to the toy sweater by stretching it as you sew. You have to look really closely to tell the

TOP: Illustration 16. *Since a sweater's ribbing draws in at the band and cuffs, it needs to be stretched out to make it straight when cutting out a Teddy Bear sweater.*

Illustration 17. *Here a sweater is stretched at the bottom ribbing band and pinned to a piece of cardboard so it is straight at the sides. Lay the toy sweater pattern on as shown and draw around it with a ballpoint pen or chalk. Remove the pins and release the sweater; then cut on the marked lines.*

difference. Ginger wears a ski sweater with sewn-on ribbing on both cuffs and bottom in *Color Illustration 4*. On the other hand, Cinnamon's cheerleader sweater in *Illustration 52* and Basic's cardigan in *Illustration 62* have the original knitted-on ribbing at the cuffs. Many commercially made sweaters have sewn-on ribbing rather than knitted-in so it really does not make that much difference — it is just a matter of choice.

When incorporating ribbing on either the sleeves or bottom, remember to stretch the ribbing so that the rows of knitting are straight and in line with rows on the body. Stretch the ribbing out and pin the sweater to a piece of corrugated cardboard or a pillow or something similar and draw around your pattern with a ballpoint pen, soft pencil or chalk. When released, it springs back, but you will know where to cut.

Measuring For The Neckband

Since knits vary in size and stretchability and bears vary in size, it is not possible to give an *exact* measurement.

The neckband should fit your bear's neck — stretched just a little bit but still relaxed, plus a seam allowance.

Measurements are for plain bands or mock turtlenecks. If you want a fold-down turtle neck, make the band wider.

Sweaters From Knee Socks

Knee socks can easily be turned into sweaters for 9in (22.9cm) Benjamin with a minimum of sewing as in *Illustration 19*. They can also be used for larger 12 to 15in (30.5 to 38.1cm) Teddy Bears when opened down the back and used flat as shown in *Illustration 23*. *For these larger sweaters, both socks of a pair are required* while only one sock is needed for very small ones as in *Illustration 15*.

When making sweaters from knee socks you cannot always utilize the ribbing for the bottom of your sweater if the design has a top-bottom position such as the hearts in *Illustration 23* or reindeer in *Illustrations 18* and *58*. With plain socks, the top ribbing can be used as the bottom of the sweater.

Sweaters From Leg Warmers

Leg warmers are ideal for Teddy Bear sweaters too. See *Illustration 21*. For 12 to 14in (30.5 to 35.6cm) bears you need only to cut armholes, sew the shoulders and then sew in the sleeves and neckband. You can even get two sweaters for 12in (30.5cm) bears from one leg warmer, and sometimes a cap as well, depending on the size. *Illustrations 50* and *73* show leg warmer sweaters.

Warmers can be used for larger bears 15 to 18in (38.1 to 45.7cm), also, if split and opened out flat as in *Illustration 22*.

Sleeves from sweaters can be used in the same way leg warmers and knee socks can as in *Illustrations 24* and *25*.

Sewing The Sweater

Use a small stitch on your sewing machine, not the tiniest, but a small one to prevent raveling. For your first sweater use a knit with medium to small size stitches rather than large, loose ones. If you find that the one you are working on is raveling badly, just sew around the edges of each piece to anchor the cut threads. Most sweaters will not require this, however.

Stretch *slightly* as you sew so your sweater will have give when being put on your bear.

1. Sew the shoulder seams; leave the body turned inside out.
2. Sew underarm seams of the sleeves and turn them right side out.
3. Slip a sleeve up inside the sweater body and place the sleeve edge around inside the armhole. Place the sleeve so that its underarm seam is in the correct position and baste or pin in place, stretching it somewhat as you sew. Sew in other sleeve in the same manner. (This method is for sweaters made from tubes such as sleeves, socks and leg warmers which have no side seams. If you are working with a sweater with cut open side seams, all you need to do is sew your shoulder seams, then sew the sleeves to the *opened* sweater body. Next, sew from the wrist along the underarm seam and down the side seam to the bottom.)
4. Fold the neckband into a loop and sew the ends together. Next, fold it over so it is double and baste the two edges together, stretching it as you baste.
5. With sweater inside out, put the neckband inside with the raw edges up even with the neck edges. Pin the neckband seam at one shoulder seam; then pin the other side of the loop at the other shoulder seam. Pin at center back and center front.
6. It is important that you *stretch* both the neckband and the neck to one and one-half to two times their size as you sew. Some knits will stretch easier than others. This will make it easy to stretch the neck over Teddy's head and keep your stitching threads from breaking.
7. Hem or add ribbing to sweater bottom and sleeve if needed.
8. Make a matching stocking cap and decorate it with a tassel or yarn pompon.

Illustration 18. *There are many knee socks, both old and new, which make great little Teddy Bear sweaters. Adult size socks can be used for bears from tiny miniature size up to 15in (38.1cm) tall.*

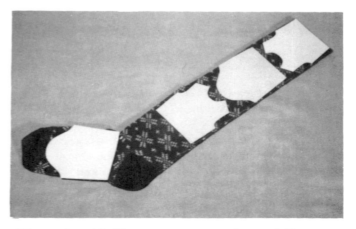

Illustration 19. *You can get two 9in (22.9cm) Benjamin sweaters from one sock.*

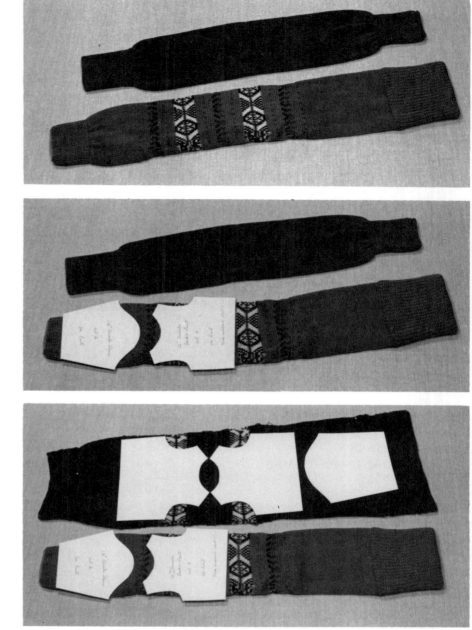

Illustration 20. Leg warmers, both plain and patterned, can be utilized for simple-to-make Teddy Bear sweaters.

Illustration 21. A leg warmer with the 12in (30.5cm) size pattern on it. There is enough room left for another little sweater like that worn by 12in (30.5cm) Cubby in Illustration 50.

Illustration 22. Two leg warmers of the same design, but of different colors, demonstrate the two different ways to make sweaters. At top, a leg warmer is cut open for a large 15 to 18in (38.1 to 45.7cm) size sweater. (The other sleeve will be cut from the end at left.) Below, a smaller 12in (30.5cm) size uses the warmer as is so the sweater has no side seams. Two of the smaller sizes can be made from one warmer.

Illustration 23. Knee socks can be opened up and used for larger sweaters, as shown. Although only one sock is shown here, both socks of a pair are needed for one 15in (38.1cm) size sweater. The ribbing had to be cut from the top of the sock and sewn onto the bottom of the sweater because the little heart design would be going the wrong way. The toe of one sock was used for a stocking cap. See Color Illustration 4.

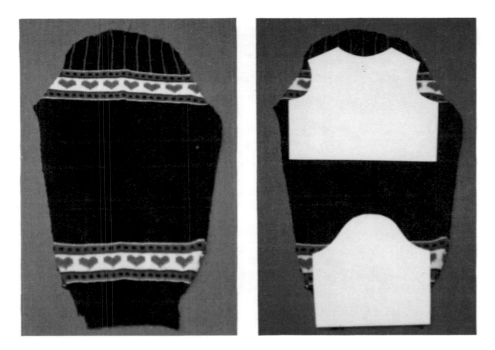

FAR LEFT: *Illustration 24. Sweater sleeves such as this one with heart designs can be used in the same manner as knee socks and leg warmers.*

Illustration 25. This is a sleeve opened out for a sweater for 18in (45.7cm) bears. It takes both sleeves for one 18in (45.7cm) size sweater.

Cardigans

Cardigans can be made easily and quickly from a cardigan sweater. *Illustration 26* shows how you can button it and then cut out the front piece utilizing the buttons and buttonholes already there. You do not even have to make any adjustments on the pattern; just treat it as a plain pullover. You may need to slide your pattern up or down slightly to make the top button come at the right place. Cardigans with buttons somewhat close together make better Teddy Bear sweaters than those with only a few widely spaced buttons. Zippered cardigans can be made from old zippered sweaters or sweat shirts. Be sure you zip the sweater so that the slide is *below* the little sweater's neckline as in *Illustration 29* or you will cut off the slide and ruin the zipper. Immediately after cutting out the sweater, take a needle and thread and go over and over the ends of the zipper track at the neck on each side so the slide will not go off the ends. When you sew on the neckband, you will catch the zipper ends in your seam and finish them off.

T-Shirts

Most any knit cloth in solids, stripes or print is suitable for little T-shirts and sweaters. Iron-on letters and decals add a touch of humor to T-shirts as well as personalize them. Seasonal messages can be used such as "Merry Christmas," "St. Patrick's Day," and birthday wishes can be ironed on, too. Children love to have their own name on their bear's shirt such as on Buddy's little T-shirt in *Illustration 64*. Cinnamon wears an alphabet design T-shirt in *Illustration 49*.

Letters and designs can be drawn on with indelible felt-tip pens or embroidered decals, like that on Basic Bear's apron, can be sewn on. Decorating ideas for shirts for bears can be as limitless as those for "people" shirts. Be creative!

Hats, Caps, Bonnets

Except for snug-fitting stocking caps, most Teddy Bear headgear will need something to help keep it from getting lost or falling off at the most inopportune times.

The most effective way to keep a hat on a Teddy Bear is with ties which are an integral part of the hat as in *Color Illustration 5*. If the hat should fall off in spite of the ties, they will usually still keep the hat hanging around the Teddy Bear's neck. The same is true of bonnet strings with a slide — if the slide is a good snug fit as in *Color Illustration 7*.

For hats that do not normally have ties as part of their design, elastic thread straps under the chin are very successful. Basic Bear's clown hat is held in place by thread elastic in *Color Illustration 9* that is practically invisible. It works well for chef caps, sailor hats and baseball caps, too.

Velcro inside a cap will help hold it in place. It can be purchased in little circle or square fasteners. Use the stiff or hook side of two *heavy duty* fasteners on the inside band of the hat. Test it first, though, by pressing it against the bear's head and moving it *sideways* to see if it grabs because some fur cloth responds to Velcro better than others.

Hats can always be sewn onto the bear's head or, in an emergency, held on with a medium size safety pin. Sometimes a safety pin can be a real help when a Teddy Bear is traveling somewhere and has a worrisome hat that keeps falling off.

Take a little extra time to help your bear find ways to keep his hat in place because bears love wearing hats — and they know they look absolutely adorable in them!

Use hat patterns included in 15in (38.1cm) Classic Ginger's wardrobe section in Chapter 6. It is a most versatile pattern for all kinds of hats for several sizes of bears.

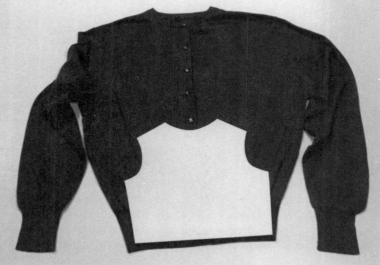

Illustration 26. *Cardigan sweaters should be buttoned, as shown, when making Teddy Bear cardigans.*

Illustration 27. *Treat a buttoned cardigan the same as you would a pullover. Position the pattern carefully so the buttons are properly placed in center. Basic Bear models a cardigan in Illustration 62.*

Illustration 28. *Zippered cardigans should be constructed by the same rules as buttoned ones except that care should be taken to prevent the zipper pull from being cut off.*

Illustration 29. *Make sure the pull is down below the top of the sweater pattern when cutting out the sweater. Use safety pins to keep the pull from sliding off the cut ends until the zipper ends are caught securely with a needle and thread.*

Rain Hat or So'wester

Make this in yellow vinyl or any yellow fabric. Ginger's rain hat was made from a shower curtain valance as was his coat in *Color Illustration 5*.

1. Cut four crown sections and four brim pieces, using the hat with 15in (38.1cm) Classic Ginger's patterns.
2. Sew two of the crown sections together, joining the single notch. Sew the other two sections; then join the first two to the second two and you have the crown. (If you use any kind of plastic material, be sure to use *very large stitches* on your machine.)
3. Sew two of the brim sections together at the ends, matching the triple notches to form a ring; then sew the other two together in the same manner.
4. Stitch the outer brim to the inner brim around the outside edges. Turn right side out and press edges with an iron.
5. When sewing the brim to the crown, matching the double notches, your brim seams should line up with two of the crown seams. This will give you a front and back and two sides to the hat.
6. To finish off the seam where the crown and brim have been joined, turn the hat inside out; press the seam up toward the crown and stitch all the way around about 1/8in (0.31cm) up onto the *outside* of the crown (which is now turned inside). This will hold the seam up inside the hat and give it a nice finished look on the outside. You can use a bias tape binding if you prefer but the row of stitching works well unless you use a loosely woven cloth that ravels badly.
7. Both the sailor and So'wester hats need to have stitched brims. Begin at the outside, 1/4in (0.65cm) in from the edge for the first row, using a *medium to large stitch*. Repeat, sewing the next row 1/4in (0.65cm) parallel to the first. Repeat the rows all the way to the inside as indicated on the pattern. (The Rough Rider and farmer hats require no brim stitching.)
8. Sew on ties for holding the hat in place "during a wind." Attach them inside at the side seams.

Rough Rider Hat

Follow directions for constructing the rain hat but use a khaki twill or poplin fabric as shown in *Color Illustration 7*. No stitching is needed on the brim as army hat brims were plain.

The ties called "bonnet strings" went across the front of the hat and through holes at each side toward the inside, to fasten under the chin. A bead or "slide" was then pushed up to hold the hat in place when necessary. The strings can just hang down in front, go in back of the head or be pulled up to the top of the crown and tied, holding the brim up on each side as shown on the hat pattern page. Shoestrings make great bonnet strings or ties for Teddy Bear hats!

Teddy Roosevelt wore a crossed sword insignia on the turned-up brim. Cubby has a Teddy Bear button on his.

Sailor Hat

Follow directions for the rain hat. For larger 18in (45.7cm) bears this pattern is appropriate for a sailor hat to perch over one ear. The old navy hats worn during the Spanish American War had a more flared brim than sailor hats of today. These new hats caused a fashion for cloth hats with stitched brims for children in the early 1900s. Made up in colors, too, they could be purchased in tan, red, navy blue, and later in patterned fabrics like the old Teddy Bear hat in *Illustration 72*. See also *Illustrations 51* and *back cover*.

Cub Scout Cap

The crown pattern for Ginger's rain hat, used with the visor, makes a little *Cub* Scout cap for 12 to 14in (30.5 to 35.6cm) bears as seen in *Illustration 57*. It will need a little bias facing around the bottom edge since the visor is only joined in the front. Put a little covered button on top where the sections meet. A diamond-shaped patch of yellow felt, sewn or glued on the cap front, serves as the scout symbol. (The kerchief is a triangle of yellow cotton, 12in [30.5cm] by 17in [43.2cm] by 12in [30.5cm].)

Baseball Cap

With the visor instead of a brim, Ginger's pattern becomes a baseball cap, too, which can be made in the colors of your favorite team. It fits the 12 to 15in (30.5 to 38.1cm) bears. You can even sew on one of those embroidered emblem patches of your favorite team.

By the way, those miniature hard plastic hats used at professional baseball games to hold snow-cones make great baseball caps for 12 to 14in (30.5 to 35.6cm) bears as in *Illustration 58*.

Beanie

Without a brim of any sort, the same crown becomes a 12 to 14in (30.5 to 35.6cm) size beanie to be worn with a school blazer or sweater. Use a bias facing to finish the edges. Souvenir pins can be pinned on as well as political buttons, school letters or any number of things.

Fancy Hats

You may find still other hats from this basic pattern by adding flowers, feathers, ribbons, chin straps or ear flaps. It can be made of most any fabric and a ruffle can serve as a brim. Also, the brim pattern can be combined with a mob cap crown.

Mob Cap, Colonial Bonnet or Night Cap

Made simply from circles of cloth, these bonnets can be drawn up to fit your bear's head. For 18in (45.7cm) bears, the circle needs to be about 15in (38.1cm) in diameter. For 14 and 15in (35.6 and 38.1cm) bears, it should measure 13in (33cm). See *Color Illustration 11*.

The easiest and fastest way to construct these bonnets is to cut them *double*, then sew around the outside edge and turn. All you have to do next is make two rows of stitching to form a casing for elastic or ribbon.

Tams

Your pattern for a 16 to 18in (40.6 to 45.7cm) bear's tam is simply two circles 7½in (19.1cm) in diameter. For the band, cut a hole 3in (7.6cm) in diameter in the center of one of them. This will give you a band about 2¼in (5.8cm) wide all the way around. Hem the inside opening of the second circle by turning the edge over once and stitching around it, stretching it just a bit as you sew to make it fit well.

Next, sew the two circles together around the outside circumference, making sure the hemmed edge of the cut out circle is facing up. Turn right side out; press with steam iron and add a bright colored yarn pompon, a ball cut from ball fringe or a shank button. See *Illustrations 50, 57* and *63*.

For smaller bears, 12 to 14in (30.5 to 35.6cm) tall, make your circle patterns 6½in (16.5cm) in diameter with the cut-out hole 2¾in (7.1cm) across.

Chef Caps

18in (45.7cm) Basic Bear models a chef cap in *Color Illustration on cover* made of unbleached muslin to match his apron.

To make the band, first cut a rectangle of muslin 11½in (29.2cm) by 4½in (11.5cm). Bring the ends together and sew them, forming a tube 4½in (11.5cm) tall. Next, fold the tube double, making it only 2¼in (5.8cm) tall. A circle 11½in (29.2cm) in diameter forms the crown when gathered onto the band.

To keep the cap crisp and stiff so it will stand up, you can line it with two or three layers of nylon net as you go. If you want an easier way to stiffen it, just stuff wadded nylon net up inside after you complete it.

For smaller chef caps for 12 to 15in (30.5 to 38.1cm) bears, cut the band 3in (7.6cm) by 8¼in (21cm) and follow directions above. The crown should be a circle 7½in (19.1cm) in diameter gathered on.

Flat Brimmed Hats

For a flat brim, your pattern should be a circle 9in (22.9cm) in diameter with a hole cut in the center 3¼in (8.3cm) in diameter. For the brim, cut two of these circles and sew around the outside edge with the usual 1/4in (0.65cm) seam. Turn and press. Mark the inside circle in four equally spaced places to be matched to the seams of the crown of Ginger's hat pattern.

Made in felt, it can become a cowboy, U.S. Cavalry or Royal Mountie hat. (Make the Rough Rider jacket in red with black trousers and boots for your Mountie Bear.)

This hat also becomes a "Scarlet O'Hara" hat with flowers and ribbon streamers as in *Color Illustration 6*, or a romantic old-fashioned bonnet with a ribbon across the top. For the bonnet, tack ribbons at the seam where the brim and crown meet and pull the brim down on each side as you tie the ribbons under the chin. These two romantic hats go with long or full skirts and lots of ribbons or lace.

You can make the hat of felt and clip it all around the edges for a ragged "Tom Sawyer" or farmer hat. The flat brim lends itself well to humorous interpretations so you probably will think of all kinds of characters to do.

Stocking Caps

Knit cloth works best, although any cloth can be used for this simple, traditional head gear. All you need to do is make a tube about the same circumference as your bear's head of any length from short to quite long. Hem the edges of one end, then sew around the edges of the other end and gather it up.

The gathered end can remain on the outside to form an old-fashioned poof or be tucked inside and covered with a yarn pompon or tassel. During the first decade of the 20th century, it was the fashion to suspend the tassel or pompon 1 to 3in (2.5 to 7.6cm) from the end of the cap as in *Illustration 4*. In more recent years, very large pompons have been the fashion.

Boots and Shoes

For rain boots *Color Illustration 5*, Rough Rider boots *Color Illustration 7* or "Santy Claws" boots *Illustration 64* start with the bear's foot pattern. Be sure to use the *pattern for the bear that is going to wear the boots* (except for Buddy Bear who wears 12in [30.5cm] Cubby's boots). Use felt for best results in the beginning, later you can experiment with all kinds of materials. *Illustration 30* shows how to make your boot pattern and then modify it for other style boots and shoes. If you have not done pattern drafting before, this

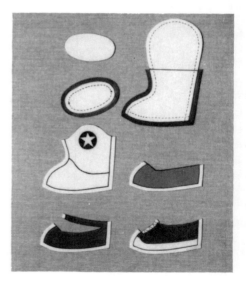

Illustration 30. Use the bear's leg pattern as a base for drafting your own boot and shoe patterns. The pattern at the top shows how to add 1/4in (0.65cm) to the leg and foot pad pattern to enlarge it for a simple boot. In the middle are cowboy boot and slipper patterns made from the new boot pattern above. At bottom, strap slippers and tennis shoes can also be created from the first simple boot pattern as well as many other styles of footwear. Use felt scraps and experiment.

exercise is so simple and requires so little investment in materials and time that you can experiment to your heart's content, having fun while you learn.

1. Measure up about halfway to the top of the leg pattern and draw a line across it to become the top of the boot, top right in *Illustration 30*.

2. Trace around the foot and lower leg *on the cutting or outside line* and then make another new line 1/4in (0.65cm) out from that one all the way around to enlarge it as indicated by the dark area. Do the same for the foot pad pattern which will become the boot or shoe sole. That is all there is to it; you have your simple two-piece boot pattern (plus the innersole described in step 3).

3. For the innersole pattern, top left, just use the bear's foot pad *as it is*. Use two layers of cardboard glued together.

4. Cut four side pieces and two soles for one pair of boots. Sew boot sides together and sew in the sole as you did when constructing your bear's legs by pinning it at each end to hold it in place.

5. Clip in several places at the front instep curve, then turn right side out.

6. Put a little glue on the bottom of the cardboard innersole to hold it in place and fit it into the boot, pulling the seams up above it.

7. Hem the top about 1/2in (1.3cm) or, if using felt, just trim off a little to your liking and make a few stitches at the seams to prevent raveling.

The sole can be made of a different color or shade as on Cuddle's slippers in *Color Illustration* 6. (You can just barely see the sole on her right slipper.) You can adapt your boot pattern for lace-up boots, tennis shoes and slippers of all styles. By sewing felt designs on the boots, you can create cowboy boots, saddle-oxfords and jogging shoes. When you make your patterns, try them out with scraps of old fabric until you perfect them. Once you make them, label them and file away for future use.

Some of the larger bears can wear infant shoes in size 1 or 2. There are many clever shoe designs which are charming or humorous on Teddy Bears. It is a good idea to take your bear with you when you shop for them so he can try them on. Remember that a bear's foot is wider than an infant's narrow foot. They may seem too nararow at first but the bear's furry foot can be gently squeezed into the shoe and the laces tightened to a really good fit. There may be a little space left at the toes; if so, a bit of wadded tissue or cotton can be pushed into the space to fill out the shoe.

Your bear can wear hand-me-down baby shoes if you have a tiny friend who has outgrown some — whose mother will give them up.

Aprons

For generations, Teddy Bears have been sitting on stools or kitchen cabinets and tasting cookies and other goodies during holdiays as well as tasting some awful things, like vegetables, their owners were made to eat. With all those hours they spend in the kitchen, every Teddy needs an apron to protect his fur. Besides, they make him look so efficient and expert.

Three sizes of bear aprons are on the same page in 18in (45.7cm) Basic Bear's clothes patterns in Chapter 7. They are marked as to which to use for the different size bears.

There are two ways to construct them; one, with bias binding around all the edges and the other, with a lining.

In *Illustration 53*, Cinnamon wears a yellow apron bound on the edges with red calico bias tape and decorated with iron-on letters. First, the binding is sewn across the bib top, then around the edges of the skirt. Next, the waist tie, neck tie and side binding are all made with one piece of binding. To sew on, match the center of the binding strip to the notch at the side of the bib and pin it into place. Sew from one end of the waist binding, forming a tie; then catch the side edge of the apron inside it as you stitch and continue onto the end of the neck tie. Repeat on the other side.

For the 18in (45.7cm) size apron, the ties should be about 28in (71.1cm) long, the 12 to 15in (30.5 to 38.1cm) size about 25in (63.5cm), and the smallest 9in (22.9cm) size about 20in (50.8cm) long.

The other, easier method is to just cut the apron double and sew across the top of the bib and around the skirt, leaving the sides open. Turn right side out and sew on the ties as shown in steps a, b and c.

The two larger aprons have a pocket 2¾in (7.1cm) square with 1/4in (0.65cm) turned under all round. The smallest one has a 1¾in (4.5cm) square pocket also turned under 1/4in (0.65cm) all around.

Embroidered decals such as the Teddy Bear on Basic Bear's apron in *Color Illustration on cover*, iron-on letters such as on Cinnamon's, rick-rack, lace, ruffles or embroidery can give individuality to your Teddy Bear's apron. Ginger's fancy apron in *Illustration 56* requires about 30in (76.2cm) of lace or self ruffle 1 to 1½in (2.5 to 3.8cm) wide. Make the apron double with the ruffle sewn between the two pieces for a nice finished look.

Chapter 5
MAKING YOUR OWN PATTERNS

It is always special when you can have fun, acquire something new and add to your store of knowledge and experience at the same time! There are so many clothes you can create for your Teddy Bears, there simply is not enough space for all those patterns. There are also a number of bear costumes that require pieces too large for the pages of a book. I can, however, in the space of just one chapter, give you an elementary course in pattern drafting that can teach you how to create dozens of clothes patterns for all your bears and, if you learn your lesson well, for doll's clothes and even for yourself, as well.*

When making adjustments for new patterns, it is important that you trace the pattern, make your desired changes on it and then label it thoroughly. (Never attempt to make adjustments directly onto your cloth.) Pin all the pattern pieces together and store in an envelope labeled with that bear's name and size. If, for instance, you adjust a pattern for three different bears, it will be wise to have an envelope with each bear's name and size. Make three different patterns, each with whatever adjustments you want and store each in its own envelope for future use. When you acquire a collection of bears, you will also acquire lots of patterns for clothes and patterns can be confusing if not properly labeled, and worse, cause costly mistakes. You may find it efficient to file each bear pattern along with his own patterns for clothes in one large envelope together.

The first rule to remember is that you must be methodical and take it one step at a time. First, concentrate, for instance, on widening a pattern piece before you begin to think about lengthening it. Take each modifying step to completion before taking the next step. Start with something simple like extending the width of a straight sleeve to become a full, gathered sleeve as in *Illustration 31*. Added width is indicated by the dark area.

When you have learned that, try your hand at making a full night gown, angel robe or pegnoir pattern from a straight coat, jacket, or pajama top pattern as in *Illustrations 32, 33* and *34*.

One rule to remember is that if you take width away from a plain sleeve, you will need to reduce the armhole size also by taking away some of the body side seam to compensate. When *adding* width to a straight sleeve you must *add* width to the armhole at the underarm seam. (When making a gathered sleeve, this need not be done.)

*For almost 20 years Estelle Worrell has designed costumes for Nashville Academy Theatre as well as for two nationally produced movies. She is the author of three books on the history of American costume and two other books on dolls and doll clothes.

If you want to reduce the body size but leave the armhole as is, start at the armhole and *angle* your side seam line in as you move toward the waist. This will reduce the body without altering the armhole.

You can make one-piece pajamas or overalls by combining top or bib with trousers. Be sure, in the case of pajamas, that the length from neck to crotch is sufficient.

It is impossible to give exact measurements and patterns for Teddy Bear clothing because every bear is different. Fur fabrics come in many varying densities and pile lengths which affect a bear's proportions as in *Illustration 1* and every reader has a unique sewing and stuffing touch so even though all may be using the same bear patterns, no two are going to be identical. Every pattern should be checked to make sure it is appropriate for your particular bear.

Pleated Skirt

This very versatile skirt can be worn with a sweater, as a Scottish kilt, with a jacket to form a suit, with a blouse or middy, with the overalls bib added to form a jumper or sun dress and, of course, attached to a bodice for a dress.

Did you know that pleating is older than gathering as a means of incorporating fullness into a garment? In the first decade of the 20th century when the Teddy Bear was first invented, pleated skirts were called kilted skirts.

The skirt waistband length should be your bear's waist measurement plus 1½in (3.8cm) for an overlap. Make it 2in (5.1cm) wide. The skirts shown in *Illustrations 50* and *52* should be cut about 48in (121.8cm) by 8½in (21.6cm) allowing for a 1in (2.5cm) hem for 16 to 18in (40.6 to 45.7cm) bears. For 14 to 16in (35.6 to 40.6cm) bears make it about 40in (101.6cm) by 7in (17.8cm) and for 12 to 14in (30.5 to 35.6cm) Teddies 36in (91.4cm) by 5½in (14cm).

For pleats, start at one end at the waist or top and measure toward the center, 3/4in (2cm). Mark a small x, then measure 1½in (3.8cm) from the x and mark a dot. Then measure 3/4in (2cm) from the dot and make an x then add another 1½in (3.8cm) and make another dot. Repeat this all the way across the top of the skirt till you get to the other end. Next, take your first dot and fold it over to meet your first x making a pleat; then bring the second dot over to meet the second x making the second pleat, continuing on across the skirt. You can practice your pleats on a piece of notebook or scrap paper or old cloth if you feel unsure at first. It is really quite easy.

Blouse

For old fashioned blouses and middies add fullness to the sleeves as in *Illustration 31* and gather to fit the armhole.

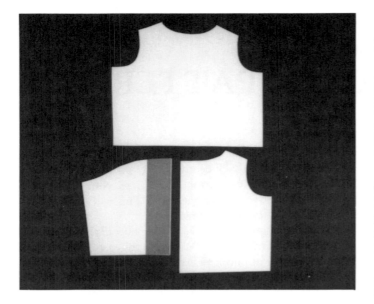

Illustration 31. Cinnamon's pajama pattern can become a blouse pattern when extra width is added to the fold edge, as shown, for a gathered sleeve.

Put on a cuff measured to fit your bear's arm at the wrist. It is especially interesting that many of the styles of Teddy's early days such as gathered sleeves, long waists and straight trousers and so on, have returned to fashion. Clothes can be both nostalgic and modern at the same time! Teddy Bear blouses were tremendously popular in 1906 to 1910, usually worn with overalls or trousers. Any of the jacket, pajama shirt, or coat patterns can be adapted for blouses.

Nightshirts

Jackets, pajama shirts and coats need only to be lengthened for simple little nightshirts. Basic Bear's night-shirt pattern is demonstrated in *Illustration 32*. Ginger's raincoat, Cubby's Rough Rider jacket and Benjamin's pajama shirt can be made ankle or floor-length and the side seam corners rounded for the most charming nightshirts.

Make a little stocking cap to match with tassel or yarn pompon to top it off and you will have a real winner!

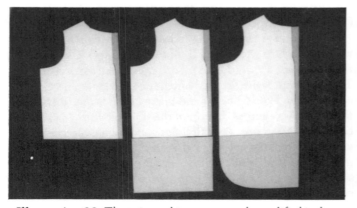

Illustration 32. The pajama shirt pattern can be modified in three easy steps to become an old-fashioned nightshirt pattern. Left, add a bit of width at the front. Next, lengthen the pattern to the desired length, and finally (right) curve the side seam corners as shown. (The finished nightshirt is in Color Illustration 10.)

Nightgowns

Use the pattern for Ginger's raincoat to make a new pattern for a nightgown for 14 to 18in (35.6 to 45.7cm) bears. Begin with the sleeve pattern as shown on the left in *Illustration 33*. Add 2in (5.1cm) down the fold edge as shown. Next, add 2in (5.1cm) to the length as shown on the left in *Illustration 34*. The finished sleeve pattern is intended to be cut on the fold as was the original sleeve.

For gown body use the raincoat body and extend 2½in (6.4cm) in width as demonstrated in *Illustration 33*, right. Next, add 2in (5.1cm) to the length as shown in *Illustration 34*, right. When adding length to a curved skirt edge, measure down at intervals close together and mark for new length making it parallel to the original length.

Extending the body and sleeve widths will allow the neckline to be gathered up. Use either Cinnamon's or Ginger's collar pattern, depending on how large you want it,

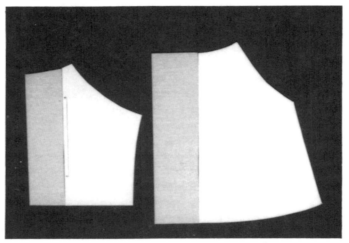

Illustration 33. Ginger's raincoat pattern can be given extra fullness for a clown suit top, smock or full dress. Add to the sleeve on the fold edge as shown, (left) and to the center back and front of the body (right). This will enlarge the neck which will then be gathered to fit the bear. (The finished clown suit top is in Color Illustration 9.)

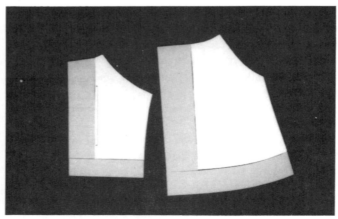

Illustration 34. For long robes, nightgowns or formals, add extra length at the bottom. Length needs to be added to the sleeve only for larger bears or for a gathered edge like that on the clown suit in Color Illustration 9.

with the nightgown or just add lace or a drawstring. Put elastic in sleeve wrists. This nightgown can open in either the front or back. It is like the one modeled by Old Timey Rosie in *Color Illustration 11*.

For 12 and 13in (30.5 and 33cm) nightgowns use Cubby's Rough Rider jacket body pattern widened and lengthened in the same manner as Ginger's raincoat described above. The sleeves can be used just as they are or extended and gathered.

For Benjamin use his pajama shirt and extend the body pattern about 2in (5.1cm) in width at the center front and back. If you want extra fullness at the sleeves, add 1in (2.5cm) to the pattern at the shoulder fold edge. After you have extended the width of both body and sleeves, you are ready to add to the length according to how long you want it to become.

Illustration 35. Bess, the feminine interpretation of Basic, is ready for her winter's nap in a homespun looking cotton gauze nightgown and mob cap. It ties at the neck in back. Ginger's coat pattern was enlarged for a new, fuller, longer nightgown pattern. Sleeves can be gathered at the wrists or left plain. Directions for the mob cap are in Chapter 4.

Clown Suits

For 14 to 18in (35.6 to 45.7cm) bears start with Ginger's raincoat pattern and follow the directions for making a nightgown pattern on pages 38 and 39. The only difference is that you do not need the extra length. It is a good idea to make a whole new clown suit top pattern instead of actually using your nightgown pattern so there will not be any confusion between the two.

Clown trousers are made from Ginger's trousers with 2in (5.1cm) more added to the outseam fold edge. They may need extra length added to fit your bear. Use elastic at the ankles and either elastic or drawstring at the waist.

For smaller Teddy Bears use the appropriate trousers, and jacket or shirt pattern and add extra width at trousers side, at center back and front of jacket, and at center of sleeve. Check your bear for the proper length.

The neck ruff shown on Basic Bear's costume in *Color Illustration 9* requires a strip of fabric 49in (124.4cm) long by 3½in (8.9cm) wide. Three rows of ribbon of coordinating colors can be added as shown. A ruff can be made of just one contrasting color or of striped cloth. Tulle or nylon net can be made into interesting ruffs as can wide satin ribbon. Pompons on front of top can be made of yarn or just taken from cotton ball fringe. Sometimes pompons are sewn onto the knees or ankles of clown trousers.

Barnum, the circus bear, has his own clown suit pattern which can also be used for the Hanimals.

Angel Robe

Use your nightgown pattern again, adding still more fullness to the body. Leave the sleeves full at the wrists instead of gathering them. Cross a length of Christmas tinsel over the chest and around the sleeves to make it sparkle. A little loop of tinsel can make a halo for this most angelic bear! If you really want to go all the way, make some little wings with Sitting Bear's guardian angel wing pattern and put him under your Christmas tree to wait for Santa. Teddy Bears only need small wings because they are not angelic *all* the time and large wings would not really be in keeping with their mischievous nature. See *Illustration 65*.

Bathrobes and Coats

Cinnamon's pajama top, Ginger's raincoat, Buddy's sleepers top, Cubby's Rough Rider jacket and Benjamin's pajama top can all be used for bathrobes or coats by just simply lengthening them. Although buttons and buttonholes can be used at the front, all that is really needed for the bathrobe is a belt and some little thread belt loops to hold it in place after the front is overlapped.

Since bathrobes come in every imaginable fabric and color, there is no limit to the bathrobes you can create for your bears as shown in *Color Illustration 8*.

Coats follow the same rules of construction as bathrobes except that they do not need as much length added.

When attaching the collar, start at center back and sew around to the front on one side, then repeat on the other side. Use a pleat at center back, like that on Ginger's

raincoat and Cubby's Rough Rider jacket for adjusting these patterns to fit different sizes of bears. What a thrill for a child to have a Teddy Bear with a bathrobe or coat made of the same fabric or color as his own!

Illustration 36. *Any jackets, pajama tops or coats can be lengthened for bathrobes, nightgowns, nightshirts, buntings and other long garments.*

Illustration 37. *Ginger's coat pattern can be decreased in size for smaller bears by taking away width at the underarm sleeve seam and the body side seam as shown. Huggy's dress was made in this manner.*

A little belt can be added across the back, and the front can be extended for a double breasted coat for variations. If you own a cloth bear without fur, you can even make him a fur coat!

The pajama tops, sleeper top and Rough Rider jacket patterns can be used for raincoat patterns, too. See Ginger's raincoat directions for sewing vinyl cloth.

Robe and coat patterns can be decreased in size by taking width away at side and underarm seams as in *Illustration 37*.

Sleepers

Designed to be used for knit cloth the sleeper pattern given with Buddy Bear will fit 13in (33cm) Huggy and 12in (30.5cm) Cubby as well.

By simply raising the buttons on the shirt and making a larger hem at the trousers waist, they can be made to fit smaller bears, too. For Hanimal and Hanimal Baby, cut 1in (2.5cm) off the sleeve length and when you sew the underarm and side seam take 1/2in (1.3cm) allowance instead of 1/4in (0.65cm). For a really nice fit for the smaller bears you can run elastic through the hem across the back of the trousers and make a little drop seat.

No matter what size bear you make these sleepers for, you will need to place the buttons so they fit his own particular size and shape. When deciding where to put the lower button on the shirt back, remember that it serves two functions; first for fastening the shirt and second, for holding up the back trousers. Try the sleepers on your bear and have him sit as well as stand so you can mark where to place the buttons.

For larger 14 to 15in (35.6 to 38.1cm) bears such as Rosie and Ginger, add 2in (5.1cm) to the top of the trousers, 2in (5.1cm) to the bottom of the shirt and 1in (2.5cm) to the sleeves as in *Illustration 38*. Try the sleepers on your bear and mark where the buttons should go.

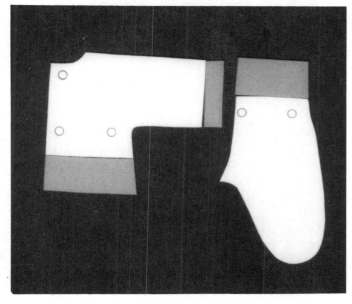

Illustration 38. Buddy's sleeper pattern can be modified for larger bears by adding to the sleeve and shirt length as shown on the left, and by adding to the top of the trousers as at right.

You can make a one-piece sleeper pattern by placing the shirt pattern onto the trousers and taping or pinning them together as in *Illustration 39*. It is important to make the back long enough so measure from your bear's neck, at the back, down his back to the center seam at the crotch where the front and back meet. Make sure the sleepers equal that length at the center back seam.

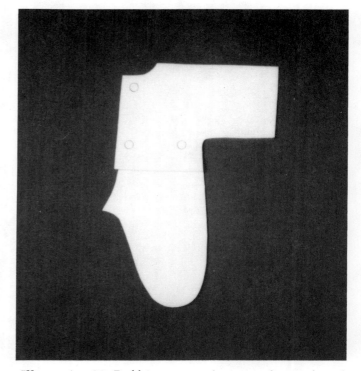

Illustration 39. Buddy's two-piece sleepers can be transformed into one-piece sleepers, long johns or snowsuits by combining the top and bottom as shown and in Color Illustration 10.

For Benjamin you need only to turn his pajama shirt so that it opens in back and tuck it inside the trousers. Add buttons for the sleeper trousers to fasten onto. If you want feet in the trousers, use a *knit cloth* and lengthen them about 2in (5.1cm) at the hem. Make them rounded like those of Buddy Bear's sleepers and, if you want, make a little dart for the foot at the front.

Pajamas

There are patterns for Cinnamon's pajamas as well as for Benjamin's.

For 14 to 15in (35.6 to 38.1cm) bears, use the pattern for Cinnamon's pajama top and cut off 1/2in (1.3cm) at the back center fold edge. Use the front pattern as is. When the pajamas are constructed, the front will overlap more than on the larger bears. Use cotton flannel, printed cottons or silk.

For 12in (30.5cm) bears, use the Rough Rider jacket pattern for a pajama top with the pajama trousers pattern for Buddy.

Buddy's sleepers pattern can be used for pajamas with long shirt and trousers without feet. They can also be used for a coat, robe, dress or overalls as demonstrated in *Illustration 40*.

The Suit

A suit for 14 to 18in (35.6 to 45.7cm) bears can be created with Cinnamon's pajama top pattern plus Ginger's trousers for either short or long pants. A blazer edged with braid is very dapper as is a tennis blazer of bold stripes. A

Illustration 40. Buddy's sleepers can be used for any number of garments such as a blouse or coat from the top or overalls from the bottoms.

navy blue blazer with a fancy gold yacht club patch or family crest can make your bear an elegant fellow indeed!

For a "Little Lord Fauntleroy" look, make the suit of velvet and add a satin and lace blouse. Benjamin's pajama pattern can be used for a frilly blouse, velvet jacket and shorts.

For feminine versions of these suits, use the pajama top pattern with a skirt. A little red or blue school blazer looks chic worn with the plaid kilt.

Baseball Suits

The ever-versatile pajama top pattern for Cinnamon is almost identical to old fashioned baseball shirts (and to some modern ones, too). Make it in the colors of your favorite team and embroider or iron on the name of the team. Ginger's trousers pattern can be shortened for baseball trousers.

Benjamin's pajamas can be fashioned into a baseball suit for him by tucking the shirt inside and shortening the trousers slightly. Any number or team name can be embroidered on the shirt.

Trousers

Trousers patterns are found in Ginger's, Benjamin's and Buddy's patterns. They can be made to fit bear's from 8 to 18in (20.3 to 45.7cm) with only slight adjustments. The Tiny Teddy and Petite Bear families have their own trouser patterns.

Trousers can be shortened for shorts or knee britches. They can be widened at the outseam for full culottes, clown trousers, knickers, bloomers and other full styles. They can become stretch pants and even leotards when width is removed from the outseam, a knit fabric is used, and a strap added to go under the foot.

Overalls need only the addition of a bib given in Cinnamon's patterns. It can be adjusted by simply adding or subtracting from the center fold edge and shortening the lower edge at the waist.

Feet can be added to any trouser at their lower edge to make sleeper bottoms like those in Buddy's patterns. Add a dart in front as shown.

Chapter 6
CLASSIC TEDDY BEARS

These classic Teddy Bears possess characteristics of both new and antique bears — those characteristics with timeless appeal. But what makes a bear desirable year after year? What makes one a classic?

Well, first of all an elegant classic Teddy Bear is usually jointed with sewn-in foot and paw pads. It takes time and effort to construct a bear with movable parts and make everything fit together properly.

Secondly, he is constructed of good quality materials. If one is going to spend more time making a Teddy Bear, that extra time should be made worth the effort.

Thirdly, the best quality bear is well proportioned so that he looks attractive from any angle, sitting or standing. He should possess some characteristics of real bears for after all, he is a toy BEAR.

Next, he is engineered so that he sits well without falling over and stands or lies down in a natural position.

Finally, he is appealing and lovable so that he is capable of touching people, reaching out and making them love him.

Classic bears wear clothes well, especially soft classics like sweaters, scarves, hats, coats of all kinds and pajamas. They can wear anything that humans can so you can let your imagination go!

Classic bears are for children of school age on up to adult collectors, mainly. Pre-schoolers, unless they are exceptional, will rarely care properly for such a fine Teddy Bear. Unless you think you can stand to see your beautiful creation maltreated without wincing, it might be best for you to make a hinged bear for the pre-schooler and save the special classic bear for the older child. On the other hand, being "loved to pieces" may not be the worse fate that can befall a Teddy Bear.

The 6 to 12-year-old crowd dearly love and appreciate these bears as do teenagers, the college crowd and adults of all ages. With prices for old Teddy Bears rising every day, and original ones becoming scarcer, these classic bears can fill a very real need for both young and old collectors.

The following directions for making the jointed bear are to be used also for the Old Timeys, Rosie and Sweetie Pie, Circus Bear, Barnum and for the Petite Bear family.

CUTTING AND SEWING THE JOINTED BEAR

1. Trace your patterns on typing paper or tracing tissue. (Cinnamon's head center pattern had to be given in half because of space but you should trace it so that you have a whole pattern.)

2. *Label each pattern piece fully*, noting not only what part of the bear it is for but what size bear and his name. This may not seem important in the beginning but you will be glad later that everything is clear as to what it is. Also, put on each piece how many you will need. For example, "18in (45.7cm) Classic Bear Cinnamon, Front body, cut 2 facing each other." It is important even if you will be making your bear immediately. If patterns are properly labeled, you can pull them out some dreary day next winter or even years from now and get right to work on a new bear without making a mistake.

3. Draw around the pattern pieces on the *back side* of fur cloth or whatever cloth you are using with a soft pencil or ballpoint pen. Remember to reverse part of your pieces as directed on the patterns. (9in [22.9cm] Benjamin and the Petite bear family should have both the sewing and cutting lines traced on the cloth. See "Constructing Tiny Teddies" page 121, steps 1 through 6.)

4. Mark the body side seams where the joining cords are to come through. Mark also any notches or dots used for matching and fitting pieces together. *Mark a dot on the arms and legs where the cords are to come through the disk center.*

5. BASTE everything together *before* sewing fur cloth or any pile fabric because it slips badly during sewing if you do not. Baste with 1/4in (0.65cm) seams as indicated on patterns. When basting across seams, do not sew them down flat, but leave them standing up so that your machine sewing will be facilitated.

6. Sew the two back pieces together at the center back seam, leaving it open for about 2in (5.1cm) at top. Sew the front center seam. When sewing the back to the front, start at the center of the crotch where the seams meet and go up one side to the neck and then up the other side. Leave *small* openings for the cords as indicated on pattern.

Leave open the tops of the arms and legs for stuffing. When sewing the head, sew the two side pieces together from the neck, up around the nose, to the dot. Next, position the point of the head center piece by pushing your needle through the middle of the dot and then going into the point where the two dots on the side pieces come together. It is a good idea to pin the center piece in place completely before basting so you know it is positioned accurately.

When positioning the foot pad in the foot, pin it at each end at the dots, matching them to the front and back seams. Sometimes the foot needs to be stretched just a bit as you sew it to the pad.

7. After sewing, *clip seams in all the curves and corners* and turn right-side-out.

Joining Cord

The four Classic Bears, the Old Timeys, Circus Bear and the Petite family are all joined in the same manner.

You can use either cord or wire. Cord should be strong cotton cord made up of smaller threads twisted together or a tough woven or braided type. It can have a plastic or waxed coating but should not be all plastic as it will stretch. If you prefer wire, use picture frame wire No. 3 which is, like cord, made up of a number of small wires twisted together. You will need a small wire snips for cutting it. For the demonstration we will use cotton cord for joining, except for *Illustration 45*.

Use two cords for miniature to 11in (27.9cm) bears, six cords for medium-sized 12 to 15in (30.5 to 38.1cm) bears and eight for 18in (45.7cm) Cinnamon.

Joining Disks

There are several different types of disks you can use for joining. Fender washers, which can be found at most hardware stores, large coat buttons with either two or four holes, wooden disks and laminated cardboard disks you can make yourself. See *Illustration 42*. For this demonstration we will use cardboard disks because they are both easy to make and easy to work with.

Cardboard disks should be made of two or three-ply board which can be cut with scissors. Use the disk indication on the pattern for size. Each bear requires eight disks. Each disk should be made of at least four layers of cardboard.

You can just find a spool, jar top, or bottle cap approximately the size of the disk you want and quickly draw around it, over and over again until you have the required number. Then get comfortable with an old pair of scissors and cut them all out. They do not have to be perfect so you can cut them out quickly.

After all are cut, glue them together, four layers each, with white liquid glue and press them till dry with a large book or board.

When dry, take a large nail and hammer and make two holes in each disk about 1/4in (0.65cm) apart. Do this over a block of wood or a vise so the nail can go all the way through the disk. Use any cardboard from the backs of school tablets to those that come from the laundry.

You also can go to your nearest frame shop and buy a sheet of two-ply board that is acid-free. Do not ask for matte board which is too thick to cut comfortably with scissors; ask for a thinner board used for mounting. You can make your Teddy Bear with the satisfaction that his joints will last for decades to come without causing any deterioration of the fur as corroded metal or acid containing board might after many years.

Unless you intend your bear to last for your grand-

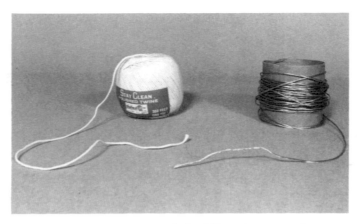

Illustration 41. *Joining cord should be a firm, twisted cotton twine. Twisted picture frame wire, about a No. 3, can be used also. Use twisted and not braided wire as the braided wire has a tendency to stretch.*

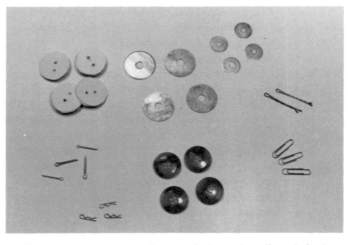

Illustration 42. *Joining disks can be layered cardboard, fender washers or large coat buttons. Joining clips can be cotter pins, button clips (for small bears), bobby pins or metal paper clips or wooden match stems.*

children, however, this should not be of great concern.

Cardboard disks are not only the easiest to work with but they also have one particular advantage that other disks do not have. You can put a few dots of white liquid glue on them on the side that presses against the fur cloth to stabilize them. This is especially important for those *inside the bear's body* because they will keep the cords from ever drooping or enlarging the holes. Be sure not to let the glue touch the cords. Cardboard disks work equally well with cord or picture frame wire.

Joining Clips or Dowels

A clip of some kind is needed for securing the cords as well as for strengthening the disk center by distributing the force.

Wooden kitchen match stems or small dowels will be used for the demonstration because they can be glued in place. Cotter pins from the hardware store, bobby pins, heavy metal paper clips and button clips work equally well.

If bobby pins are used, bend the ends so they do not extend past the disk's edges.

ASSEMBLING THE JOINTED BEAR

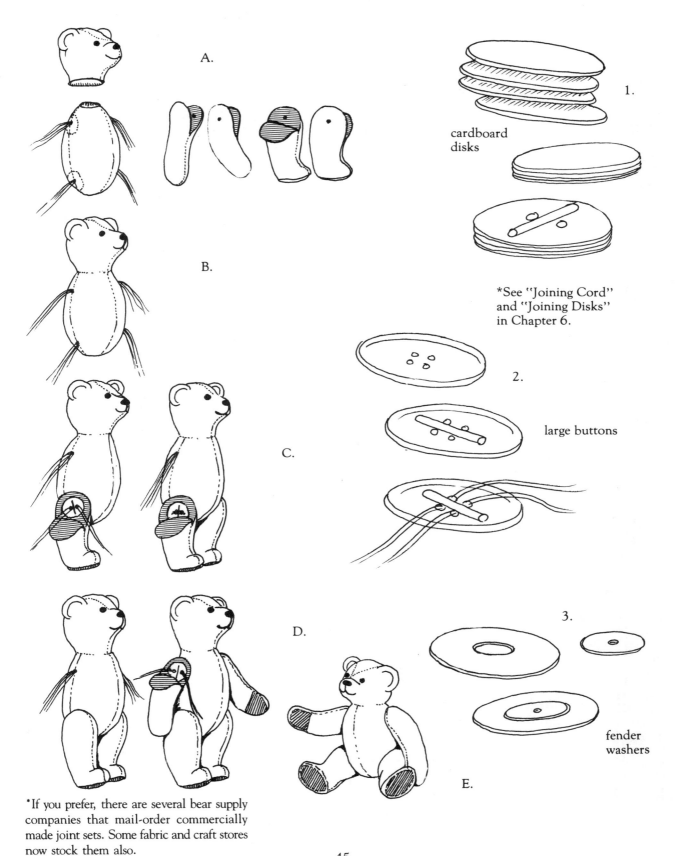

A.

B.

C.

D.

E.

1.

cardboard
disks

*See "Joining Cord"
and "Joining Disks"
in Chapter 6.

2.

large buttons

3.

fender
washers

*If you prefer, there are several bear supply
companies that mail-order commercially
made joint sets. Some fabric and craft stores
now stock them also.

STUFFING AND ASSEMBLING YOUR JOINTED BEAR

For best results, use a polyester filling. A slender dowel for pushing the filling into the bear will be a great help but you can use a new, *unsharpened* pencil if you do not have a dowel.

1. If you want your bear's feet to be flat on the bottom, cut two layers of cardboard for inside each foot. Use the foot pad pattern, cutting on the inner or *sewing* line instead of the outer line. Glue two layers together and place them into the foot, making sure the seams are pulled up out of the way. Stuff the feet firmly. Stuff the legs about two-thirds of the way up and leave them open at the top. Most of the bears in this book do not have stiffening in their feet. It is just a matter of personal preference.

2. Stuff the paws *lightly*, then fill the arms firmly up two-thirds of the way and leave them open at the top also.

3. Stuff the lower body *firmly* with polyester filling, bringing it up to a little above the small openings left for the leg joining cords.

4. Place your cords inside the body going through the cardboard disks and out through the leg holes as shown in step A on page 45. Put a few dots of glue on the *outer* side of each disk (next to the fur cloth) and press it against the cloth.

Finish filling the body *firmly* up to the arms and repeat for the arm cords and disks. Fill the body up to the neck opening and then stitch up the center back seam which was left open a couple of inches to facilitate stuffing. Tie or take a safety pin and fasten cords to the body to keep them out of your way as in *Illustration 44*. This also keeps them from accidentally being pulled out.

Illustration 43. Cords should be put through the body and the disks during stuffing, then the head sewn on.

5. Stuff the head firmly, filling out snout and cheeks fully. Turn under the bottom edge and baste a small hem. Leave the face blank or go ahead and create the face at this point. You will notice by now that the opening at the top of the body is smaller than the neck opening at the base of the head. You have not made a mistake — it was designed that way! The head should fit *out beyond* the body opening. It gives you leeway to position the head in one of many possible attitudes.

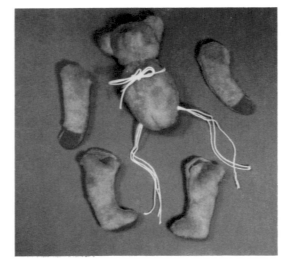

Illustration 44. A bear with the head sewn on and the legs ready to be attached. The arm cords should be tied or pinned out of the way until needed to prevent being accidentally pulled out.

With three or four *large* pins experiment with various head positions. If you want the head to look down, turn more hem under in front; if you want him to look up, turn more under at the back. The head can also be made to tilt to either side in the same way. Not only can you tilt it, but you can turn or pivot the head making your bear look to the side. When you practice a bit, you will find that you can both turn and tilt the head at the same time. The "looks" and the personality of your bear will begin to emerge at this point. He will help you make some of the decisions concerning his true character. When you decide the time is right to sew on the head, use a *large* needle and four strands of sewing thread. Sew with a blind stitch, going sideways into the neck, then a horizontal stitch in the body, then again in the neck and so on. When you have sewn about three-quarters of the way around, stop and push some extra filling into the neck to make the head stand up firmly unless, of course, you prefer it a bit floppy. Finish sewing around the neck. Pull your thread firmly after every two or three stitches. Go around at least one more time to insure that the head is attached securely as in step B.

6. Punch a *small* hole in one leg at the dot where the cord is to go through. Use a crochet hook to pull the cords through the hole; then divide the cords pulling half through one disk hole and the other half through the other hole. (Be sure you have the foot facing forward.) Tie the cords with square knots over the match stem or dowel as in step C.

7. Pull the cords at the bear's other side. Test them, by pulling hard, to see if they are fastened well. Next, pull them through the other leg and disk as you did the first as in step C, right. When you are ready to tie the cords, it will help on your first bear if someone can assist you for a few moments.

Squeeze the bear's body by pressing the leg disks on each side — *hard enough to compress the stuffing inside.* Have someone pull the cords *tightly* and tie them over the match stem and disk. You will learn to do this without assistance as you make more bears.

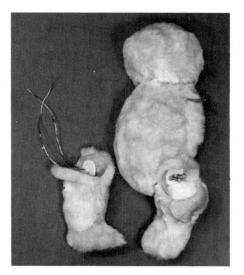

Illustration 45. *A bear with the legs being joined with picture frame wire and cardboard disks.*

8. Add filling to the top of the legs and whip or blind stitch them closed. Just before you close the leg completely, push a last bit of stuffing in to fill out the form, step D, left.

Your stitches can be made virtually invisible by picking the fur pile caught in the seam with a large pin or needle and freeing it so that it stands up again. You can do this to the seams on the tummy and face, also, to make them less noticeable.

9. Fasten the arms in the same manner as the legs, step D, right. Complete their stuffing and blind stitch them closed.

10. Your finished jointed Teddy Bear as in step E.

Note: If you, by chance, made the legs or arms too loosely joined, there are two simple remedies. First, if they are only slightly loose, try just placing your thumbs on the bears tummy and your fingers on his rump and gently squeeze. This usually makes the legs move as they should. For the arms, squeeze his chest in the same manner.

The second remedy for more serious problems is to open the bear's center back seam 1 or 2in (2.5 or 5.1cm) and, with a dowel, push in more stuffing at the lower body to tighten the leg cords, the upper body to tighten the arm cords. Whip stitch the hole closed.

THE BEARS
CINNAMON (18in [45.7cm])

Cinnamon is the largest of the classic jointed bears. Since a quality commercially-made bear this large is usually quite expensive, you will feel a special pride in making him.

Illustration 46. *A bear with his limbs joined. His arms are completed; his legs are joined and need only to be sewn closed at the top. More stuffing will be added during closing.*

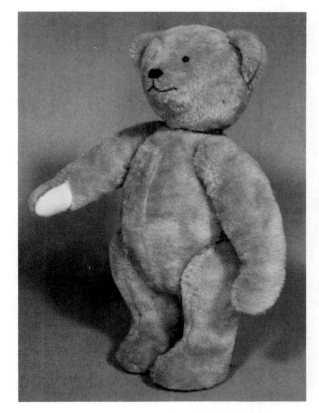

Illustration 47. *Cinnamon with small black shoe-button eyes, a felt nose and suede cloth paws is made of 3/8in (0.9cm) pile fur cloth. A classic bear in every way!*

CINNAMON

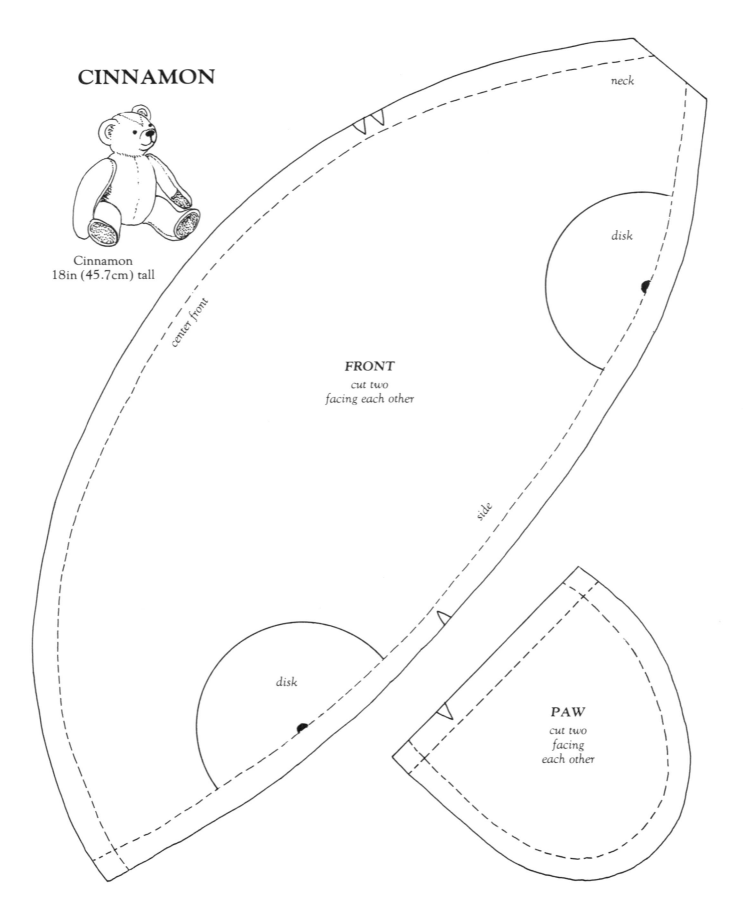

Cinnamon
18in (45.7cm) tall

neck

disk

center front

FRONT
*cut two
facing each other*

side

disk

PAW
*cut two
facing
each other*

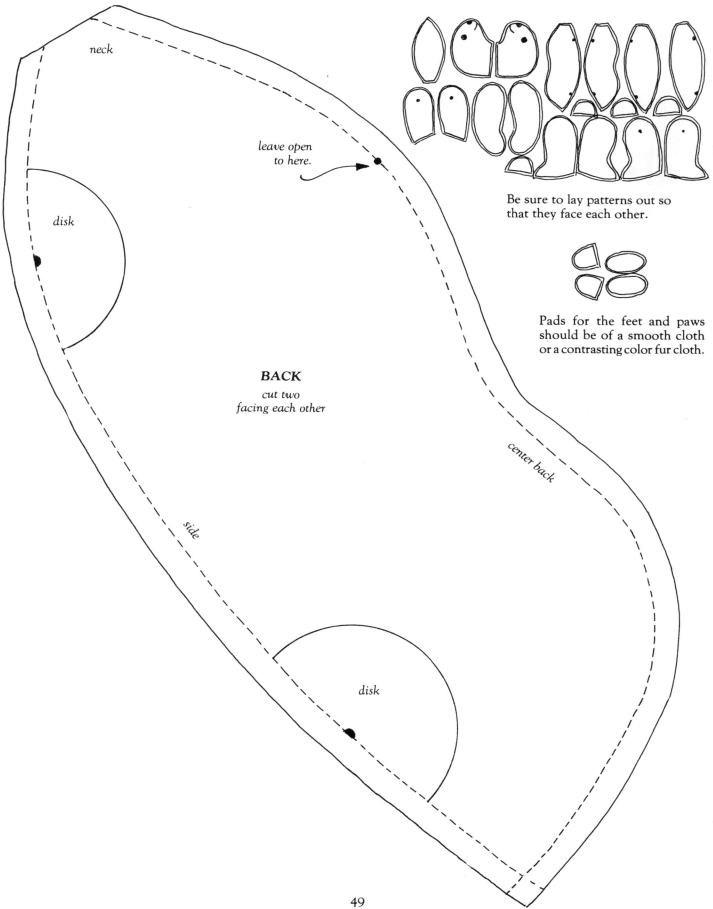

CINNAMON

Be sure to lay patterns out so that they face each other.

Pads for the feet and paws should be of a smooth cloth or a contrasting color fur cloth.

neck

leave open to here.

disk

BACK
cut two
facing each other

center back

side

disk

49

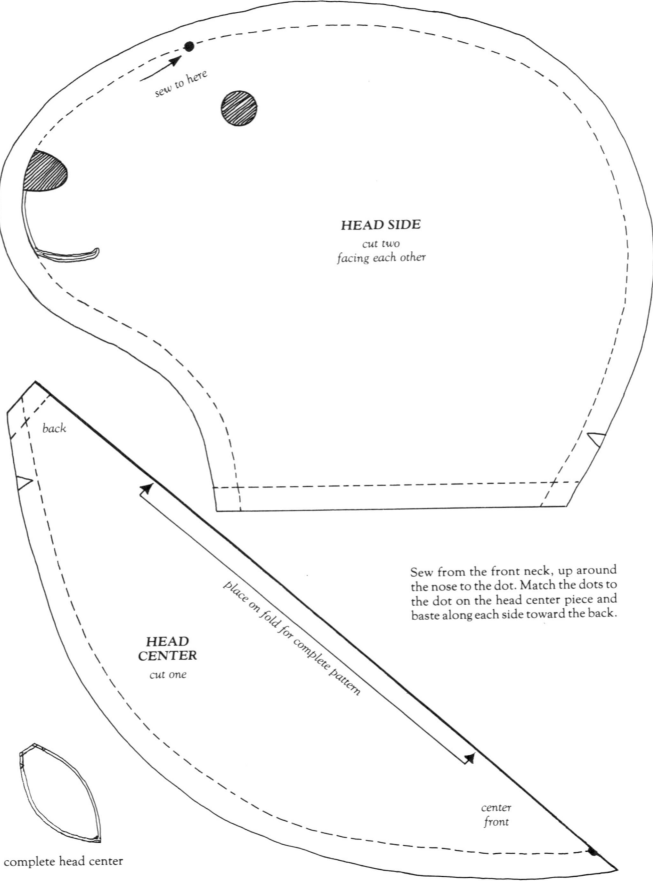

CINNAMON

HEAD SIDE

cut two
facing each other

sew to here

back

Sew from the front neck, up around the nose to the dot. Match the dots to the dot on the head center piece and baste along each side toward the back.

place on fold for complete pattern

HEAD CENTER

cut one

center front

complete head center

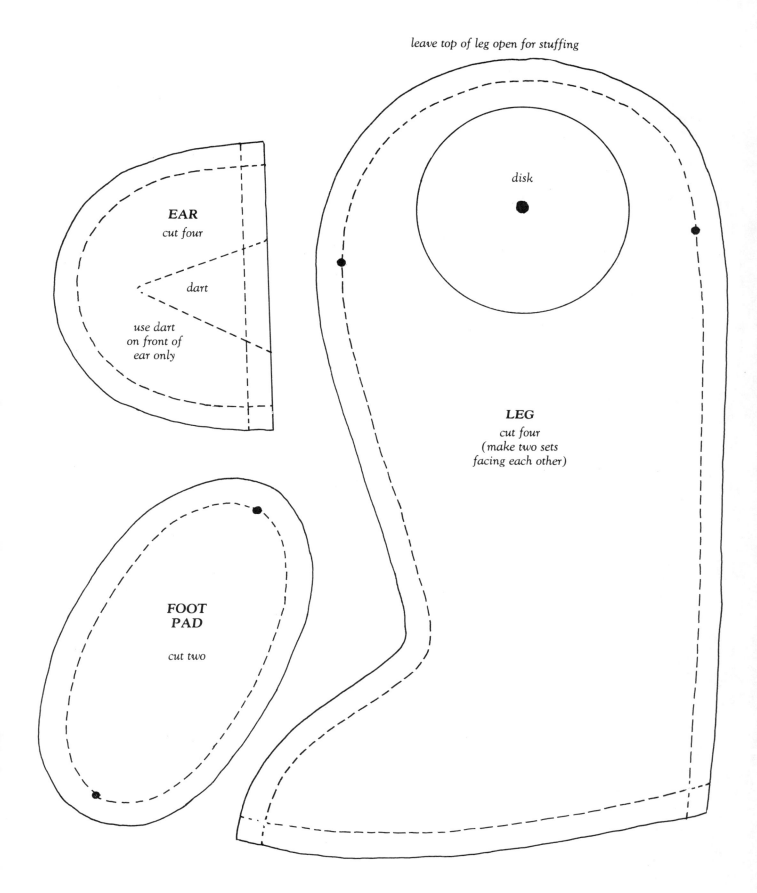

leave top of leg open for stuffing

EAR
cut four

dart

*use dart
on front of
ear only*

disk

LEG

*cut four
(make two sets
facing each other)*

**FOOT
PAD**

cut two

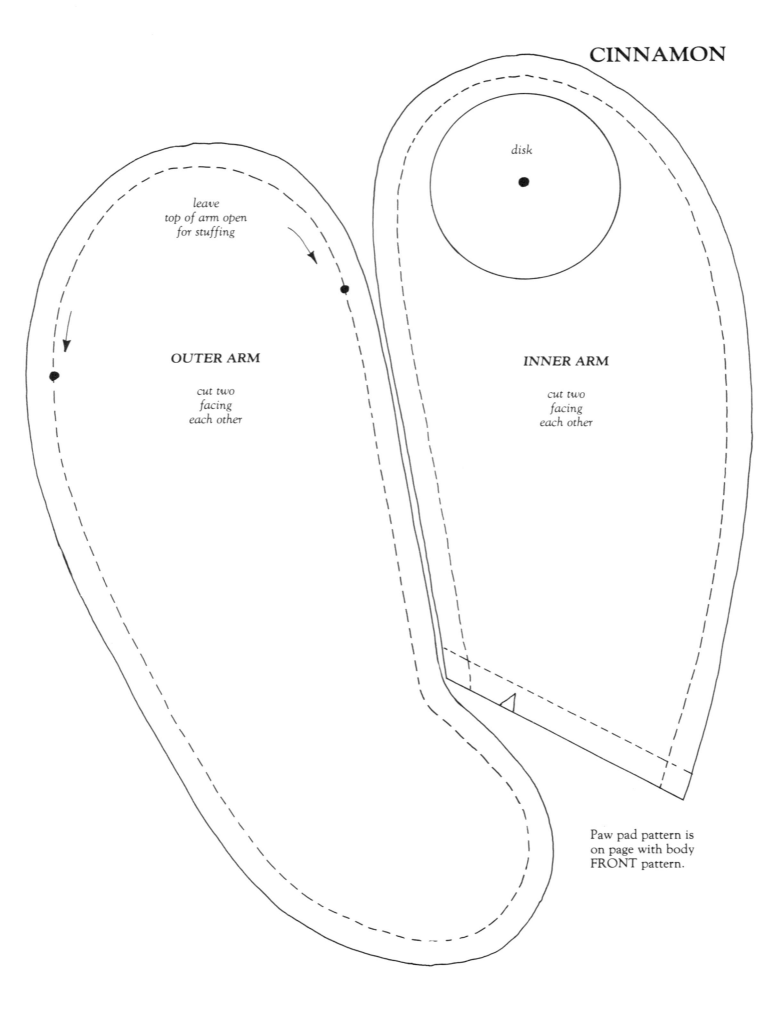

CINNAMON

*leave
top of arm open
for stuffing*

OUTER ARM

*cut two
facing
each other*

disk

INNER ARM

*cut two
facing
each other*

Paw pad pattern is
on page with body
FRONT pattern.

CINNAMON'S CLOTHES

Pajamas

The pattern for Cinnamon's pajama trousers is with Ginger's patterns. Follow directions on pattern concerning size.

The shirt pattern is for both the front and back as well as for front and back facings. For pajamas use the curved front pattern and its curved facings as diagrammed. The back and back facing should be cut on the fold as indicated.

You may have other Teddy Bears in your collection that you wish to use this pattern for. Adjustments can easily be made by making a pleat at the back like that on Ginger's coat or Cubby's Rough Rider jacket.

An aqua and pink cotton flannel was used for these classic little pajamas with pink bias tape edging and decorative frog closings. The tape was sewn into three loops for a simplified frog as shown in *Color Illustration 3*. For the "Teddy Bear collector who has everything" — make them of silk and purchase elegant ready-made frog closings.

Overalls

Use the bib pattern with Ginger's trousers. Make straps about 12in (30.5cm) by 1½in (3.8cm), fold over and sew. Use buttons for fastening the straps in front or use overall fasteners or gripper snaps. If you want a kerchief pocket for either the front or back, make it 2½in (6.4cm) by 2½in (6.4cm) and turn under 1/4in (0.65cm) all around.

Slender bears may need elastic at the back waist or a little button at the back seam. Fatter bears may fill them out nicely.

Cinnamon's T-shirt, made with the sweater pattern, was made of an old wool shirt with rows of ABC's in shades of browns, reds and creams.

Illustration 49. Cinnamon in an alphabet patterned T-shirt worn on the outside of his overalls for a modern little boy look. Anne Rogers Collection.

Illustration 48. Cinnamon in an old fashioned blouse, red cravat and overalls. The blouse was made from his pajama shirt pattern with extra width added to the sleeves so they could be gathered. Anne Rogers Collection.

Illustration 50. Cinnamon is a dashing Scotsman in his kilt, tartan and tam — of Royal Stewart plaid, of course. A costume jewelry pin holds his tartan at the shoulder and he sports a little red fur sporran. He is made of a 1/2in (1.3cm) pile white fur cloth. Cubby, beside him, is snug and warm in his ski sweater and cap made from a leg warmer, as in Illustration 21.

Illustration 51. A white Cinnamon models his blue sailor suit with red and white striped vestee across the neck and an anchor on the sleeve. His middy was fashioned from his pajama shirt, his sailor hat made from Ginger's hat pattern.

Kilt, Tartan and Tam

Use directions for the pleated skirt in Chapter 5, "Making Your Patterns" and add a tartan scarf to match, as in *Illustration 50.* Cinnamon's kilt is of a Royal Stewart tartan with a little red fur cloth sporran fastened with a chain. He always carries three pennies in it.

His tartan scarf is fastened together at the shoulder with a costume jewelry pin, but a fancy button will do as well. To keep the scarf from sliding off the shoulder there is a small safety pin at the kilt waistband on the opposite side to hold it in place. The scarf should be 5in (12.7cm) by 30in (76.2cm), hemmed at the sides, and fringed on the ends.

For tam, see *Hats* in Chapter 4.

Sailor Suit

The very versatile pajama pattern, with a sailor collar added, was used for Cinnamon's sailor suit. Ginger's rain hat pattern makes a sailor hat for 18in (45.7cm) bears. Red or white were as popular in 1906 for children's sailor suits as was blue.

If you want to make an old fashioned middy for your bear, extend the sleeve width, as demonstrated in *Illustration 31* and add gathers at the shoulder. Make a little cuff to catch the fullness at the wrists and add a pocket to hold a whistle. The pocket should be 2½in (6.4cm) by 2½in (6.4cm); turn under 1/4in (0.65cm).

For a feminine version, use the middy with either a matching or white pleated skirt.

Sweater

Cinnamon's sweater in *Color Illustration 1* was made from a new white adult sweater with lavender Teddy Bears

continued on page 60

Illustration 52. A thick beige fur Cinnamon with brown suede cloth paws shows off her cheerleader outfit consisting of a white pleated skirt and baby blue sweater. The "T" stands for Teddy University. Allison Smith Collection.

Illustration 53. Cinnamon loves to make gingerbread men and ginger bears for little Benjamin. His apron is bright yellow with red calico edging and BEAR in red iron-on letters in front. Benjamin wears a little gingham apron to keep his sweater clean as he helps Cinnamon. Both apron patterns are in Basic Bear's patterns, Chapter 7. Benjamin, Frances Bayer Collection.

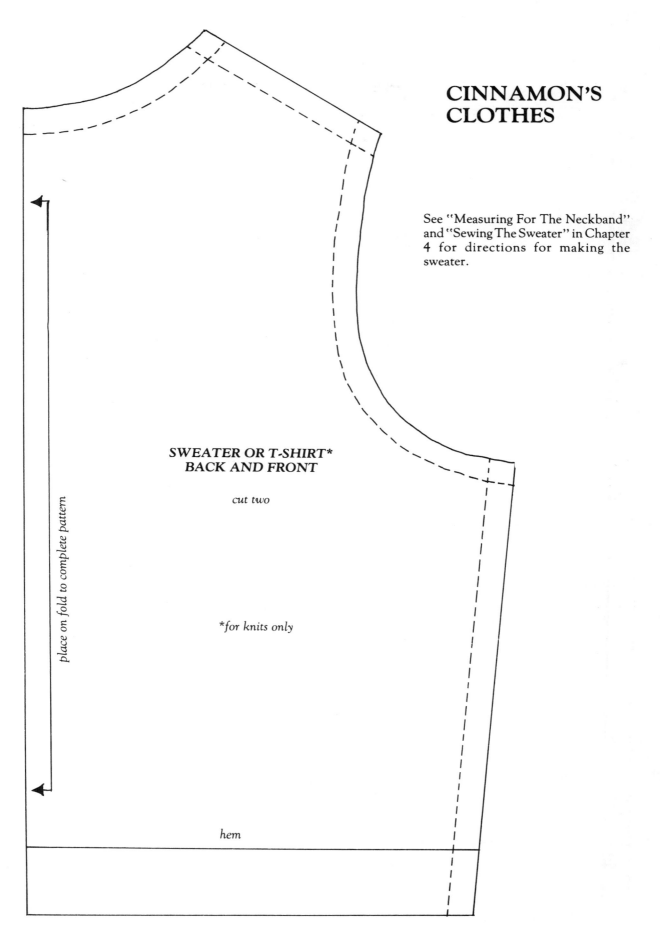

CINNAMON'S CLOTHES

See "Measuring For The Neckband" and "Sewing The Sweater" in Chapter 4 for directions for making the sweater.

SWEATER OR T-SHIRT*
BACK AND FRONT

cut two

*for knits only

place on fold to complete pattern

hem

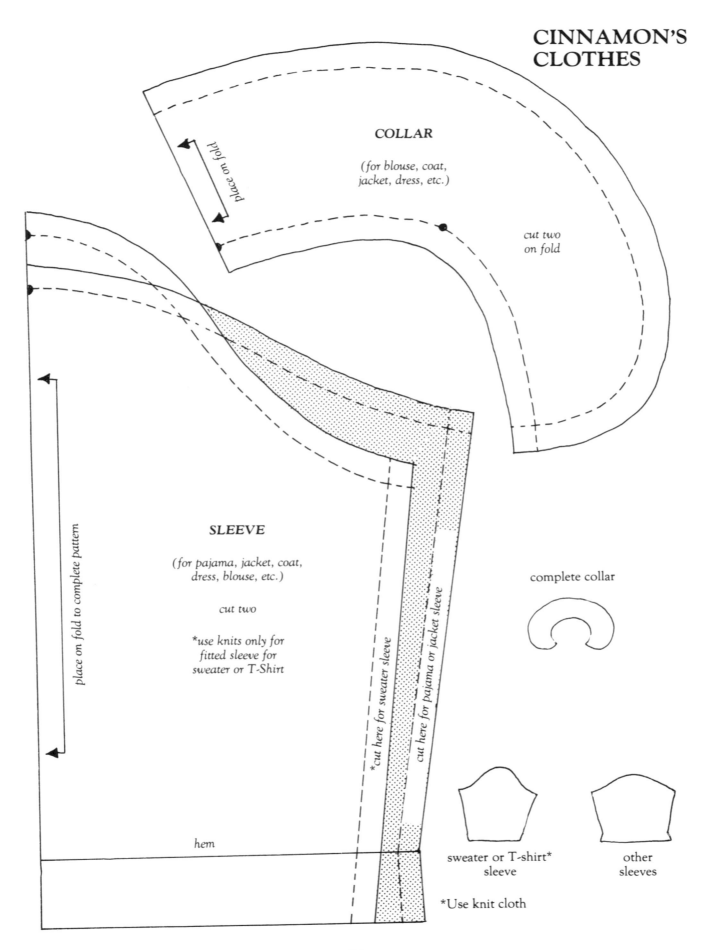

CINNAMON'S CLOTHES

COLLAR

(for blouse, coat, jacket, dress, etc.)

place on fold

cut two
on fold

complete collar

SLEEVE

(for pajama, jacket, coat, dress, blouse, etc.)

cut two

*use knits only for
fitted sleeve for
sweater or T-Shirt

place on fold to complete pattern

*cut here for sweater sleeve

cut here for pajama or jacket sleeve

hem

sweater or T-shirt*
sleeve

other
sleeves

*Use knit cloth

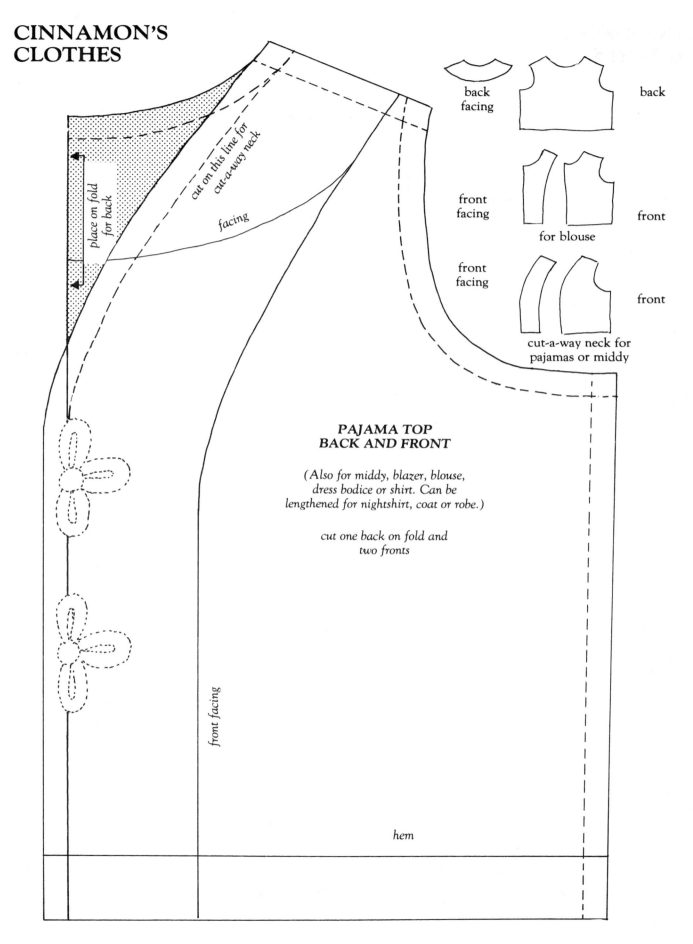

CINNAMON'S CLOTHES

back facing

back

front facing

front

for blouse

front facing

front

cut-a-way neck for
pajamas or middy

place on fold
for back

cut on this line for
cut-a-way neck

facing

PAJAMA TOP
BACK AND FRONT

*(Also for middy, blazer, blouse,
dress bodice or shirt. Can be
lengthened for nightshirt, coat or robe.)*

*cut one back on fold and
two fronts*

front facing

hem

CINNAMON'S CLOTHES

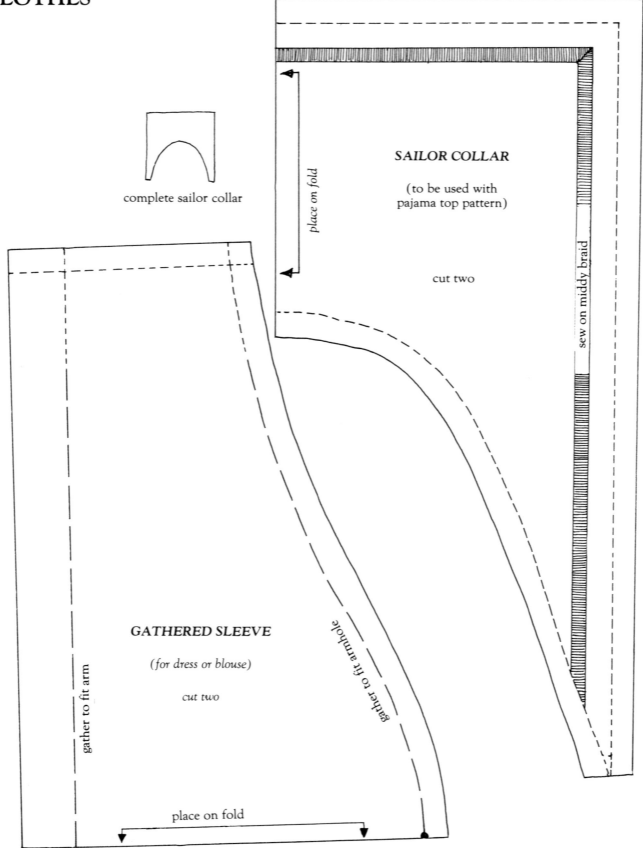

complete sailor collar

SAILOR COLLAR

(to be used with
pajama top pattern)

cut two

place on fold

sew on middy braid

GATHERED SLEEVE

(for dress or blouse)

cut two

gather to fit arm

gather to fit armhole

place on fold

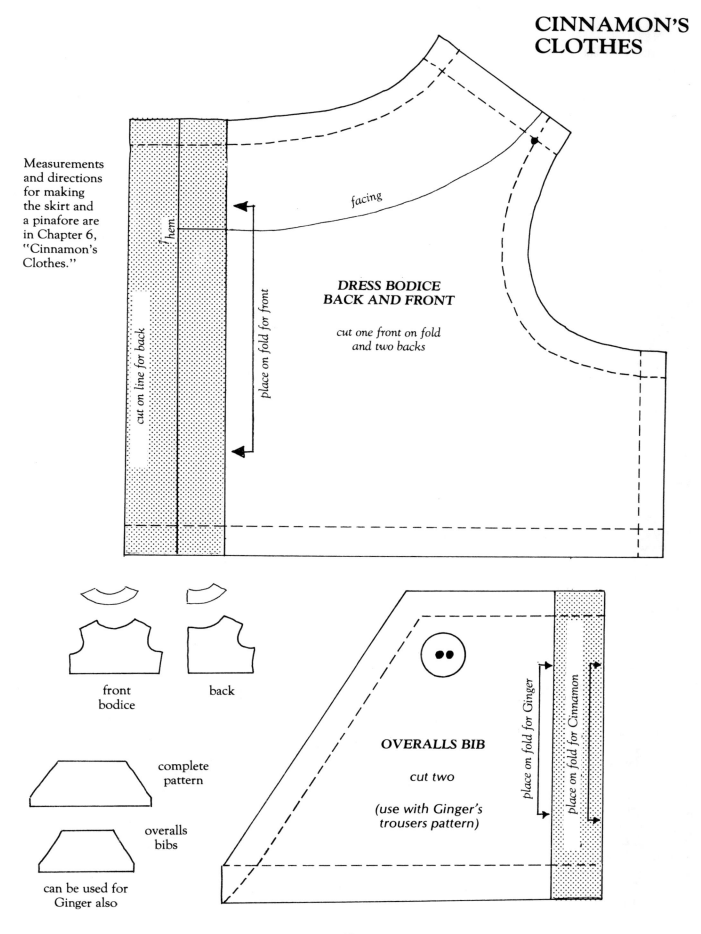

Measurements and directions for making the skirt and a pinafore are in Chapter 6, "Cinnamon's Clothes."

cut on line for back

hem.

facing

place on fold for front

DRESS BODICE BACK AND FRONT

cut one front on fold and two backs

front bodice

back

complete pattern

overalls bibs

can be used for Ginger also

OVERALLS BIB

cut two

(use with Ginger's trousers pattern)

place on fold for Ginger

place on fold for Cinnamom

across the chest and around the sleeves. (See *Sweaters* in Chapter 4 for directions for making it.) The original adult size sweater is shown in *Illustration 12* at center back. Since the Teddy Bear designs were high on the body of the sweater, Cinnamon's little garment had to be cut without ribbing. Ribbing from the same sweater was later added to both the bottom and sleeves.

Cheerleader Outfit

Use the pleated skirt directions given in Chapter 5, "Making Your Patterns." Sweater directions are in Chapter 4.

The fun of making a cheerleader outfit is, of course, that you can make it in the colors of your favorite school with the school letter on front. Cut the letter out of felt. You can cut a fat letter with a slender letter glued or sewn on top to give an outline like professional letters or just use one. If you cannot draw the letter freehand, there are letter stencils you can buy at most discount stores. It should be about 2½ to 3½in (6.4 to 8.9cm) high.

Pompons can be made of 1/4in (0.65cm) wide strips of tissue or crepe paper attached to small dowels.

For a really spectacular cheerleader outfit, you might top it all off with real baby tennis shoes or saddle oxfords from your local discount or department store. Cinnamon wears a size 1 but you should take your bear with you to try them on when you go.

Dress

Use the bodice and dress sleeve from Cinnamon's own patterns. The skirt should be about 8½in (21.6cm) by 40in (101.6cm). Gather it onto the bodice. For the neckline, use either the collar or a self ruffle about 12in (30.5cm) by 2in (5.1cm). For best results, it should be cut on the bias and folded double. Lace 1/2 to 1in (1.3 to 2.5cm) wide can be used instead, if you prefer, and a band of matching lace around the skirt hem is charming, too. Cinnamon's dress can be seen in *Color Illustration 2*.

Pinafore

Use white eyelet batiste, cotton broadcloth or any plain white fabric. Printed batiste with dainty little patterns works well, too.

The skirt should be about 7in (17.8cm) by 40in (101.6cm) with the waistband/sash about 2in (5.1cm) by 45in (114.3cm). Visually divide the 45in (114.3cm) waistband into three sections of 15in (38.1cm) each and make a mark at each point. Gather and attach the skirt to the middle 15in (38.1cm) section, leaving a 15in (38.1cm) sash at each end for tying.

For the bib, cut a rectangle of cloth 5in (12.7cm) high by 3in (7.6cm) wide. Fold this over making a bib 3in (7.6cm) wide and 2½in (6.4cm) high. Cut two straps, each about 10in (25.4cm) long by 1¼in (3.2cm) wide; fold over and sew. Sew the straps to the sides of the bib rectangle and then attach the whole thing to the center of the waistband by placing it behind the band and topstitching across it. It can be whip stitched from behind, if you prefer. The straps can be used plain or with ruffles added. About 1½yd (137cm) of eyelet ruffling or self ruffles is required. Graduate the ruffle in toward the waist on the front as in *Color Illustration 2*. Attach the ends of the straps in back to fit your bear and tie it on over a bright colored dress.

A plain little apron bib with button-on straps can be made from the overalls bib pattern. This can be used for a sundress also.

Other Clothes

Other clothes can be created from these basic patterns. A nightshirt can be made from the pajama shirt pattern, as can a bathrobe. All kinds of blouses as well as a little blazer or suit jacket will go with either skirt or trousers. They can be adjusted to fit bears you already have. See Chapter 5 for directions for drafting your own new patterns from these basic outfits.

Cinnamon can also wear some newborn size baby clothes if the sleeves and legs are made shorter. He can wear Basic Bear's clothes, too, as in *Illustration 53*.

GINGER

Being one of the larger bears, yet small enough to be easy to sew clothes for, makes Ginger a very popular and versatile size.

He has large glass eyes instead of buttons as described in Chapter 2, "Your Bear's Face."

Illustration 54. *Ginger of a 1/2in (1.3cm) cream fur cloth with embroidered nose, large glass animal eyes and suede cloth paws —personality plus!*

60

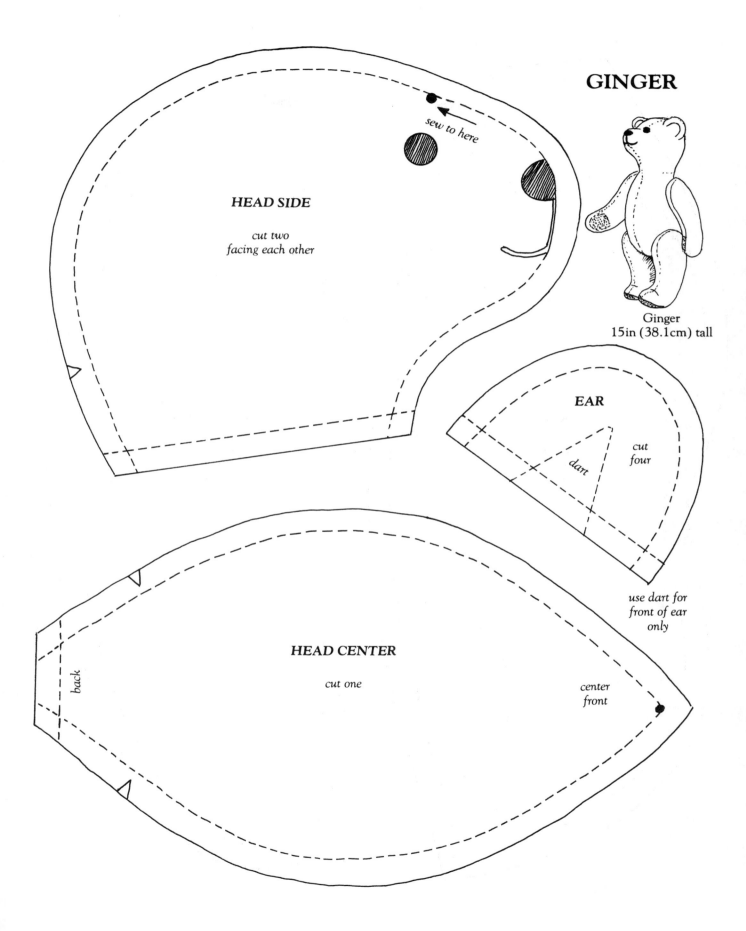

GINGER

HEAD SIDE

cut two
facing each other

sew to here

Ginger
15in (38.1cm) tall

EAR

dart

cut
four

use dart for
front of ear
only

HEAD CENTER

cut one

back

center
front

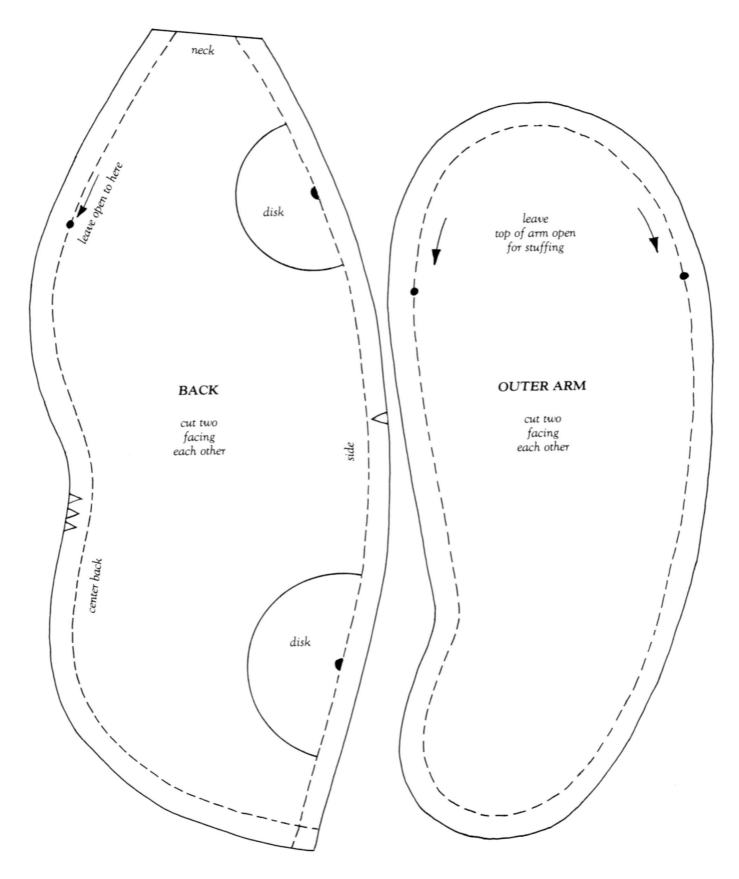

neck

leave open to here

disk

BACK

*cut two
facing
each other*

side

center back

disk

*leave
top of arm open
for stuffing*

OUTER ARM

*cut two
facing
each other*

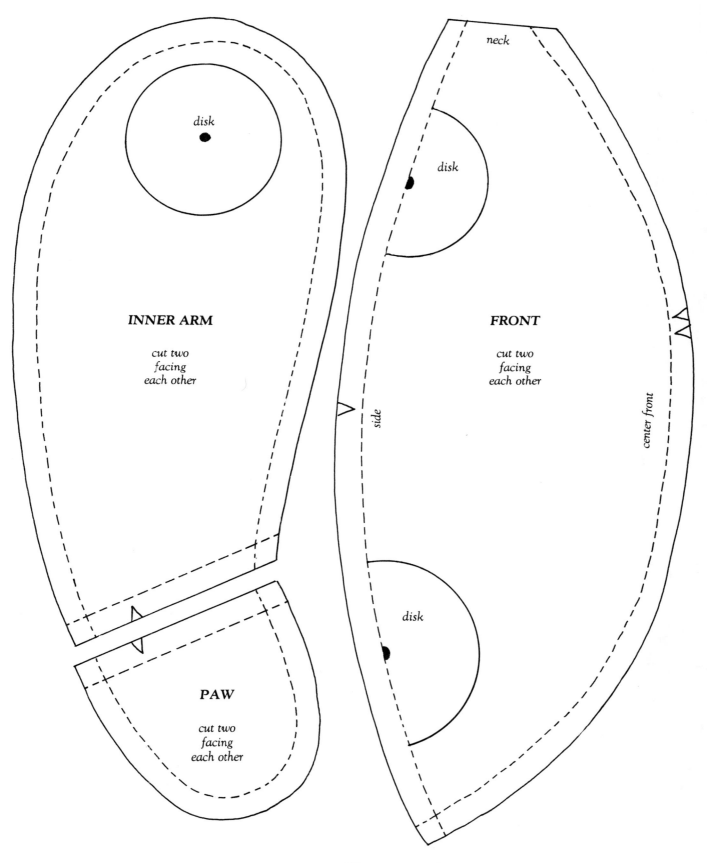

disk

INNER ARM

*cut two
facing
each other*

PAW

*cut two
facing
each other*

neck

disk

FRONT

*cut two
facing
each other*

side

center front

disk

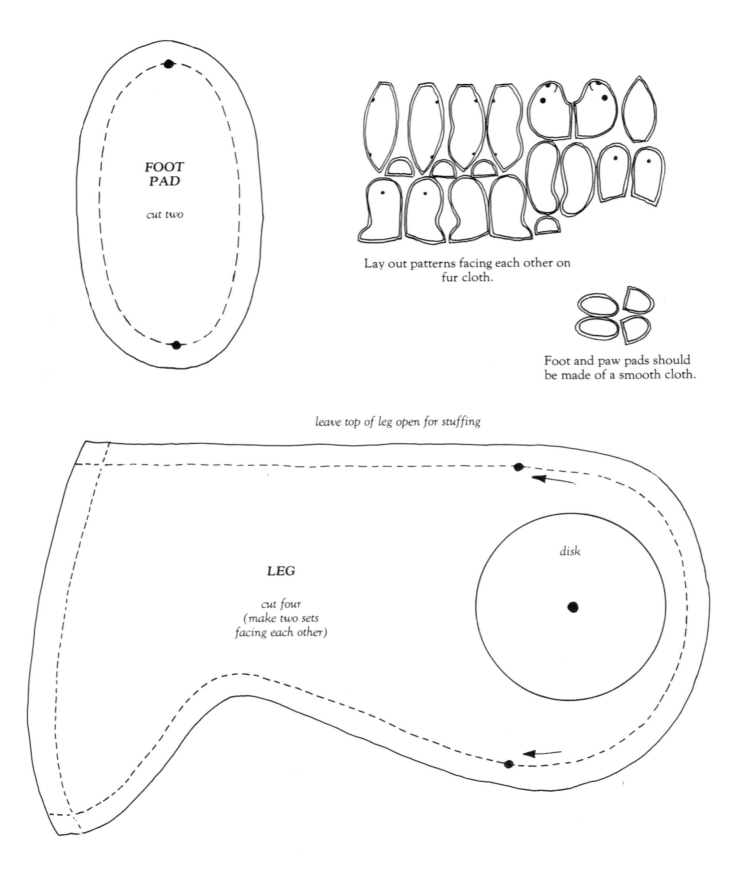

FOOT PAD

cut two

Lay out patterns facing each other on fur cloth.

Foot and paw pads should be made of a smooth cloth.

leave top of leg open for stuffing

LEG

*cut four
(make two sets
facing each other)*

disk

GINGER'S CLOTHES

Sweater

Ginger's sweater in *Color Illustration 4* was made from a new pair of adult size knee socks with little heart designs. For this size bear, both socks must be cut down the center back and opened out as shown in *Illustration 23*. A cap was made from the foot of one of the socks, the neck and sleeve bands from the other foot. A pompon of coordinating yarns tops off a very classy sweater and cap set. Directions for making Teddy Bear sweaters are in Chapter 4.

Another Ginger sweater, modeled in *Illustration 55*, was cut from a white adult-size sweater. A tri-color knit binding at the V-neck makes a charming tennis sweater.

Cardigan

The adult size argyle knee socks used for this argyle bear sweater were also cut down the center back and opened up as demonstrated in *Illustration 23*. This size sweater requires a *pair* of socks.

After the sweater back and front were sewn together, the front was cut down its center with coordinating binding used to cover the cut edges.

Overalls

Brushed blue denim was used for overalls made from Cinnamon's bib pattern plus Ginger's trousers, *Illustration 56*. Straps should be about 11in (27.9cm) by 1½in (3.8cm)

RIGHT: Illustration 55. *A honey-colored Ginger (left) models his white tennis sweater with tri-color braid at its V-neck and a jaunty white cotton hat. At right, Ginger shows off an argyle cardigan made from a pair of adult-size knee socks.*

BOTTOM: Illustration 56. *A feminine Ginger, left, is the perfect hostess in her ruffled, flowered apron (made from Basic Bear's pattern). At right, Ginger sports overalls and a plaid shirt made from Cinnamon's pajama shirt pattern.*

folded double. Ginger sports a Rob Roy plaid cotton flannel shirt made from Cinnamon's pajama shirt pattern.

Teddy Bear outfits of 1906, consisting of large collared blouses and overalls, were labeled "Little Farmer Suits." A large bow was usually tied at the neck. Such a blouse can be fashioned from the raincoat pattern, shortened a bit.

Raincoat or Coat

Ginger's raincoat, shown in *Color Illustration 5*, was fashioned from a newly purchased shower curtain valance of yellow vinyl. The buttons are brown Teddy Bears!

When sewing plastic material use a *large* size stitch on your sewing machine because if the stitches are too close together, they will cut the plastic. Everything was machine-sewn on the coat except the buttonholes which work best when done by hand. Make pockets 2½in (6.4cm) square and turn under 1/4in (0.65cm) all around for hem and seams.

If you have a cloth, preferrably knit, that matches the vinyl, it makes a really good facing for the front and the underside of the collar.

Clear plastic can be used over a print or plain cotton cloth. Be sure the plastic or vinyl cloth is soft but heavy enough to withstand sewing.

This little ragland sleeve coat pattern is charming made up in wool for a car coat, or a dressy coat for girl or boy bears. It can be velvet with a fur collar or tweed with a velvet collar. It makes up well in plaid or checks, too.

The little pleat at the back of the neck can always be used to adjust the size to fit whatever bear you are sewing for.

So'wester Rainhat

Made of yellow shower curtain vinyl, the hat matches the raincoat. For directions for constructing it, see HATS in Chapter 4.

Apron

See Chapter 4, "General Directions For Clothes" for directions for Ginger's apron shown in *Illustration 56*. It is made of a cream colored print with tiny red and pink roses. The most feminine of all the aprons, it has a ruffle around the skirt.

If your bear needs a chef cap, see Chapter 4 under "Hats."

Nightgown

With some simple modifications, the raincoat pattern becomes a nightgown pattern as described in Chapter 5, "Making Your Own Patterns." The nightcap or mob cap is described in Chapter 4.

Ginger's nightgown in *Color Illustration 11* is being worn by Old Timey Rosie who has taken it over as her own. It is made of batiste printed with Teddy Bears holding pink and green balloons. The buttons are pink hearts from the baby button section of a fabric store.

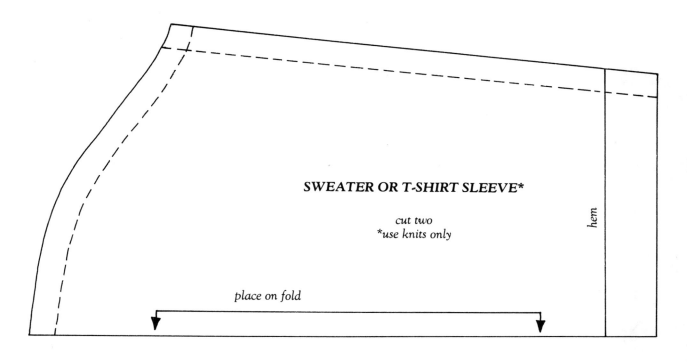

SWEATER OR T-SHIRT SLEEVE*

cut two
**use knits only*

place on fold

hem

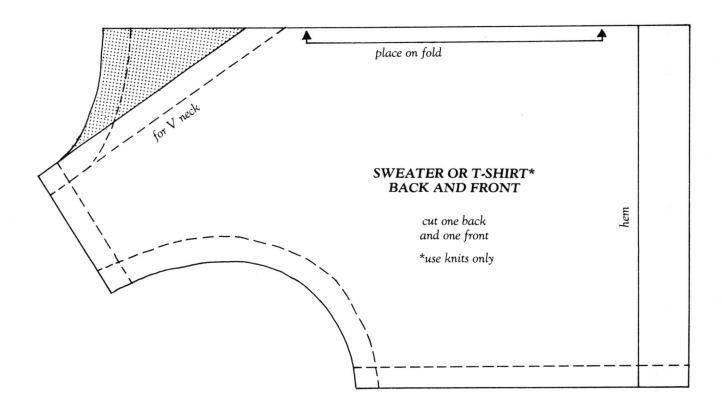

place on fold

for V neck

SWEATER OR T-SHIRT*
BACK AND FRONT

cut one back
and one front

**use knits only*

hem

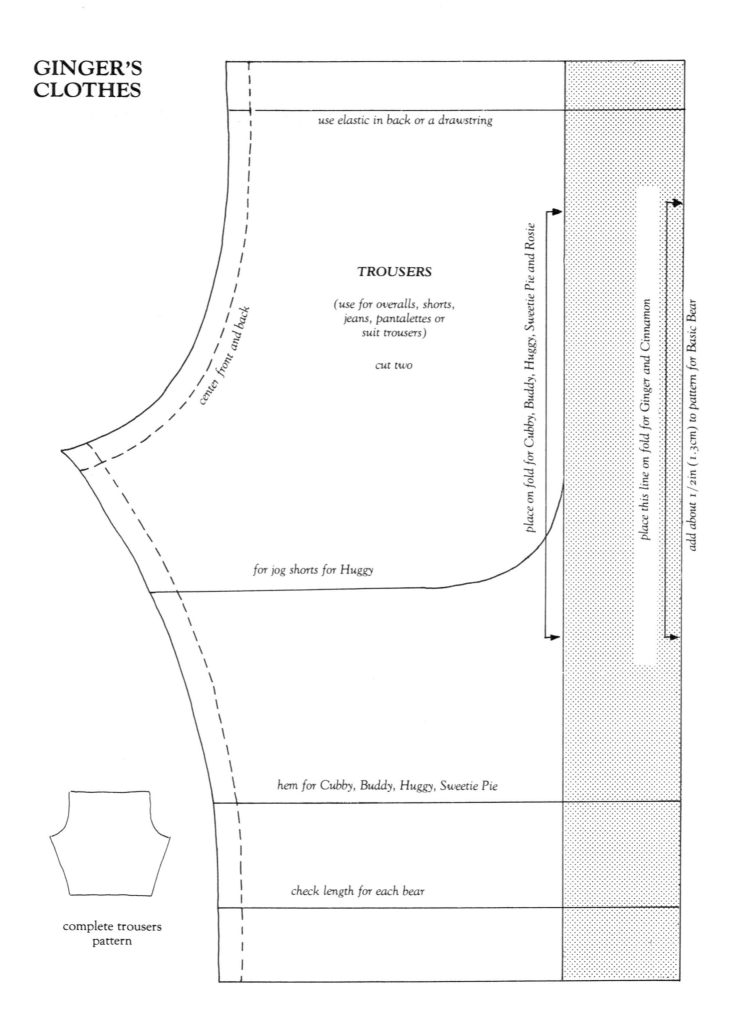

GINGER'S CLOTHES

use elastic in back or a drawstring

TROUSERS

*(use for overalls, shorts,
jeans, pantalettes or
suit trousers)*

cut two

center front and back

place on fold for Cubby, Buddy, Huggy, Sweetie Pie and Rosie

place this line on fold for Ginger and Cinnamon

add about 1/2in (1.3cm) to pattern for Basic Bear

for jog shorts for Huggy

hem for Cubby, Buddy, Huggy, Sweetie Pie

check length for each bear

complete trousers
pattern

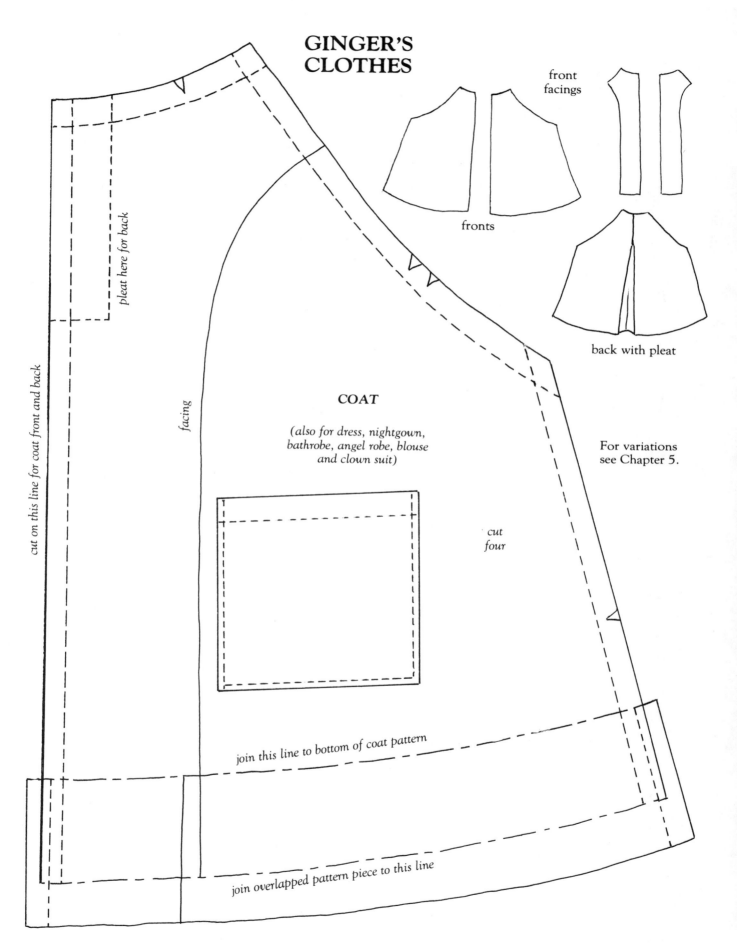

GINGER'S CLOTHES

front facings

fronts

cut on this line for coat front and back

pleat here for back

facing

COAT

(also for dress, nightgown, bathrobe, angel robe, blouse and clown suit)

cut four

back with pleat

For variations see Chapter 5.

join this line to bottom of coat pattern

join overlapped pattern piece to this line

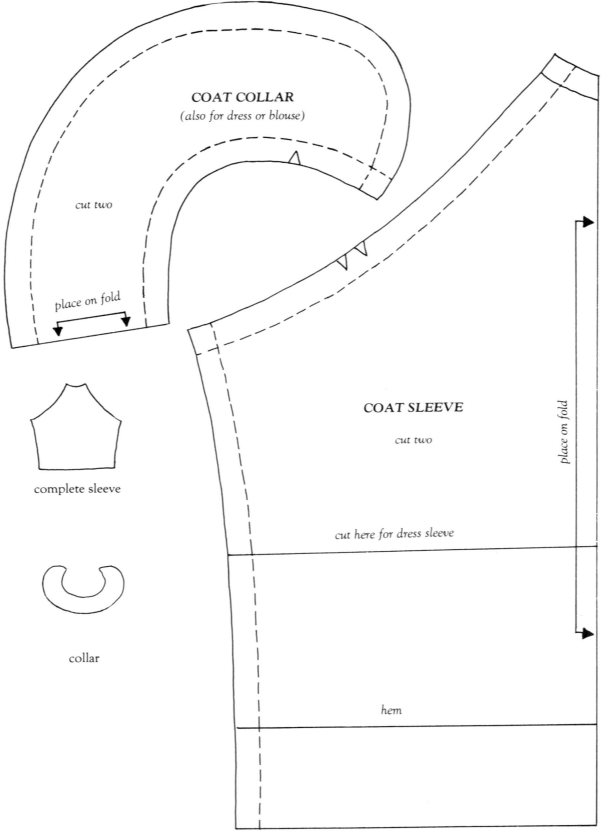

COAT COLLAR
(also for dress or blouse)

cut two

place on fold

complete sleeve

collar

COAT SLEEVE

cut two

place on fold

cut here for dress sleeve

hem

70

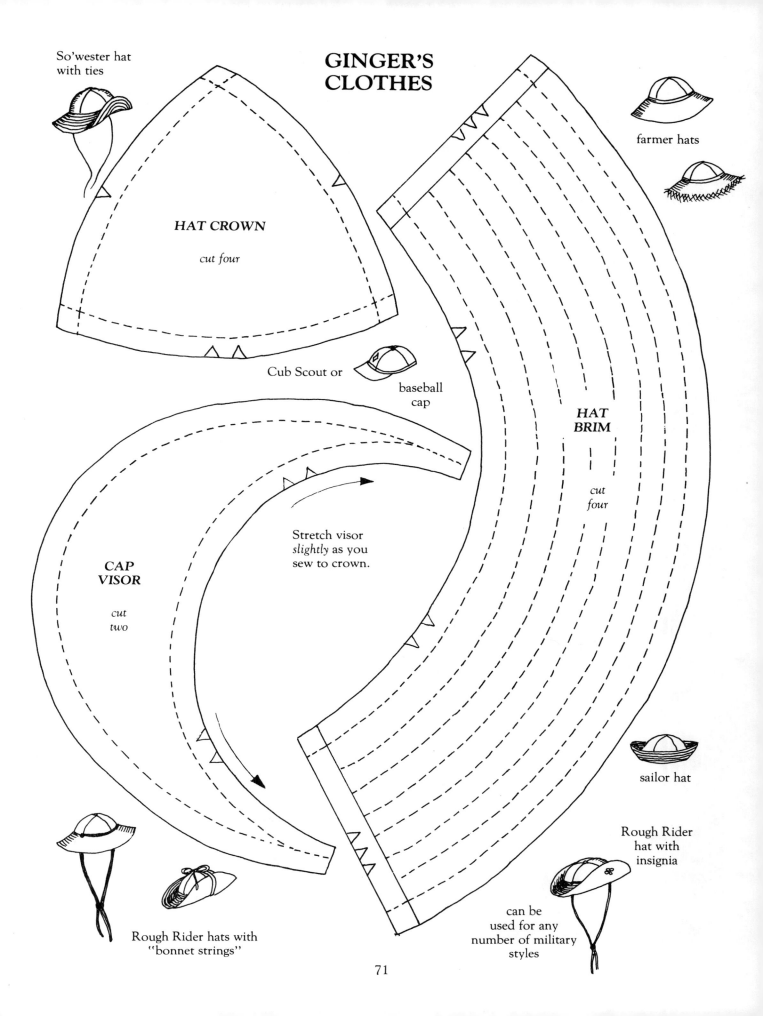

So'wester hat with ties

GINGER'S CLOTHES

farmer hats

HAT CROWN

cut four

Cub Scout or

baseball cap

HAT BRIM

cut four

CAP VISOR

cut two

Stretch visor *slightly* as you sew to crown.

sailor hat

Rough Rider hat with insignia

Rough Rider hats with "bonnet strings"

can be used for any number of military styles

71

CUBBY

If you plan to make only one jointed Teddy Bear — let it be Cubby! He is a most pleasing size for either adults or children. During the great Teddy Bear craze of 1906 to 1910, the 12in (30.5cm) bear was obviously the most popular model. Virtually every old Teddy Bear advertisement lists a 12in (30.5cm) size. He can wear so many doll clothes that you will be able to find clothes for him quite easily. He is a good size to sew for also. He can be seen in three different versions in *Illustrations 1* and *2*.

CUBBY'S CLOTHES

Rough Rider Suit

Khaki twill was fashioned into an authentic Spanish American War military jacket like that made famous by Teddy Roosevelt. The pockets are authentically pleated; the epaulettes and neckband are blue felt for dismounted cavalry. Brass buttons add military "spit and polish" to an already spiffy outfit shown in *Color Illustration 7*.

The Rough Rider hat, of a slightly darker khaki twill, was made from the hat pattern with Ginger's clothes.

Instead of the traditional crossed swords insignia pinned on the brim, Cubby has a Teddy Bear button — of course. Holding on the hat, a tan shoestring serves as the "bonnet strings" while a wooden bead is used as the "slide."

For trousers to go with the jacket, use the pattern for Ginger's trousers and follow the directions for 12in (30.5cm) bears.

For variations on the uniform theme, make a jacket and trousers of dark blue instead of khaki, with yellow trim for a U.S. Cavalry uniform. Use red for a jacket with black trousers and hat and Cubby will become a Royal Canadian Mountie. A gray jacket over light blue trousers with a yellow stripe will make Cubby a Confederate soldier and if you make him a large gray hat to go with it, he will be a dashing officer — maybe General Robert E. Bear or Colonel Teddy B. Ravenall. Most any 19th or 20th century military uniform can be created with this little jacket pattern and a bit of imagination!

Sweater

Made from a leg warmer, Cubby's ski sweater is described in Chapter 4 under "Sweaters." Tan with geometric designs across the body, it has a matching hat with a pompon of coordinating colors shown in *Illustration 50*.

Since the design was in the middle of the leg warmer, the ribbing could not be utilized for the bottom of the sweater. Ribbing was cut from the top of the leg warmer and added later. The sleeves, however, were cut so that they utilized part of the ribbing at the hem.

In *Illustration 58*, Cubby models another sweater, with little reindeer, made from a pair of old socks.

Illustration 57. A 1/2in (1.3cm) pile fur Cubby, left, is ready for an outing in his green plaid wool tam and fringed scarf. At right is a genuine CUB Scout in his little visored blue cap and yellow neckerchief. This was his very first outfit and the reason he took the name "Cubby" for himself.

CUBBY

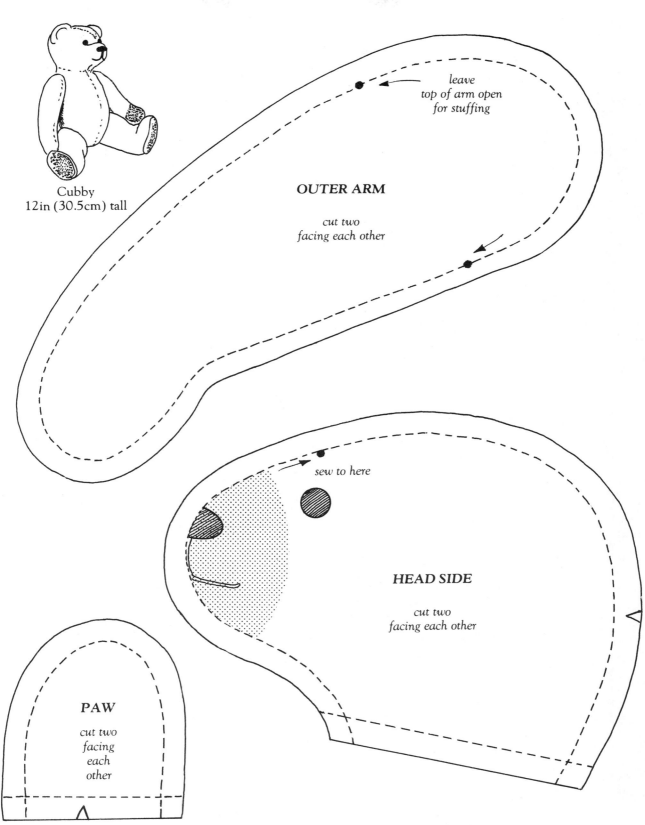

Cubby
12in (30.5cm) tall

OUTER ARM

cut two
facing each other

leave
top of arm open
for stuffing

HEAD SIDE

cut two
facing each other

sew to here

PAW

cut two
facing
each
other

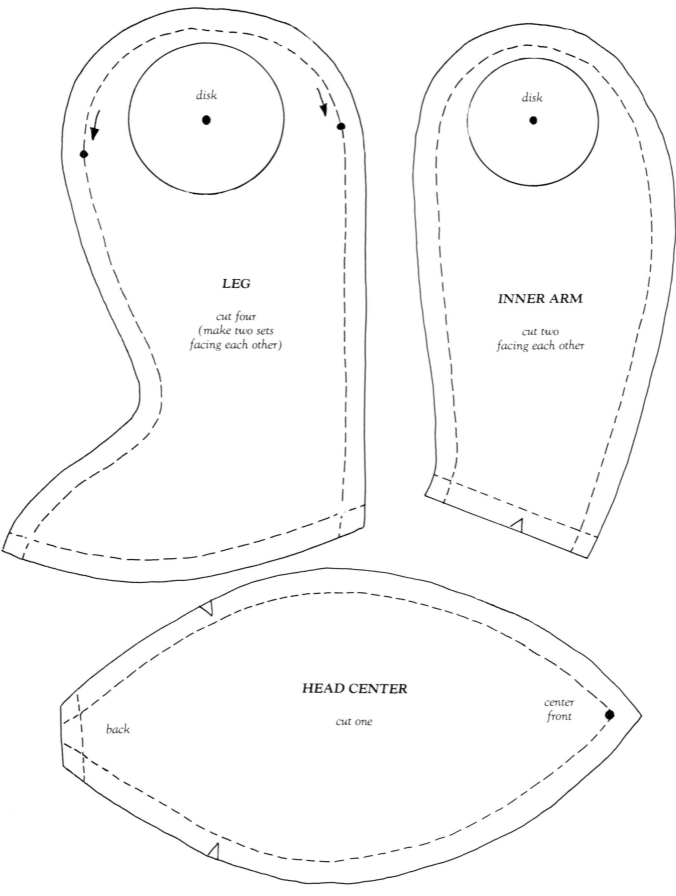

disk

LEG

*cut four
(make two sets
facing each other)*

disk

INNER ARM

*cut two
facing each other*

HEAD CENTER

cut one

back

*center
front*

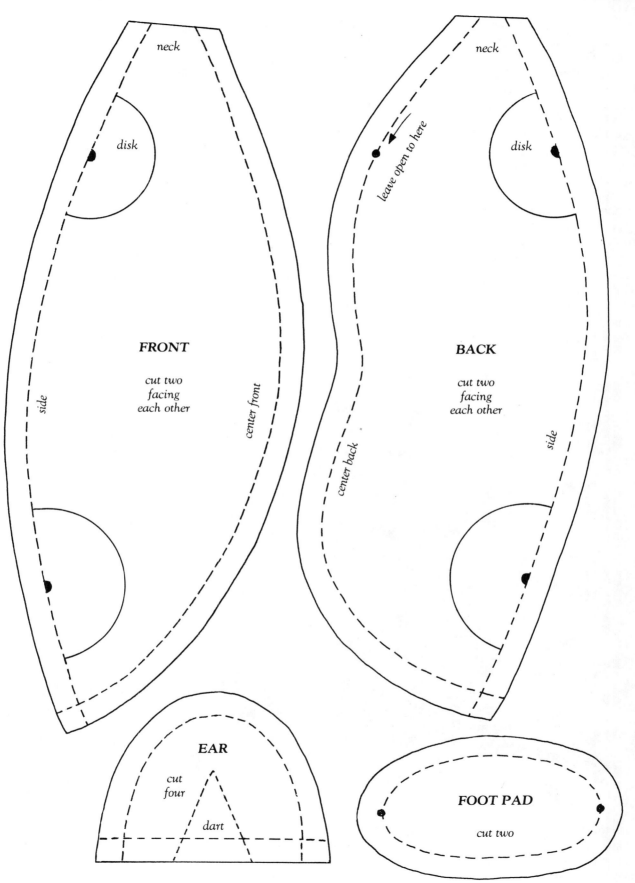

Dress

Every girl, especially, will want at least one feminine outfit for her bear for special occasions such as birthday parties or shopping trips to the toy store. What could be more feminine than the yellow nylon dotted swiss number with lace at the neck and a taffeta petticoat shown in *Color Illustration 6*? For jewelry, Cuddles wears a koala bear pin (really a button) on the bodice. Her romantic, garden party hat has flowers and ribbon streamers in back.

The skirt should be about 6in (15.2cm) by 40in (101.6cm); a puffed sleeve pattern is with Cinnamon's clothes.

Cub Scout Cap and Kerchief

Did you know that the modern Cub Scout uniform is much like the U.S. Cavalry uniform made famous in the American west? The blue shirt and trousers with the yellow kerchief is still a dashing outfit for any age.

Cubby, who is a real *cub* scout, wears a triangular scarf 12in (30.5cm) by 12in (30.5cm) by 17in (43.2cm) with a little billed cap included in Ginger's clothing patterns. A diamond-shaped patch of yellow felt serves as the scout emblem on its front in *Illustration 57*, right.

Sleepers

Made from the sleeper pattern for 13in (33cm) Buddy Bear, these yellow sleepers fit Cubby very well, *Color Illustration 3*. They are of a soft knit cloth which has plenty of give when he sits. Some general rules for making sleepers are in Chapter 5, "Making Your Own Patterns."

Scarf and Tam

The scarf in *Illustration 57* should be 24in (61cm) by 4½in (11.5cm). Use woven cloth; fringe the ends and make a narrow hem down each side.

For instructions for the tam, see *Hats* in Chapter 4.

Cubby can also wear the scarf, hat and mitten set described in Sitting Bear's clothes in Chapter 9.

Overalls/Trousers

Cubby's overalls bib, made from Cinnamon's pattern, was used with Ginger's trousers pattern. Follow the directions for Cubby's size on the pattern.

With his overalls, Cubby models a very old and battered doll straw hat as he plays by an old garden swing in *Illustration 58*. On the right another Cubby sports khaki shorts with his reindeer sweater and baseball cap.

Illustration 58. *A 1/8in (0.31cm) pile fur Cubby, dressed for play, has donned demin overalls and an old battered doll straw hat. His playmate, the original Cubby, right, is dressed in khaki shorts and his favorite reindeer sweater made from a pair of socks, one of which is shown in Illustration 18. It required both socks of the pair, opened out flat as in Illustration 23. The plastic baseball cap is one of those souvenir snow-cone containers sold at many professional ballgames.*

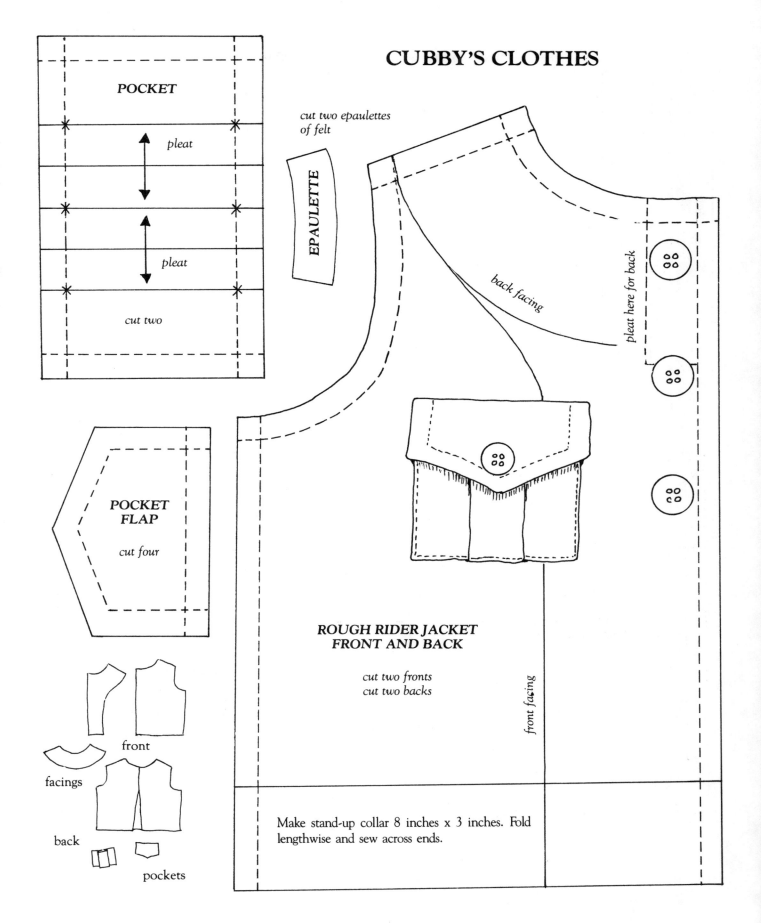

CUBBY'S CLOTHES

POCKET

pleat

pleat

cut two

cut two epaulettes of felt

EPAULETTE

back facing

pleat here for back

POCKET FLAP

cut four

ROUGH RIDER JACKET FRONT AND BACK

cut two fronts
cut two backs

front facing

Make stand-up collar 8 inches x 3 inches. Fold lengthwise and sew across ends.

front

facings

back

pockets

77

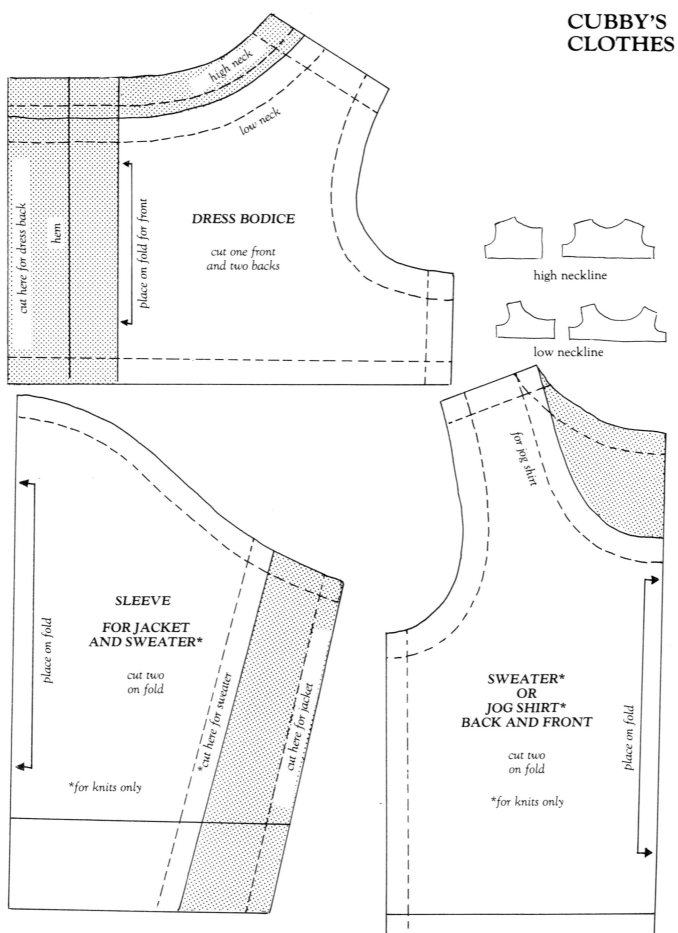

high neck

low neck

DRESS BODICE

*cut one front
and two backs*

cut here for dress back

hem

place on fold for front

high neckline

low neckline

SLEEVE

**FOR JACKET
AND SWEATER***

*cut two
on fold*

*for knits only

place on fold

*cut here for sweater

cut here for jacket

for jog shirt

SWEATER*
OR
JOG SHIRT*
BACK AND FRONT

*cut two
on fold*

*for knits only

place on fold

BENJAMIN

HEAD SIDE

*cut two
facing each other*

sew
to
here

**HEAD
CENTER**

cut one

back

center
front

PAW

*cut two
facing
each
other*

leave
top of
arm open
for stuffing

**OUTER
ARM**

*cut two
facing
each
other*

disk

**INNER
ARM**

*cut two
facing
each other*

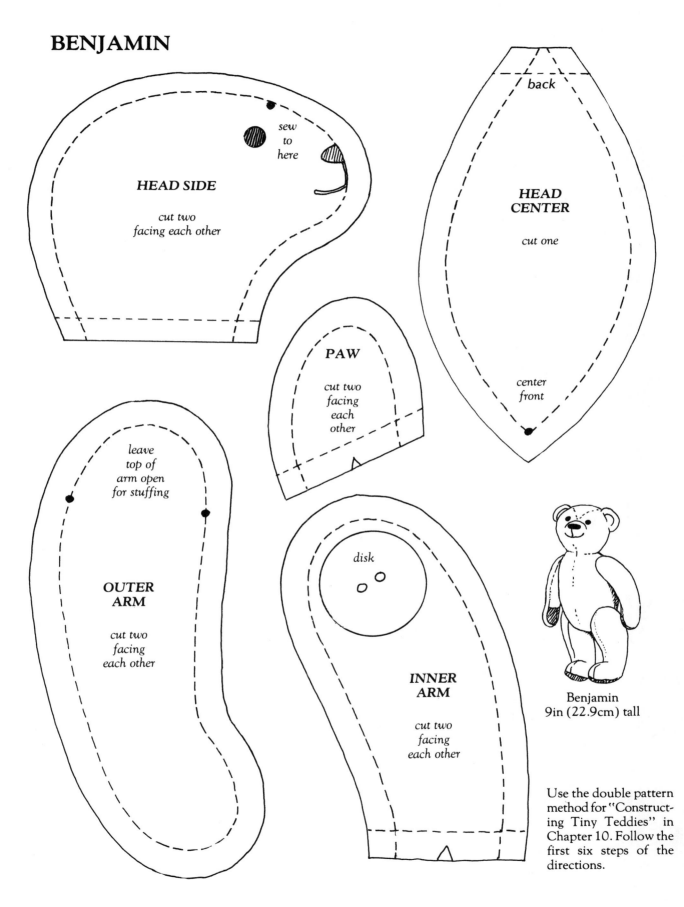

Benjamin
9in (22.9cm) tall

Use the double pattern
method for "Construct-
ing Tiny Teddies" in
Chapter 10. Follow the
first six steps of the
directions.

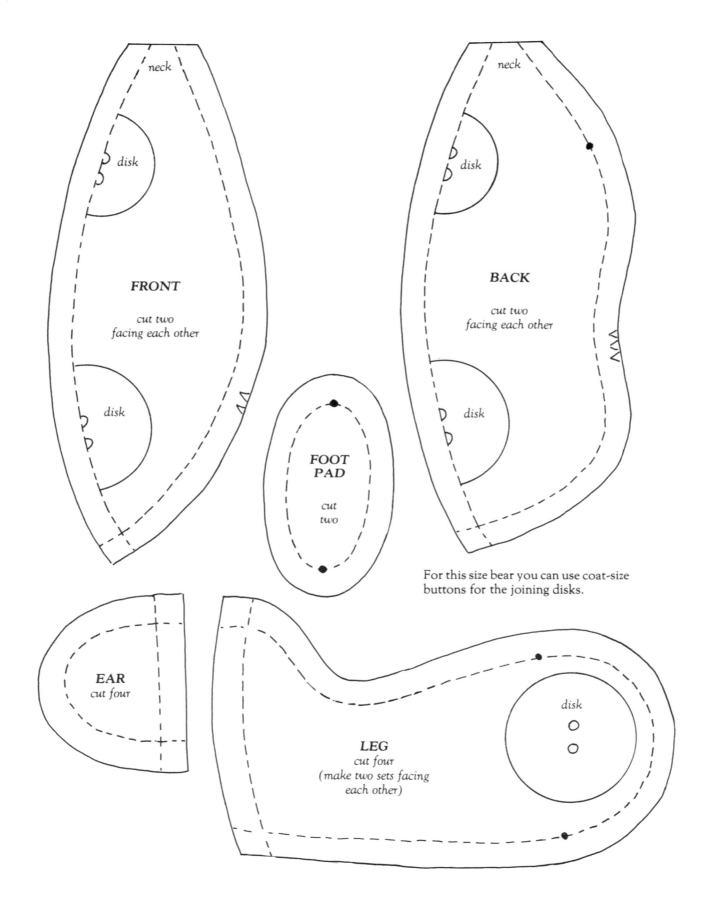

neck

disk

disk

FRONT

*cut two
facing each other*

neck

disk

BACK

*cut two
facing each other*

disk

**FOOT
PAD**

*cut
two*

For this size bear you can use coat-size
buttons for the joining disks.

EAR
cut four

LEG
*cut four
(make two sets facing
each other)*

disk

BENJAMIN

Big enough to be easy to sew clothes for, yet small enough to require only small bits of fabric, Benjamin possesses the qualities and charm of both big and miniature bears — he is a real love! He can be seen in *Illustrations 7* and *10*.

You can make him a whole wardrobe of clothes from his pajama pattern. By varying the length of his shirt and trousers and the types of fabrics used, you can fashion everything from velvet britches and lacy shirt to blue jeans and western shirt. Put drawstrings in the legs, sleeves and shirt bottom for a nifty sweatsuit for jogging. For tennis, make him white shorts and shirt. There is no end to the number of outfits you can create with just a little imagination.

BENJAMIN'S CLOTHES

Pajamas

A cream-colored cotton with authentic brown Teddy Bears and tiny sprigs of holly makes the most charming pajamas for Benjamin as seen in *Color Illustration 8*. Striped or plain cotton, silk or cotton flannel works well, too. Use the pattern as is.

This little pajama pattern can be used for many other outfits such as a Rough Rider suit, a coat (when the jacket is lengthened about 1½in [3.8cm]), a nightgown (when fullness is added as shown in Chapter 5), a Santa suit, overalls and numerous other things.

See Chapter 5 for directions for making sleepers for Benjamin.

Sweaters

Sweaters can be made of any knit cloth but those made from adult-size knee socks are particularly attractive and sometimes whimsical. Benjamin wears a green embroidered ski sweater and cap in *Illustration 15* made from a knee sock. Follow directions for making sweaters in Chapter 4.

Sunbonnet

The Benjamin pattern becomes a Becky when dressed in a red-checked and lace-trimmed sunbonnet shown in *Color Illustration 6*. There are buttonholes worked for ears to poke through — making it a "poke bonnet," perhaps?

Illustration 59. *Tennis anyone? A very perky mohair Benjamin models his blue and white tennis or jogging shirt made from a terry sweat sock top. Being elasticized, it stretches beautifully for putting on or taking off. His little navy shorts have a drawstring at the waist. (That is a Barbie® tennis racket.) To his right, a more serious Benjamin sports an aqua gingham shirt and gray wool trousers.*

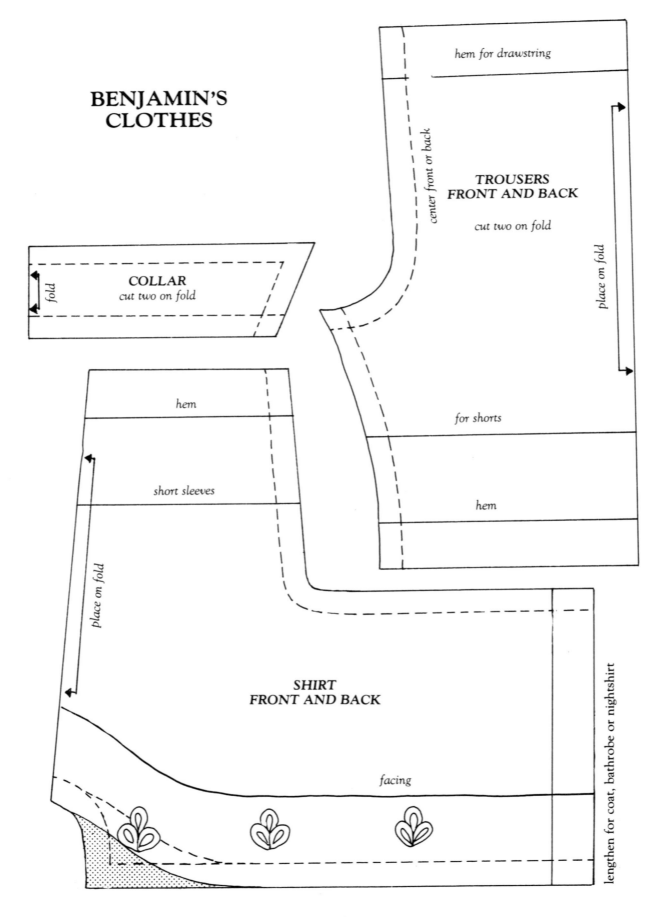

BENJAMIN'S CLOTHES

COLLAR
cut two on fold

fold

hem for drawstring

center front or back

TROUSERS FRONT AND BACK

cut two on fold

place on fold

for shorts

hem

hem

short sleeves

place on fold

SHIRT FRONT AND BACK

facing

lengthen for coat, bathrobe or nightshirt

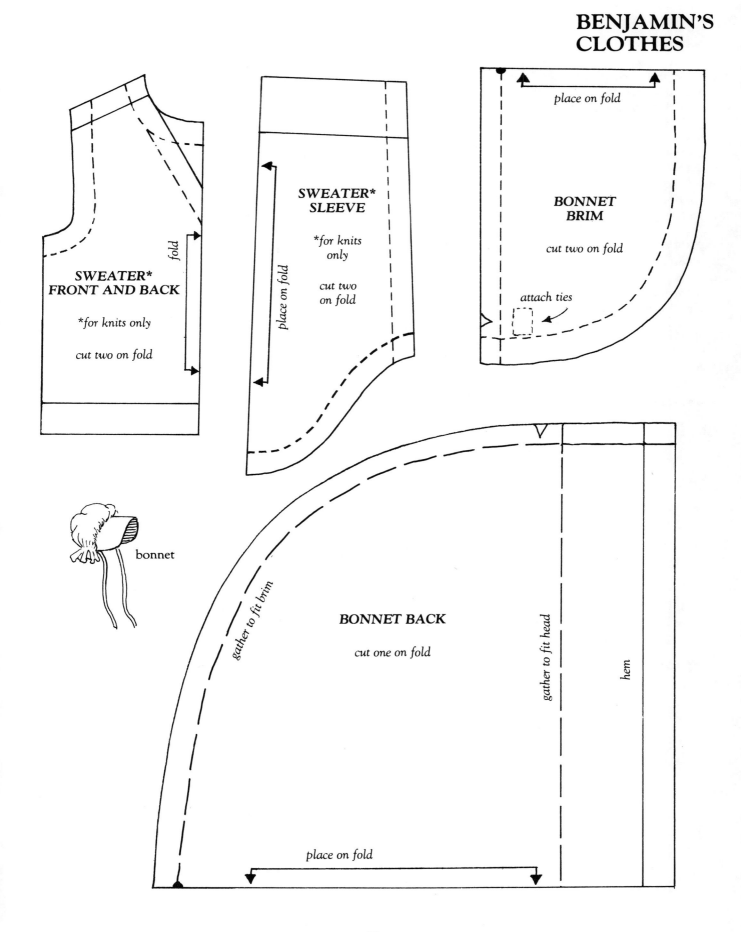

SWEATER*
FRONT AND BACK

*for knits only

cut two on fold

fold

SWEATER*
SLEEVE

*for knits
only

cut two
on fold

place on fold

BONNET BRIM

cut two on fold

place on fold

attach ties

bonnet

BONNET BACK

cut one on fold

gather to fit brim

gather to fit head

hem

place on fold

Dress

Actually, a matching skirt and blouse, Becky's dress can be seen in *Color Illustration* 6. Benjamin's pajama shirt, buttoned in back, becomes a blouse with lace sewn around the shoulders forming a yoke.

The matching skirt is hemmed at the waist with elastic run through it. The skirt should be 20in (50.8cm) by 5in (12.7cm). If you want a long skirt, add 2in (5.1cm) to the length.

There is a collar pattern included which can be used for a front buttoned blouse and the sleeves can be shortened, making it a versatile pattern.

Apron

You will find Benjamin's apron pattern superimposed on Basic Bear's apron in Chapter 7. General directions for constructing aprons are in Chapter 4. Benjamin's apron is made of orange and white checked gingham with a little pocket for a handkerchief or secret treasures just barely visible over the rolling pin in *Illustration* 53.

Jog Suit

Shorts can be made from the pajama trousers pattern and a jog shirt with the sweater pattern. This blue and white striped terry shirt was made from the top of a crew sock, using the V-neck style in a sleeveless version. Since these socks have stretch tops, the little shirt is easy to take on and off and always fits Benjamin snugly. The shorts have a drawstring at the waist (*Illustration* 59.)

Shirt and Trousers

Aqua gingham was used for the shirt with gray flannel trousers for a "little boy" look in *Illustration* 59. Made in satin, lace and velvet, the outfit can become a "Little Lord Fauntleroy" suit.

This checkered shirt has a nice country look when paired with denim trousers or overalls. It is made from the versatile pajama shirt pattern which can also be shortened to become a suit jacket.

Bathrobe or Coat

Of green silk; Becky's bathrobe in *Color Illustration* 8 was fashioned from the pajama shirt pattern with 2in (5.1cm) added to the length. A coat can be made in the same manner with 1in (2.5cm) added. A variety of fabrics can be used for both coat and bathrobe.

For directions for robes, nightshirts and nightgowns, see Chapter 5, "Making Your Own Patterns."

Chapter 7
HINGED TEDDY BEARS

Did you know live bears have their hair parted in the middle — that is correct; there is a definite part on the forehead that looks as though someone had taken a comb and brush and made a perfectly straight part! The part is particularly evident on grizzly bears.

The non-jointed Teddy Bears in this chapter have a center front seam giving a certain authenticity to their faces. These hinged bears are designed so they have the look of jointed Teddy Bears because their arms and legs are attached to the body at an angle which gives them a silhouette similar to bears with arms and legs joined to the torso with strings, wires or clips. Their arms place the paw in a natural position instead of awkwardly pointing out or up in the air like most other hinged bears. If you leave space at the top of the legs and arms when you stuff these bears, they will move and sit easily.

Another feature not usually found on non-jointed bears is their rump or seat. This gives a more rounded silhouette from the side and at the same time enables them to sit down. After all, how can a Teddy Bear sit if he has no rump?

Hinged bears are ideal for very young arctophiles (bear lovers) because they can take more abuse than jointed bears. They actually are softer to hug and sleep with, anyway, because there are absolutely no hard parts on them. And, if that is not enough reason, their arms and legs will *bend in any direction*, making them easy to dress and undress and, therefore, recommended for very young children as well as adults.

It is interesting that the more complicated bear patterns, with lots of pieces, actually can look easier on the pages of a book than easier patterns. The reason is, of course, *that fewer pieces mean larger pieces* and larger patterns have to be broken apart in order to give them in their actual size. Basic, Buddy and Huggy all have some pattern pieces that had to be cut apart and used on two separate pages. Once you combine the pieces for your complete patterns, you will see how really simple and practical these hinged Teddy Bears are.

The three bears in this chapter are proof that a bear does not have to be jointed to be charming and of fine quality. They have plenty of charm in their own right and consistently draw as much attention as jointed bears when they appear on television and in museum exhibits.

BASIC BEAR

One winter day when I sat down to my drawing table to draft a new bear, I said, "I'm going to design a good basic bear." Well, the bear I turned out several hours later was anything but ordinary but by then, my family was already asking, "Is this your basic bear?" He soon became "Basic"

Illustration 60. Basic with a very real bear-like face just being his old lovable self and showing you how he looks without his clothes. He is constructed of a beige 1/2in (1.3cm) pile fur cloth.

Illustration 61. Another Basic with a very sweet look, showing his appliqued red felt heart.

BASIC BEAR

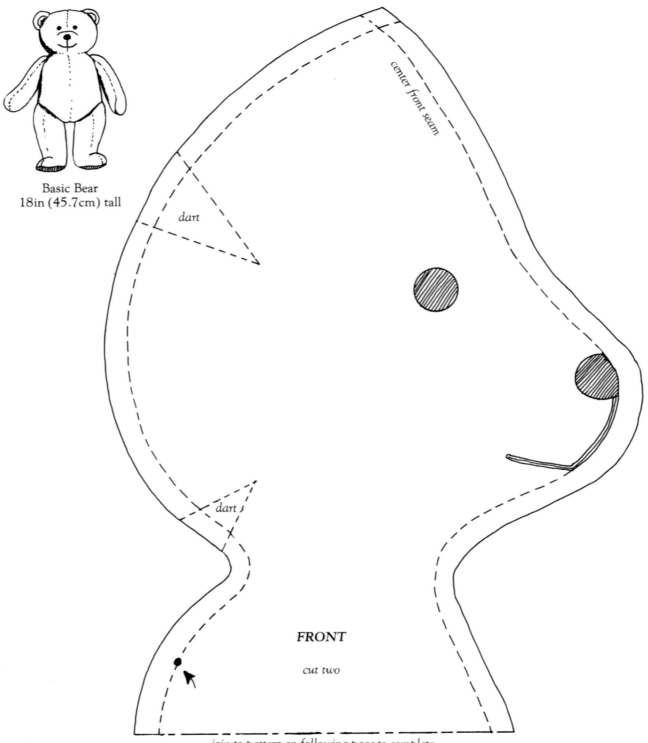

Basic Bear
18in (45.7cm) tall

center front seam

dart

dart

FRONT

cut two

join to pattern on following page to complete

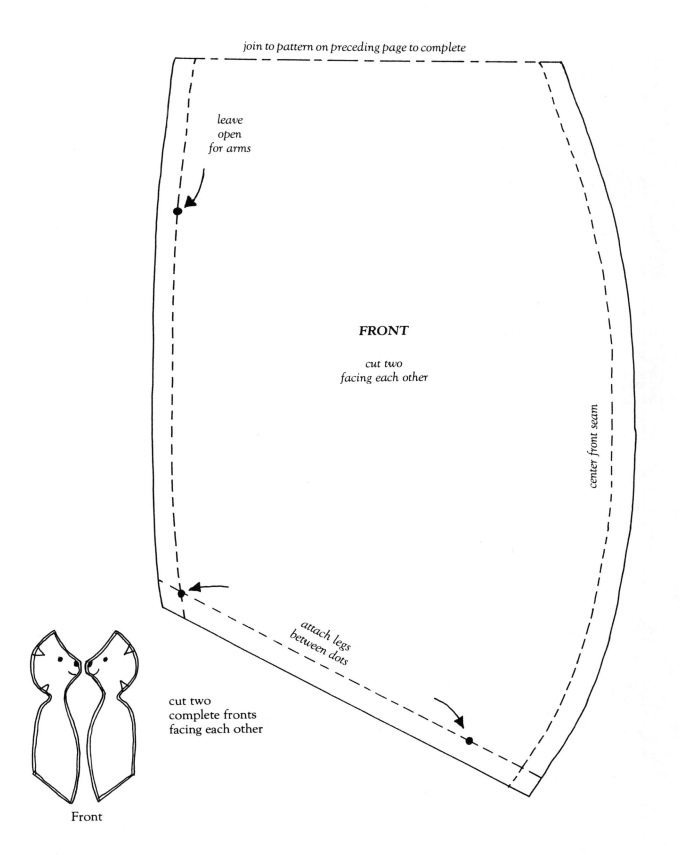

join to pattern on preceding page to complete

*leave
open
for arms*

FRONT

*cut two
facing each other*

center front seam

*attach legs
between dots*

cut two
complete fronts
facing each other

Front

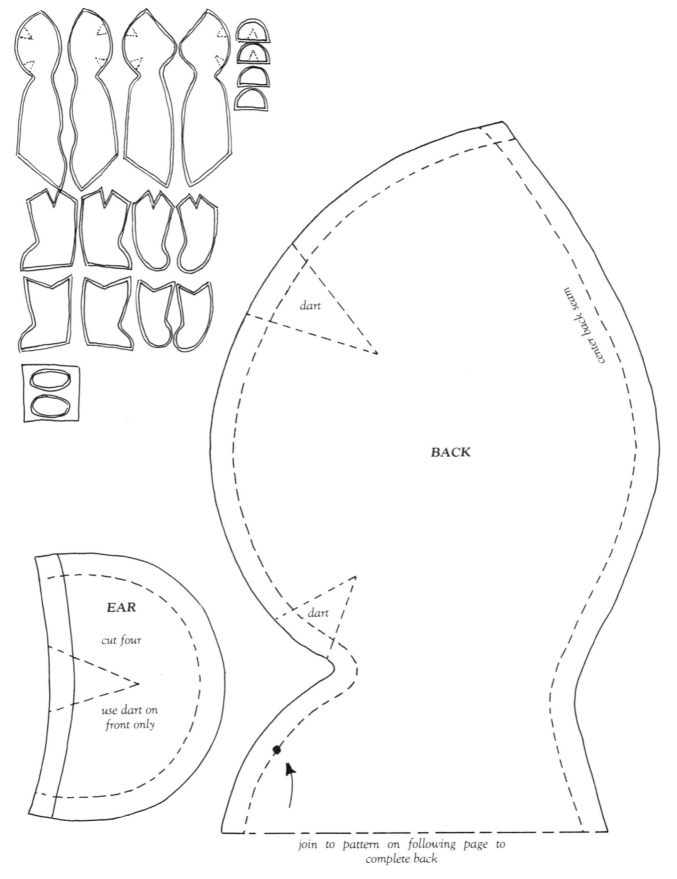

BACK

center back seam

dart

dart

EAR

cut four

use dart on
front only

*join to pattern on following page to
complete back*

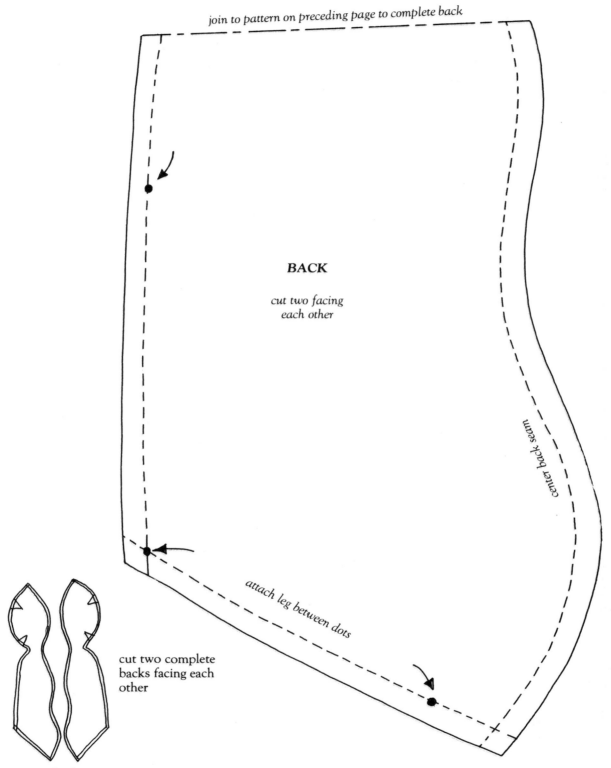

join to pattern on preceding page to complete back

BACK

*cut two facing
each other*

center back seam

attach leg between dots

cut two complete
backs facing each
other

Back

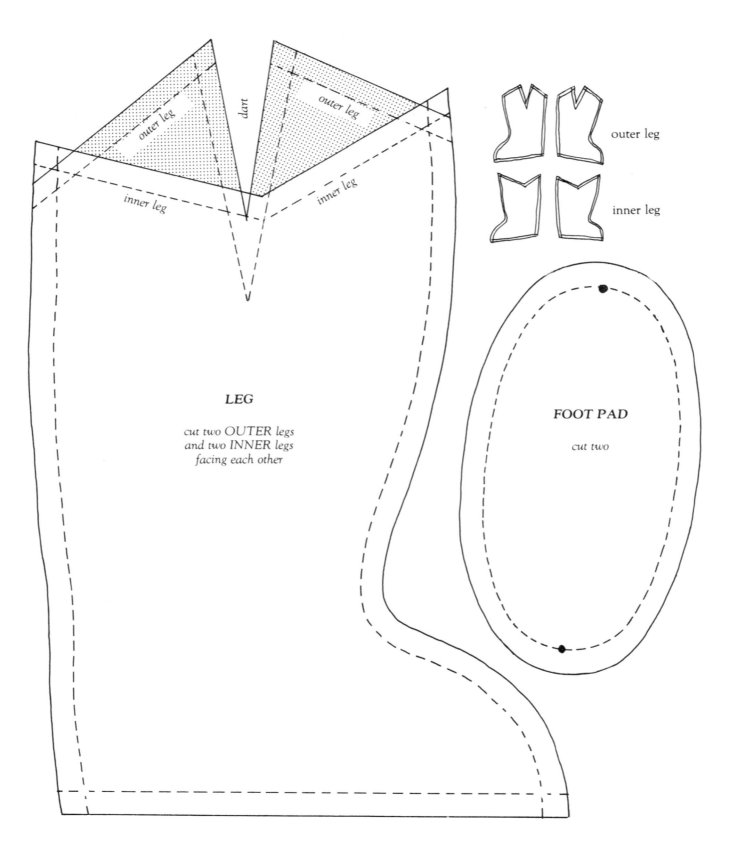

outer leg

dart

outer leg

inner leg

inner leg

outer leg

inner leg

LEG

*cut two OUTER legs
and two INNER legs
facing each other*

FOOT PAD

cut two

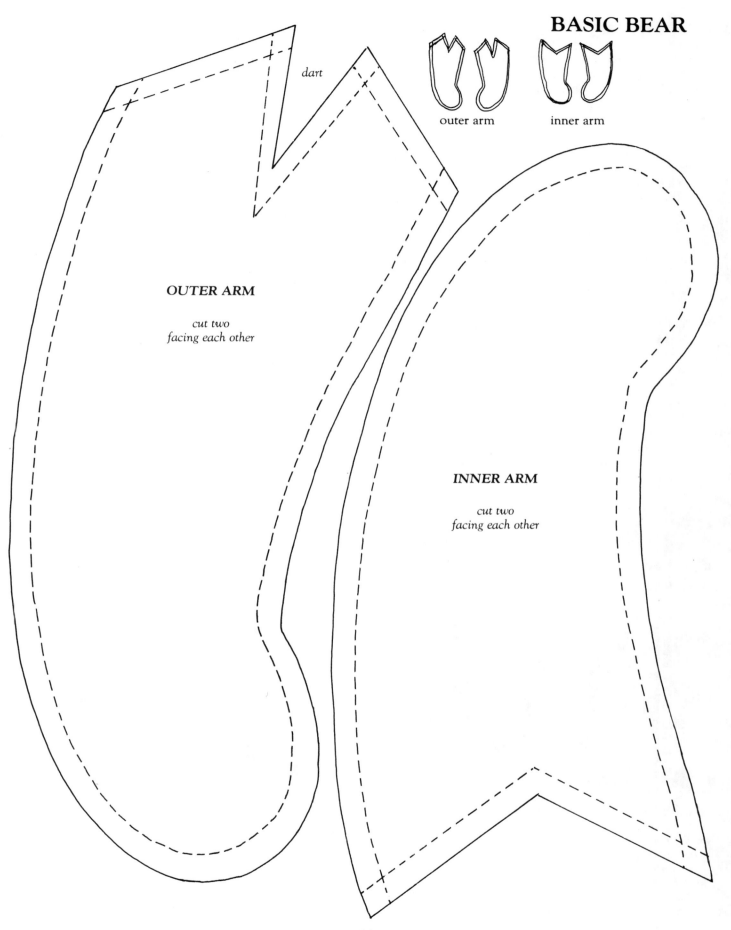

BASIC BEAR

outer arm   inner arm

dart

OUTER ARM

cut two
facing each other

INNER ARM

cut two
facing each other

91

by name and turned out to be one of my personal favorites as well as one that seemed to attract other people. He has so much personality packed into that fat body, lovable face and big feet, and his character is so strong that we would not think of changing a hair on his body or putting any other face on him. It was useless to even try to call him by any other name because *he* had already decided who he was!

CONSTRUCTING BASIC BEAR

1. There are eight pieces in the BASIC BEAR pattern. Since the front and back pieces were too large for the page, they had to be broken in half and put on two pages each. Join the sections to form complete patterns as shown.
2. Cut out patterns and draw around them onto the *back side* of fur cloth, fleece, velour (not stretchy), velvet or wool. Fur cloth pile should be about 1/4in (0.65cm) to 1/2in (1.3cm) in length. If the pile is over 1/2in (1.3cm), you will have a shaggy bear which will require a great deal of trimming. Be sure to reverse the patterns as directed so your pieces will face each other as in the diagram.

   The body front and back pieces should be placed so that the pile goes down. It should go down on the legs, if possible, or at an angle as on the arms and ears.
3. Baste everything, sewing the head darts first, then the center front and back seams. Sew the leg and arm darts just before you clip and turn the legs and arms. Leave openings in the torso for the arms and legs as indicated on the pattern.

4. When stuffing, fill the head and body firmly. The feet and lower legs should be firmly packed also. Arms should be softly filled and ears need no stuffing at all. Stop the filling 1in (2.5cm) or more from the top of the legs and arms to allow them to move easily after being attached to the body.
5. Sew arms, legs and ears on by hand with about four strands of thread and a large needle. Attach the limbs to *the front of the body first*; then fold under the edge of the back piece and whip it to the back of the arms and legs. Remember, the seams of the legs and arms should be facing front and back.
6. Basic's snout may need to be trimmed before you sew on his nose and mouth. See Chapter 2, "Your Bear's Face" for suggestions.

BASIC BEAR'S CLOTHES

Basic can wear most of Cinnamon's clothes as well as his own. It is, however, a good idea to check the patterns carefully to make sure they are large enough since he is a bit fatter in places than Cinnamon. He also can wear some small size baby clothes and baby shoes. Be sure to take him with you when you shop for him so he can try things on.

Clown Suit

A traditional French style, Pierrot, costume was fashioned of red cotton with blue, green and yellow stars in *Color Illustration 9*. The top was constructed from Ginger's raincoat pattern with width added as demonstrated in "Making Your Patterns" in Chapter 5, *Illustration 33* and page 40.

Illustration 62. *A very light beige 1/4in (0.65cm) pile fur gives this Basic (left) a bit more delicate appearance. His sweater was made from an old sweater. The Santy Claws hat looks so great with the bright red sweater, he decided to borrow it for the photograph. On the right, the Basic of Illustration 61 shows off his baby blue cardigan made from a girl's sweater, utilizing the buttons and buttonholes already on it. It also has sleeves cut so they use the original ribbing. His pastel ski cap was once a child's scarf.*

Illustration 63. *Dapper indeed is this Basic bear in his checked vest with bow tie and watch chain! Another Basic, right, wrapped in a navy, red and yellow muffler is ready for a trip with his owner. His matching tam has a red yarn pompon on top.*

Illustration 64. *Buddy, dressed appropriately for a visit with "Santy Claws," models red and white striped wool knit muffler, stocking cap and little mittens (from Sitting Bear's clothes). The set matches his white "Buddy" shirt and red trousers. Who better than dear lovable Basic should get to wear this red velour and white fur Santa suit! It is complete with red trousers, hat, black belt and even black boots.*

Illustration 65. *Was there ever a more angelic Teddy Bear than this Basic in his angel robe? It was made from Ginger's coat pattern as described in Illustrations 33 and 34. Gold tinsel and wire make the halo — heavenly!*

Also from Ginger's clothes, the trousers pattern had 2in (5.1cm) extra width, instead of 1/2in (1.3cm) added at the outseam to give them fullness. They were lengthened at top and bottom to fit.

Basic's red nose, a large button painted with nail polish, gives him a professional clown appearance.

His hat, of the same ribbons and cloth as his ruff, was just a rectangle sewn into a cylinder or tube and gathered at the top. A yarn pompon tops it off while a piece of elastic thread holds it on.

Apron and Chef Cap

Basic's apron of unbleached muslin is simply hemmed at the neck and around the skirt with neck and waist ties made of the same fabric in *Color Illustration on cover.* A charming embroidered Teddy Bear decal was sewn to the bib and little pocket added for holding important recipes, implements or a kerchief. For directions, see Chapter 4, "General Directions For Clothes."

His chef cap is described in Chapter 4 under "Hats."

Cardigan and Sweater

Teddy Bear cardigans can be made quickly and easily from "people" cardigans as described in Chapter 4 under "Sweaters." Basic's blue cardigan in *Illustration 62* utilized ribbing already on the sweater sleeves as well as the buttons and buttonholes on the front.

BASIC BEAR'S CLOTHES

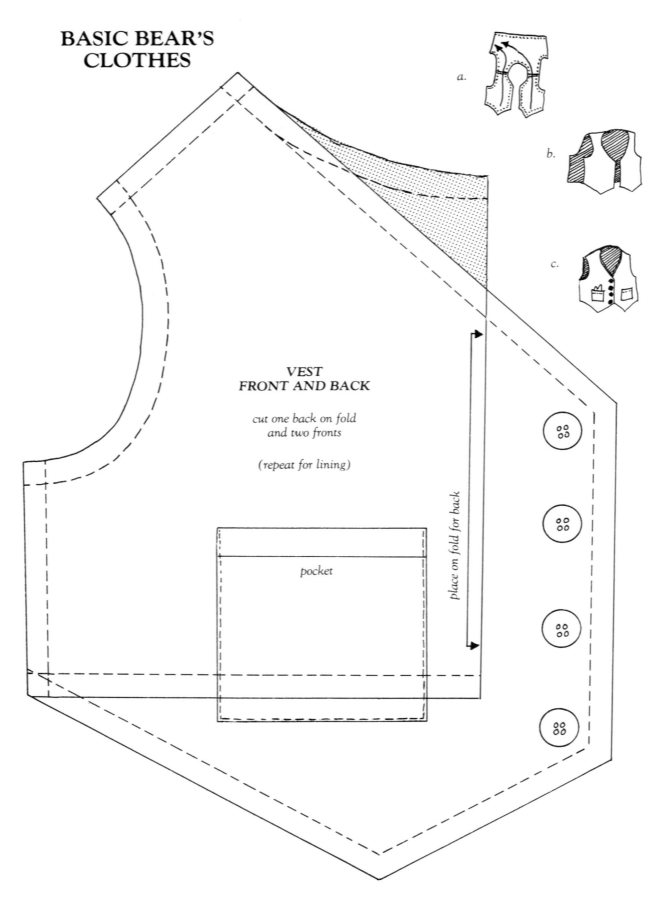

a.

b.

c.

VEST
FRONT AND BACK

*cut one back on fold
and two fronts*

(repeat for lining)

place on fold for back

pocket

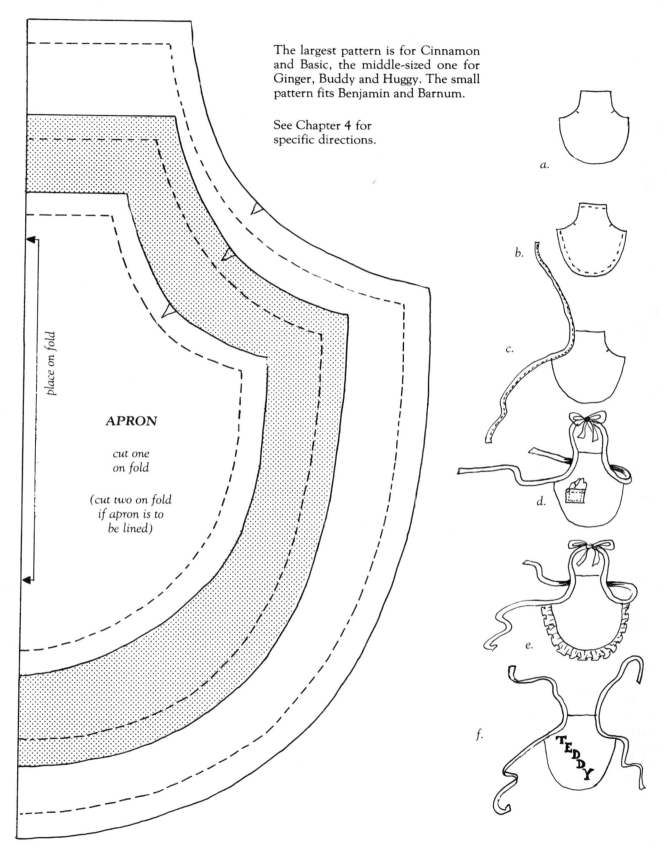

The largest pattern is for Cinnamon and Basic, the middle-sized one for Ginger, Buddy and Huggy. The small pattern fits Benjamin and Barnum.

See Chapter 4 for specific directions.

place on fold

APRON

*cut one
on fold*

*(cut two on fold
if apron is to
be lined)*

a.

b.

c.

d.

e.

f.

TEDDY

These little sweaters look charming worn by themselves or with overalls, trousers or skirt. They can be worn over any other clothes, in fact.

Night Shirt

Brown Teddy Bears being carried by yellow, red and blue balloons decorate a soft knit nightwear fabric selected for Basic's old-fashioned nightshirt in *Color Illustration 10*.

Cinnamon's pajama shirt pattern was lengthened and widened slightly at the front to make the pattern as described in Chapter 5, "Making Your Own Patterns." Red bias tape was used for the neck binding and decorative frog fasteners.

Red knit cloth makes the stocking cap with its suspended pompon. For directions, see Chapter 4, under "Hats."

Tam-O-Shanter and Scarf

Use a woven fabric for a nice fringe. Make it about 5in (12.7cm) by 30in (76.2cm); hem it down each side, and make from 1/2in (1.3cm) to 1in (2.5cm) fringe at each end. Plaid is particularly charming as in *Illustration 63*, right, but solids and stripes are nice, too. If you use a knit fabric, either hem the ends and leave them plain or add matching upholstery fringe across the ends.

See "Hats" in Chapter 4 for directions for making the matching tam.

Vest

It is really easier to make a lined vest than to hem one. This black and red McGregor Rob Roy plaid vest in *Illustration 63* is lined with a solid red velour, making it reversible and very elegant. Use vest pattern.

1. Sew only the shoulder seams of the vest and then its lining. Sew on the pockets.
2. Spread the vest out flat, right side up; then place the lining on top of it, right side down and pin in place.
3. Begin sewing at the back of the neck, go down one side of the front and across the bottom to the side edge. Repeat on the other side as shown on pattern diagram.
4. Next, sew across bottom of the back.
5. Finally, sew around each arm hole.
6. Clip all curves and corners; then turn right side out by pulling both front points through *one side* of the back as shown in step a.
7. Iron the vest so it is nice and flat.
8. Now all that is left to do is sew the side seams. Blind stitch the side seams together if your vest is to be reversible.
9. Sew buttons and buttonholes.
10. Add a little watch chain and make a black grosgrain ribbon bow tie for a very snappy outfit!

"Santy Claws" Suit

Use Cinnamon's pajama shirt pattern for Santa's red jacket in *Illustration 64*, making the neck high rather than cut away. Cut white fur; trim about 2in (5.1cm) wide. You will need about 2-2/3yd (2.43cm) for jacket and hat plus a small circle to be drawn up and stuffed for the ball on the hat.

Sew the fur trim on like a *facing in reverse*. Fold it around onto the front side and sew in place by hand. Take a miter tuck at each front corner at bottom and at neck, making the fur lie flat. Sew on snaps at neck and waistline. An old belt can be cut down for a Santa belt or use a black ribbon 1½in (3.8cm) wide.

The trousers pattern is with Ginger's clothes.

For directions for Santa's boots, see "Boots and Shoes" in Chapter 4.

Angel Robe

The nightgown in *Illustration 35* was made from Ginger's coat pattern as described in Chapter 5. It becomes an angel robe with the addition of a gold tinsel sash crossed over the chest and a wire and tinsel halo in *Illustration 65*.

This angelic Basic spent Christmas of 1984 atop the large Teddy Bear Tree at Cheekwood Art Galleries' Christmas exhibit in Nashville, Tennessee. He was the hit of the exhibit as he reigned over the entire show from his perch!

BUDDY BEAR

Buddy was named for a friend who was candidate for the United States Congress two years ago. I designed a simple little Teddy Bear easy enough for a local seamstress to produce to be given away or sold during the campaign. Since my friend's name is Buddy, I designed a little T-shirt with "Your Buddy" on the front and, "Perry for Congress" on the back.

Buddy Bear became known all around the Fourth Congressional District of Tennessee because he was quite popular with the news media and got his picture in the paper a number of times. Everyone began calling him Buddy Bear and the name seemed so right for him, it stuck.

He is especially soft and huggable and makes a nice gift for a child. He likes to wear doll clothes because so many of them fit him.

If a zipper is put in his center back seam and his torso left empty, he makes a Teddy pajama bag.

1. Join legs to the body to complete your patterns as shown on pattern pages.
2. Cut two backs facing each other and two fronts facing each other. Cut four arms, making two sets facing each other.
3. Remember to BASTE everything before sewing. Sew the darts in both front and back feet. Sew center fronts together at center seam from the top of the head to the crotch. Sew backs together in the same manner.
4. When you sew the front and back together, start sewing at the top of the head and go down one side all the way around the leg and up to the crotch. Repeat on the other side. Remember to leave openings for the arms. You can leave one arm opening a bit larger than the other for putting in the stuffing.
5. Clip and turn right side out.
6. Sew across ears before stuffing or just put in a safety pin to keep stuffing out of the ears until sewing.

Illustration 66. *Buddy of 1/4in (0.65cm) pile fur cloth shows his very simple construction, even easier than that of Basic but still with the look of a much more complicated jointed bear.*

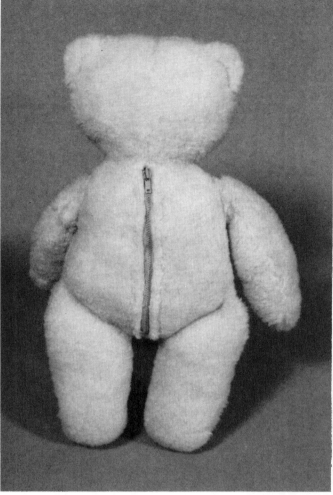

Illustration 67. *When a zipper is sewn into his back seam, he becomes a pajama bag and therefore qualifies as an Overtime bear along with those in Chapter 9.*

7. Stuff the head firmly.
8. Stuff legs, leaving about 1in (2.5cm) at the top. Stitch across stitching lines by hand as indicated on pattern.
9. Stuff torso firmly.
10. Stuff arms up to about 1in (2.5cm) from the top. They should be basted across the top so the *seams are at front and back* of the arms instead of top and bottom. This will make the arms curve naturally toward the front with the paws in the correct position as in *Illustration 66.* Sew them into the openings left for them.

BUDDY BEAR'S CLOTHES

Buddy can wear most of Cubby's clothes and some of 15in (38.1cm) Ginger's with slight modifications. Since his foot and leg patterns do not lend themselves well for making boots and shoes, he should wear those made from Cubby's leg pattern as described in "Boots and Shoes," Chapter 4.

Buddy loves to wear Sitting Bear's scarf, cap and mitten set described in Chapter 9.

Sleepers

Buddy's sleepers are of bright pink knit cloth with pearl buttons, shown in *Color Illustration 10.* He has his own little security blanket of batiste with a design of pastel colored chickens.

Make the blanket about 21in (53.3cm) with ribbon or lace edging. If you enjoy handwork, you might crochet an edge around it or perhaps make it double with a print on one side and a solid on the other.

In the same illustration, another Buddy wears red one-piece sleepers or "long-johns" described in Chapter 5.

Sweater

Buddy loves to wear sweaters made from leg warmers, socks, sweaters or ski caps as described in Chapter 4. Use Cubby's sweater pattern.

T-Shirt and Trousers

Buddy's shirt was made from a man's white undershirt but any light-weight knit will do. Red iron-on letters spell

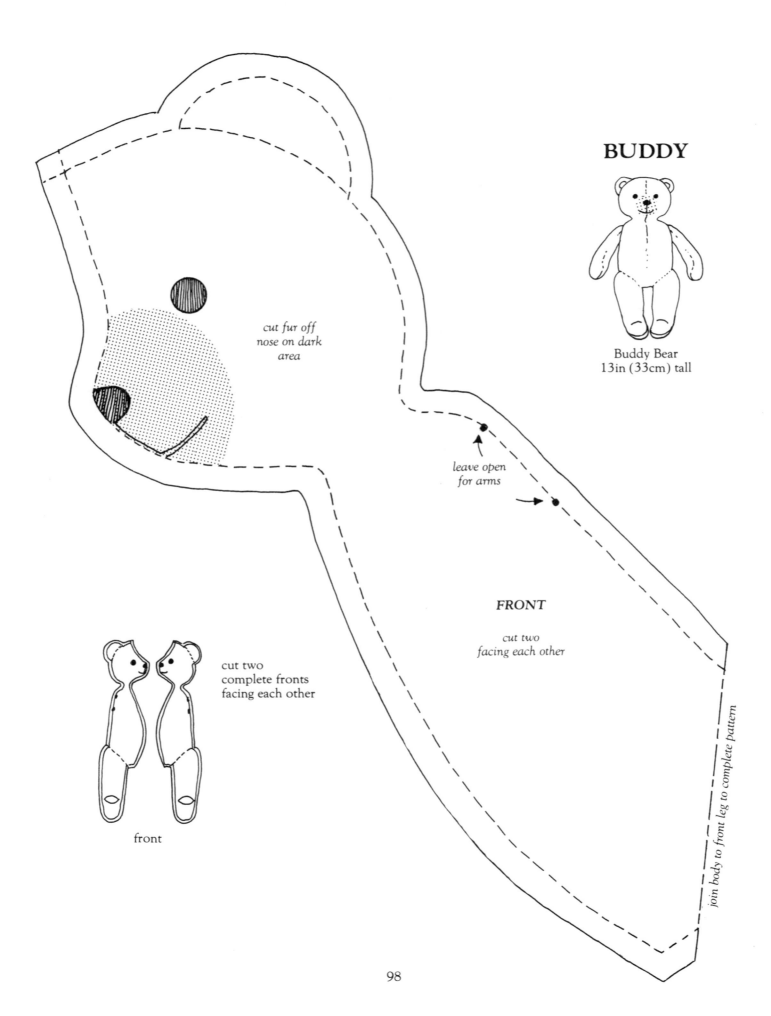

BUDDY

Buddy Bear
13in (33cm) tall

cut fur off
nose on dark
area

leave open
for arms

FRONT

cut two
facing each other

join body to front leg to complete pattern

cut two
complete fronts
facing each other

front

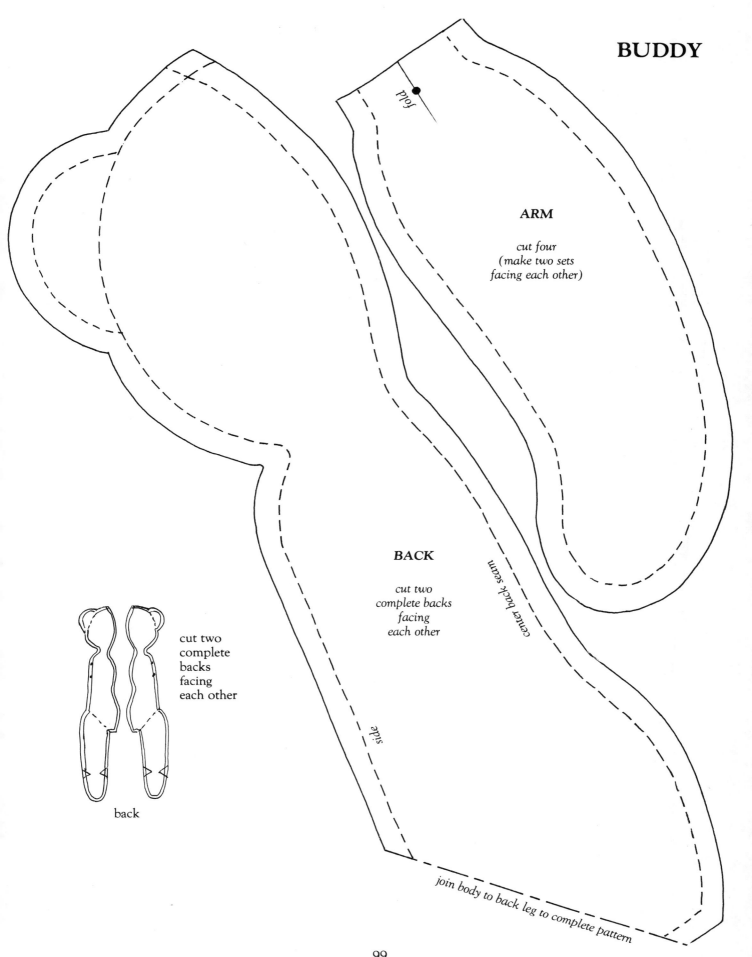

BUDDY

ARM

*cut four
(make two sets
facing each other)*

fold

BACK

*cut two
complete backs
facing
each other*

center back seam

side

cut two
complete
backs
facing
each other

back

join body to back leg to complete pattern

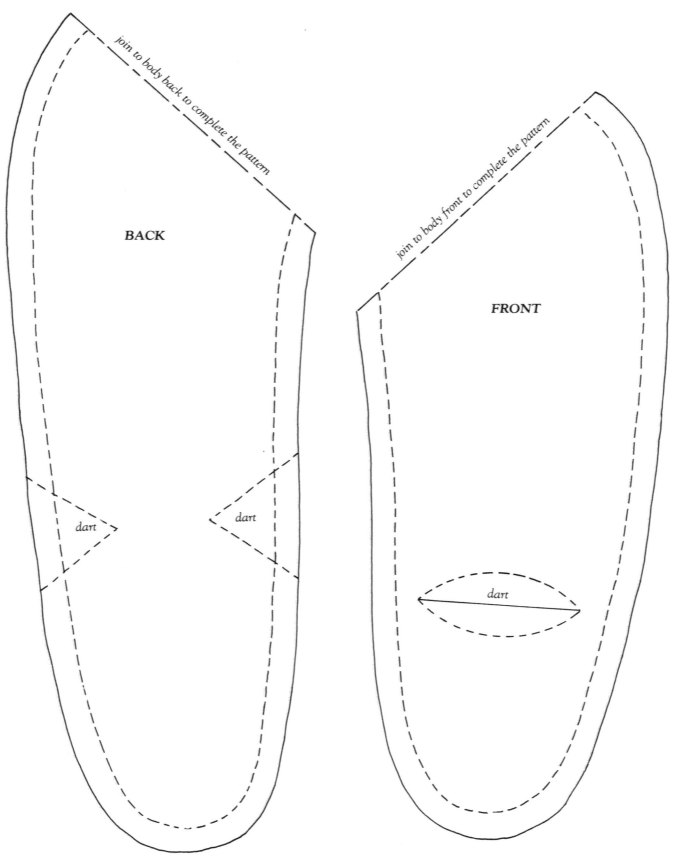

BACK

join to body back to complete the pattern

dart

dart

FRONT

join to body front to complete the pattern

dart

BUDDY

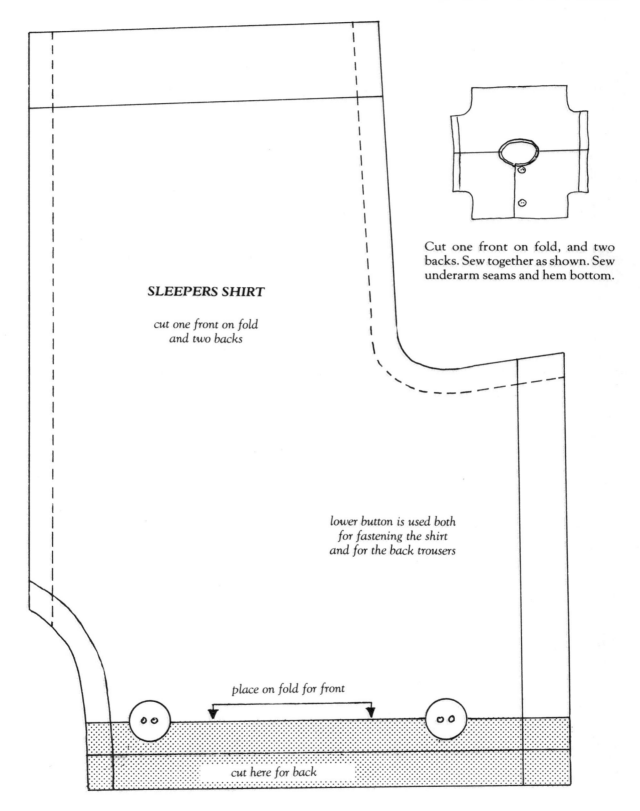

Cut one front on fold, and two backs. Sew together as shown. Sew underarm seams and hem bottom.

SLEEPERS SHIRT

*cut one front on fold
and two backs*

*lower button is used both
for fastening the shirt
and for the back trousers*

place on fold for front

cut here for back

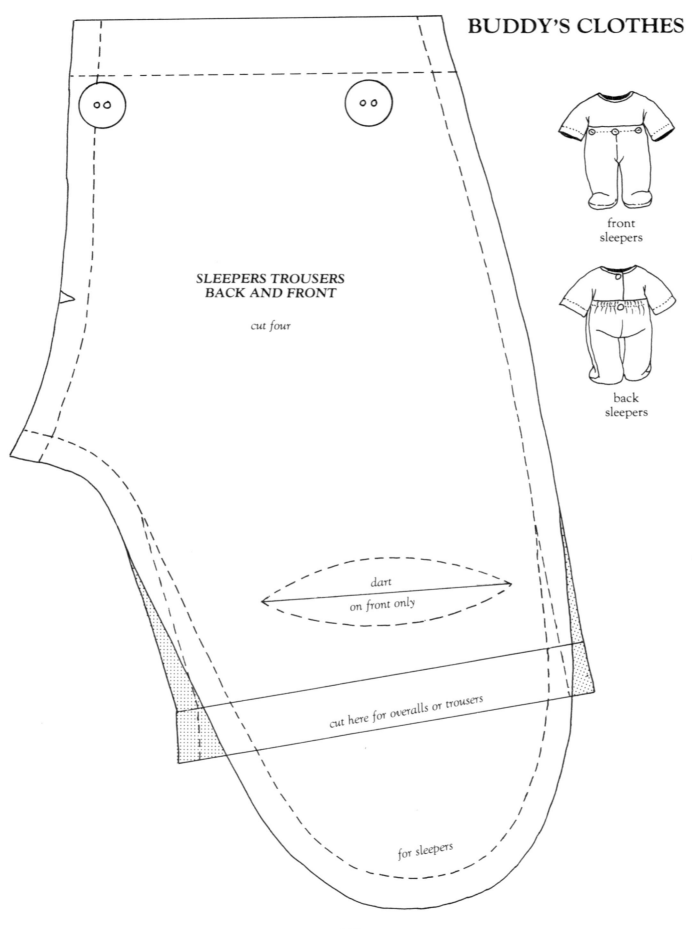

BUDDY'S CLOTHES

**SLEEPERS TROUSERS
BACK AND FRONT**

cut four

dart

on front only

cut here for overalls or trousers

for sleepers

front
sleepers

back
sleepers

Illustration 68. *Huggy just loves everybody! With his smiling face and outstretched arms, he is a joy to cuddle. His nose is appliqued felt, his fur of 1/4in (0.65cm) pile.*

out "Your Buddy" in *Color Illustration 9* and *Illustration 64.* These letters can be found in many discount and variety stores. Use 12in (30.5cm) Cubby's sweater pattern and follow the directions for making sweaters and T-shirts in Chapter 4.

Matching red trousers were made from Ginger's pattern. They can be made any length. Elastic in the hems will make sweat pants and braid or ribbon down the side will make very classy jogging pants.

Dress

A patchwork printed cotton dress made from Cubby's pattern has a country look barely visible in *Color Illustration 9.* Several different sleeves in several lengths can be used with this versatile little bodice. The dress, too, can be fashioned in any length for a nightgown, pegnoir, ice skating costume or formal outfit.

HUGGY BEAR

Just one look at him and you know why his name came to be Huggy. His outstretched arms seem to say, "Hug me," and he hugs you back, too! When you hold Huggy close to you, his little arms go right around your neck. He is the perfect huggable bedtime bear for a youngster and his happy face makes him a great daytime friend as well. Although outstretched, his arms bend easily in any direction for dressing and then spring back to their original position.

HUGGY'S CLOTHES

All of Cubby's clothes will fit Huggy as will Buddy's sleepers. Sitting Bear's scarf, hat and mittens can be worn, too, either by themselves or with a sweater on cold days.

Jog Suit

Huggy's jogging shirt pattern can be found with Cubby's patterns. It is the low neck version superimposed on the sweater. His shirt is yellow knit with red binding on the sleeves and neck in *Color Illustration on cover.*

The little shorts were made from Ginger's trousers pattern. Of red with yellow trim, they have a drawstring in the waist.

This little outfit can be made in any school or team colors for a basketball or track uniform as well as boxing or swim shorts.

Dress

To make your pattern, begin with Ginger's raincoat pattern. Cut 1/2in (1.3cm) from the underarm seam of the sleeve pattern and 1/2in (1.3cm) from the coat side seam as in *Illustration 37* in Chapter 5, "Making Your Own Patterns." Use either the short or long versions of the sleeve.

The finished dress in *Color Illustration 9* was made of a green, red and pink calico with tatting trim around the white collar and a pink bow tied at the neck. Red heart-shaped buttons fasten the dress in front.

This simple dress can be made of most any fabric with a variety of trims added to it.

HUGGY

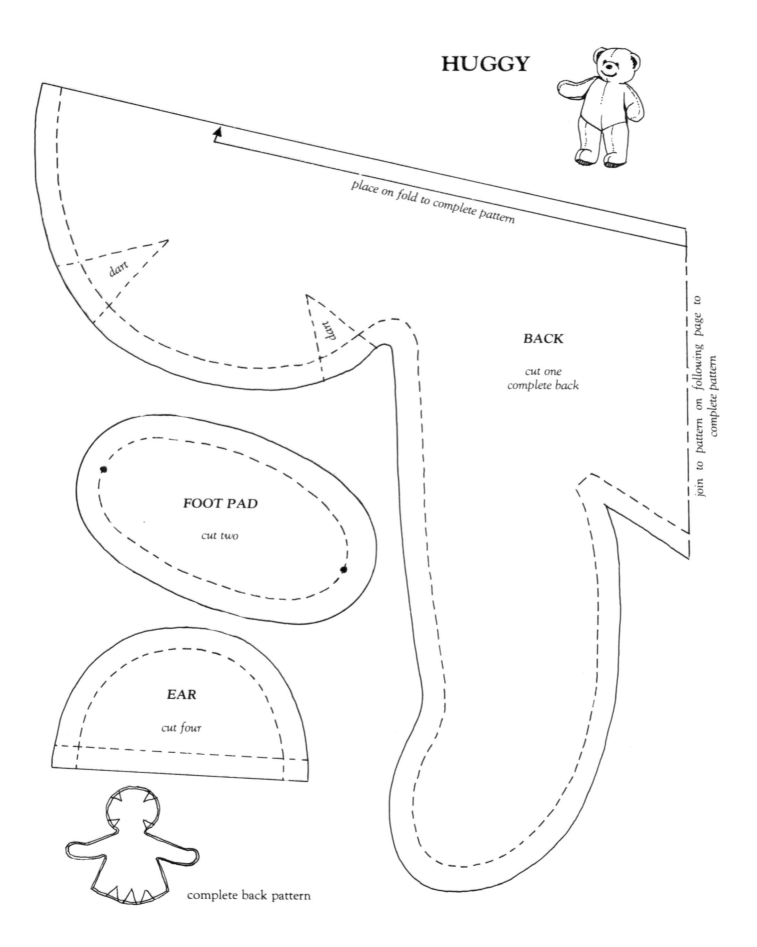

place on fold to complete pattern

dart

dart

BACK

*cut one
complete back*

join to pattern on following page to
complete pattern

FOOT PAD

cut two

EAR

cut four

complete back pattern

HUGGY

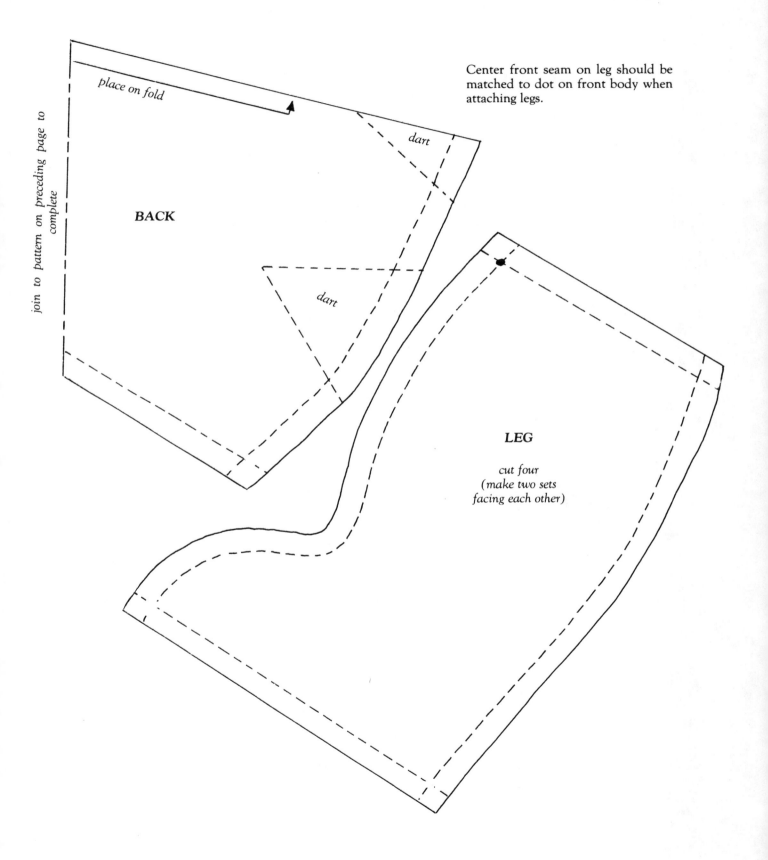

place on fold

join to pattern on preceding page to complete

BACK

dart

dart

Center front seam on leg should be matched to dot on front body when attaching legs.

LEG

*cut four
(make two sets
facing each other)*

HUGGY

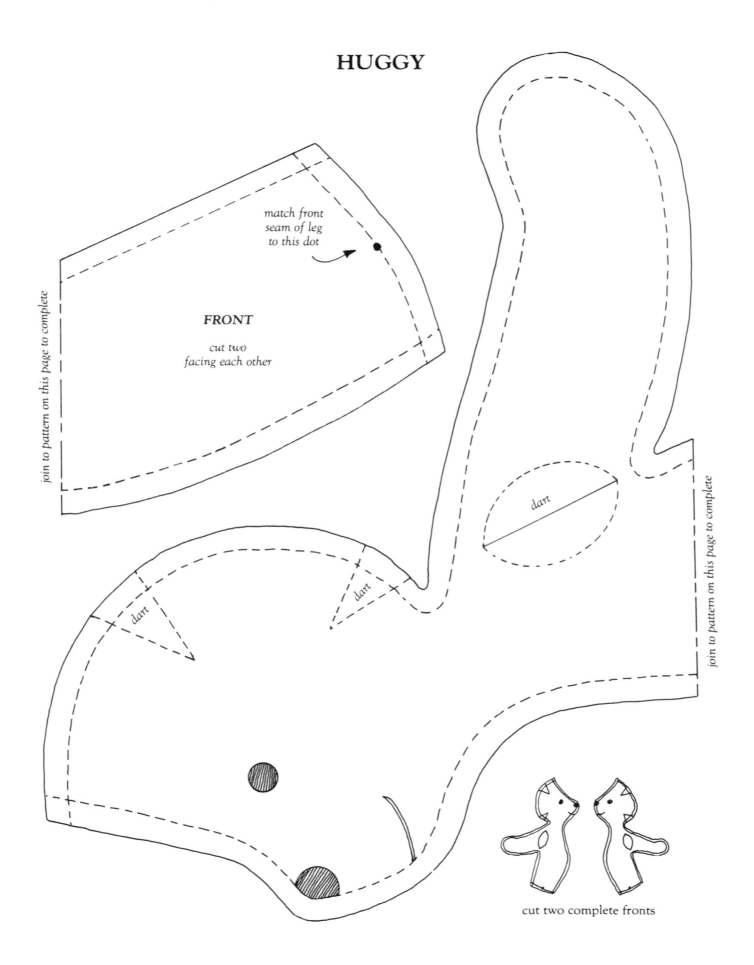

match front
seam of leg
to this dot

FRONT

*cut two
facing each other*

join to pattern on this page to complete

join to pattern on this page to complete

dart

dart

dart

cut two complete fronts

106

Chapter 8
OLD TIMEY TEDDY BEARS

Several years ago I had the rare opportunity of being with my sister-in-law, Merrill, when she and her childhood friend, "Teddy," were re-united. Her parents were leaving the large home they had lived in for many years to go to a small apartment and were going through their attic storage.

We stood over "Boo," her mother, and watched her remove first, Merrill's *Shirley Temple* doll, then her *Henry* doll, then a rare Effanbee *Luv-Ums* and toy blankets, pillow cases and quilts and other treasures to dazzle any doll collector! Suddenly Merrill lunged forward, reached down into the huge trunk and ever-so tenderly lifted a dingy squashed 12in (30.5cm) Teddy Bear. Tears welled up in her eyes as she held him to her cheek. "I, I didn't know you still had him," she whispered, still quite emotional.

During the last few years Teddy has lived with me — he is not mine, he is still Merrill's bear but he lives with me and all my bears. He can be seen in *Illustration 8*. There were heavy things on top of him in the trunk for four decades that squashed his nose to one side. To this day we have not been able to straighten it.

One day as I sat working at my desk with Merrill's old friend sitting near my notebook looking at me, I began to think about all the other bears who had spent a decade or two, or more, squashed in a trunk or box. Sure enough, when I began to look at other old bears and photographs of old bears, I saw the results of years of staying in the same position with things stored on top of them.

I set out to design some Teddy Bears, not so much like old bears were *originally*, but as they are now after years of hibernation.

I must, at this point, offer a confession to my friends. When I started the Old Timey designs, I was thinking of bears that would be more like caricatures of antique bears —something humorous. They did turn out whimsical but instead of laughing at them, my inclination was to hug them! In fact, my first reaction to the one I had labeled Old Timey "A" was, "Oh, what a sweetie pie you are!" My Old Timey "C" was originally to be named Roosevelt but became "Rosie" in a very short time.

To give your bears an old timey look, use fur cloth with a dull or grayish cast to the color, like that used for Rosie. Merrill's bear is quite dark gray-brown on his furless head and paws but under his little pink pajamas and white silk socks, he has beautiful golden blonde wool plush fur. The moths had long ago eaten the fur off his head and lower arms. You might clip your Old Timey's face and ears more than your other bears to give him a worn or moth-eaten look. You, of course, do not want to deceive anyone that a new bear is really old but you will want to recapture some of the lovable characteristics of the dear, real old timeys.

Rosie and Sweetie Pie can be lovable models for displaying old Teddy Bear or doll clothes and accessories as in *Color Illustration 12* and *Illustrations 70* and *72*.

Follow the directions for making jointed Classic bears in Chapter 6. There is a slight difference in the head construction since the Old Timey head center piece comes all the way down to the nose tip instead of stopping at the base of the snout as on the Classic bears.

There is a slight difference, also, in sewing the body or torso of both Rosie and Sweetie Pie. Stitch the two back pieces together and then the two fronts. Next, join the side seams and finally, sew across the crotch.

To achieve the floppy feel of antique bears, you may want to join each limb individually rather than use the wire or cord all the way through the body.

14in (35.6cm) ROSIE

Rosie, short for Roosevelt, was designed with the very long arms and large back hump of some antique Teddy Bears. This bear's nose is pushed up, giving her a perpetually "uppity" attitude. Rosie's feet are cut in a "pushed-up" position, making her stand on her heels while a grayish-tan fur cloth was selected to give her a dusty look. She does have an alternate, shorter paw for those who prefer a little more modern look.

Illustration 69. *Old Timey Rosie was constructed of a grayish beige fur to give her the dusty, old look of antique bears. Her arms are extremely long and her feet were cut so they look like they were bent up from years of being packed in a trunk. (Her pattern gives an alternate, somewhat shorter arm for a little more modern look.) She has claws embroidered on all her paws as do many antique bears — which, of course, is why she is an Old Timey Bear.*

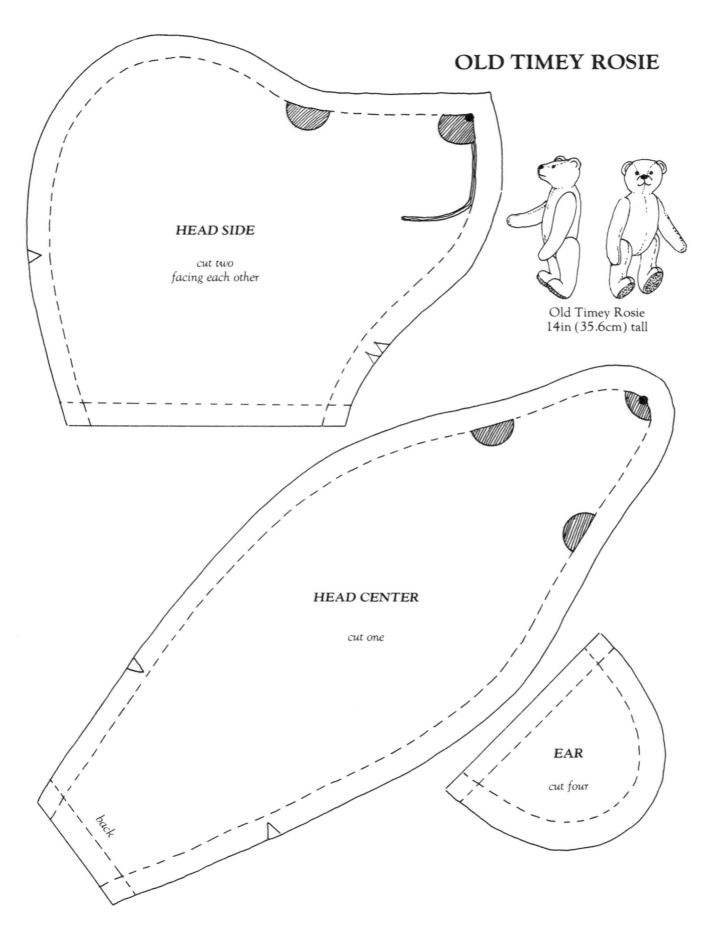

OLD TIMEY ROSIE

HEAD SIDE

cut two
facing each other

Old Timey Rosie
14in (35.6cm) tall

HEAD CENTER

cut one

back

EAR

cut four

108

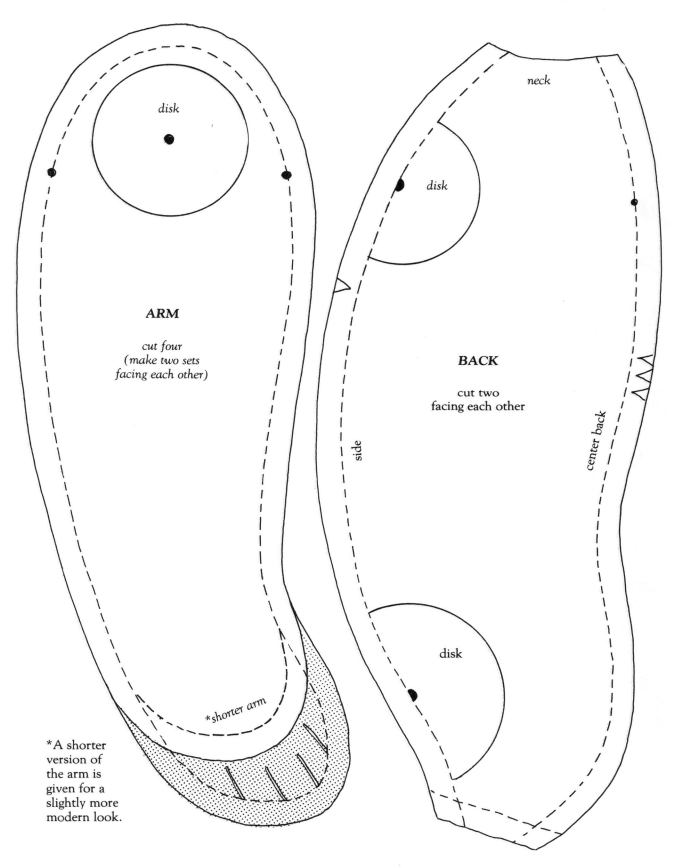

disk

ARM

*cut four
(make two sets
facing each other)*

*shorter arm

*A shorter
version of
the arm is
given for a
slightly more
modern look.

neck

disk

BACK

cut two
facing each other

side

center back

disk

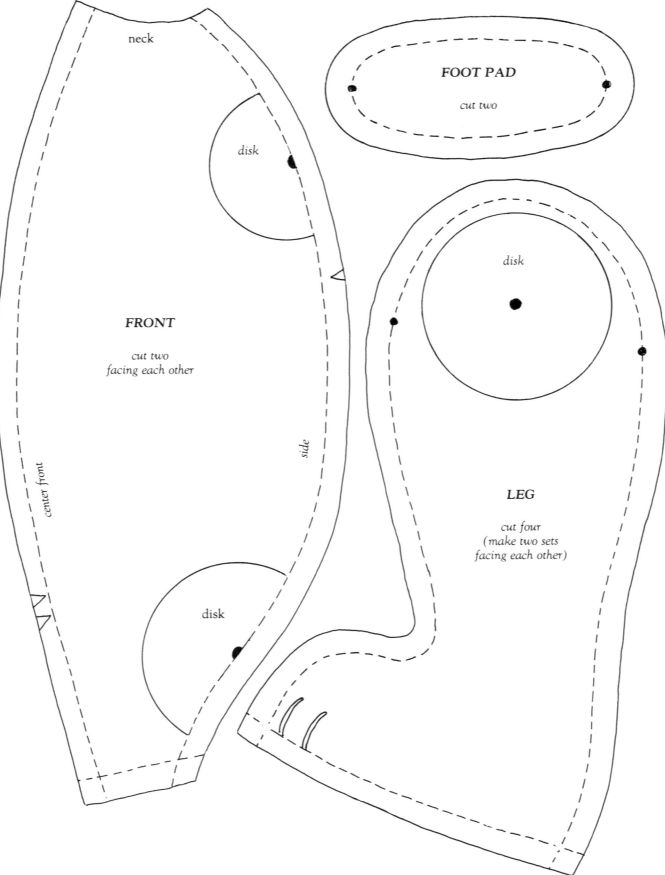

OLD TIMEY ROSIE

FOOT PAD

cut two

neck

disk

FRONT

cut two
facing each other

center front

side

disk

disk

LEG

cut four
(make two sets
facing each other)

Illustration 70. *Rosie sits beside a set of antique Teddy Bear sheets, pillow cases and an old satin pillow. She wears a very special Teddy Bear dress made by the author at age ten with a good deal of assistance from Mother. Of navy and yellow printed cotton, it has yellow grosgrain ribbon trim.*

Illustration 71. *Old Timey Sweetie Pie also has the characteristics of many antique Teddy Bears with her very large feet and squashed-down, demure looking snout. Her snout was trimmed so close to the pile "roots," it has the time-worn or moth-eaten look of a much loved very old bear. Her paws have embroidered claws. Her total look is timid and vulnerable, making everyone want to hold and talk to her.*

ROSIE'S CLOTHES

Rosie can wear Ginger's clothes, Sitting Bear's scarf, hat and mitten set, Buddy's sleepers and most of Cubby's things. Remember that Rosie has long arms so check the sleeve length of whatever pattern you use.

She wears Ginger's nightgown in *Color Illustration 11* and a sweater and cap made from Cubby's pattern in *Color Illustration on back cover.*

SWEETIE PIE

Sweetie Pie possesses long arms, too, but she has paws that curve more sharply to the front than Rosie's do. She has the very large feet of some antique bears. To give her the "hibernated" look, her nose was designed to have a "squashed down" look. Her big feet and timid downward snout give her the vulnerable, totally innocent look of a little cub.

SWEETIE PIE'S CLOTHES

All of Cubby's clothes patterns fit Sweetie Pie as do Buddy's sleepers. *Color Illustration on back cover* shows her in a coat made with Cubby's Rough Rider jacket pattern and a corduroy hat made with Ginger's pattern. Sitting Bear's scarf, hat and mittens described in Chapter 9 will fit her also.

Illustration 72. *Here Sweetie Pie shyly shows off a 50-year-old doll dress that was also worn many times by a much loved Teddy Bear. The 56-year-old Teddy Bear hat was the inspiration for Ginger's hat pattern. It even has its own original hat box (shown in Color Illustration 12).*

OLD TIMEY SWEETIE PIE

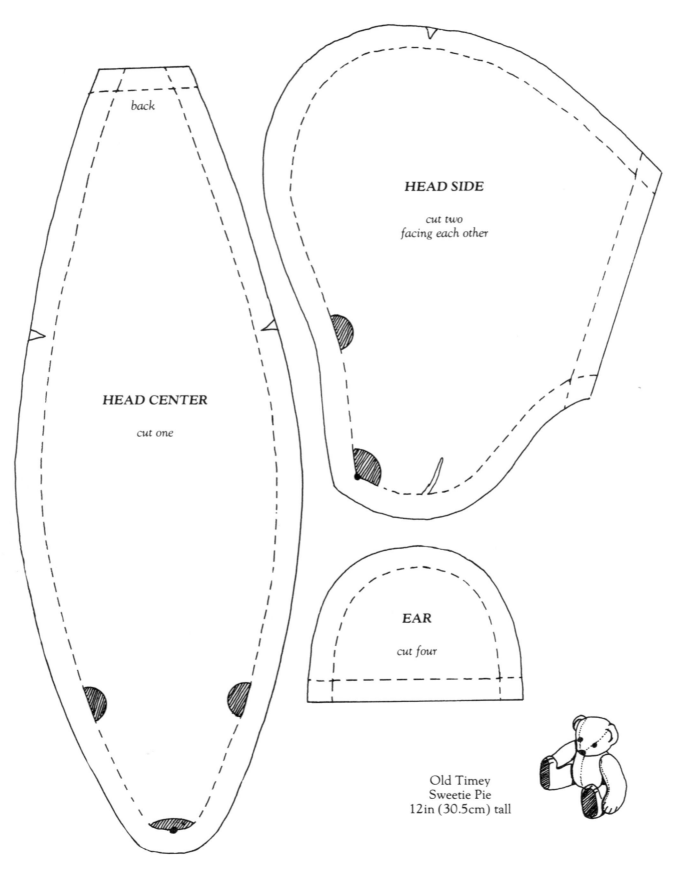

back

HEAD CENTER

cut one

HEAD SIDE

cut two
facing each other

EAR

cut four

Old Timey
Sweetie Pie
12in (30.5cm) tall

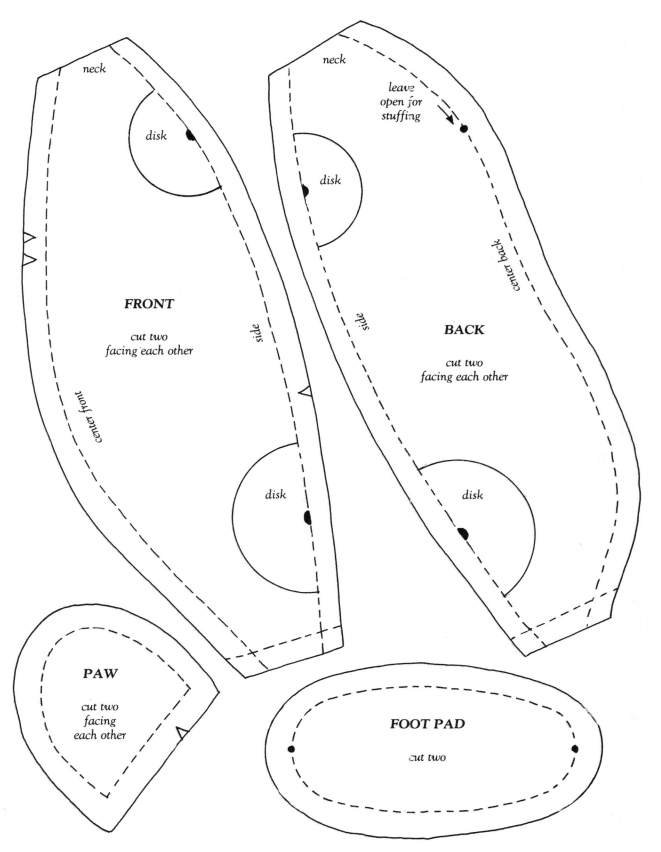

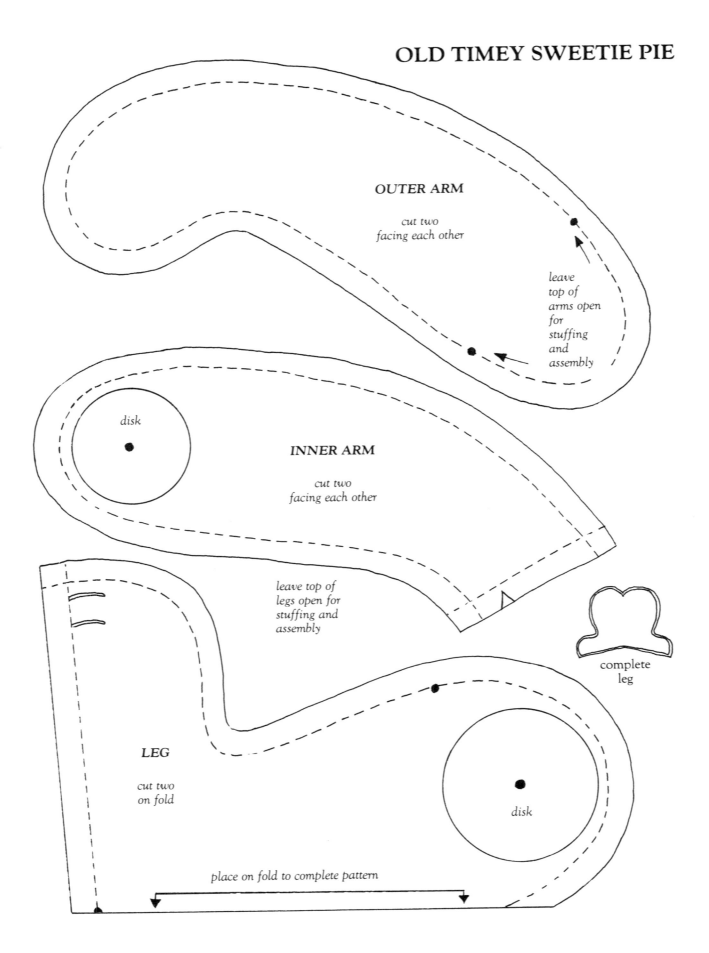

OLD TIMEY SWEETIE PIE

OUTER ARM

*cut two
facing each other*

*leave
top of
arms open
for
stuffing
and
assembly*

disk

INNER ARM

*cut two
facing each other*

*leave top of
legs open for
stuffing and
assembly*

complete
leg

LEG

*cut two
on fold*

disk

place on fold to complete pattern

Chapter 9
OVERTIME BEARS

Requiring only a minimum number of pieces, these three bears are quite simple to construct. They can be made of washable materials and serve a number of roles other than being loved and giving love to others. Of course, everyone knows that loving's all a bear has to do, that it is his reason for being, but Teddy Bears *can* have other purposes, too. Both Sitting Bear and Bea Bear are available for "overtime" work like being a throw pillow, an autograph collector, a bean bag, bath sponge, baby rattle or guardian angel.

These bears are modern and work well when constructed of modern materials. You can use just about any fabric from calico, corduroy, terry cloth or velour, to velveteen and fur cloth.

Although Buddy Bear is in Chapter 7, "Hinged Bears," he can qualify as an Overtime bear, too, when a zipper is put into his center back seam to make him into a pajama bag as in *Illustration 67*.

Buddy can also share a secret — you can hide whatever you want in his body. One young friend of mine who was told she was too old for her old security blanket ("Baa") cleverly folded it up, stored it inside her Buddy and took him everywhere with her. Nobody cares if you take a bear with you after you grow up. When she felt the need to hold her "Baa," she would unzip the zipper and reach in and hold the blanket.

Buddy helped her through a bad time which could otherwise have been traumatic.

SITTING BEAR

Constructed with only two main pattern pieces, plus an ear, Sitting Bear is deceiving because, at first glance, he looks like a jointed bear. He is surprisingly huggable and wears clothes well. He never falls over and can sit just about anywhere.

When made of a smooth fabric like muslin, cotton polyester or cotton twill in a light color, he becomes Autograph Bear. Be sure to stuff him firmly to fill out his form well for writing. Use bright colored felt tip, ball point or laundry marking pens for the signatures and messages. Such a keepsake will appeal to teenagers, kids and college students. Autograph Bear makes a unique gift for wedding or baby showers, farewell parties and birthdays. Students will love him with a scarf and cap of their own school colors.

Sitting Bear loves to sit among the throw pillows on a bed or sofa when he is made of calico, gingham or real patchwork to fit your room's decor.

Aside from collecting autographs or sitting among the pillows, Sitting Bear loves to work at another *very important overtime* job. He is particularly good at sitting in the corner of

a crib and keeping watch over a baby. His triangular shape makes him especially well suited for sitting in corners and he is a nice soft cushion for a wee one's head. Made of pink, blue, yellow or white fur cloth with his little wings added, he is a clever "Guardian Angel Bear" baby gift as in *Illustration 75*.

Illustration 73. *He wears clothes well in spite of his permanent sitting position. Here hs is dressed for play in Cubby's overalls and dark red ski sweater and cap. Autograph Bear, right, looks charming in a patchwork print dress made from Cubby's pattern.*

Illustration 74. *Sitting Bear is very simply constructed from only two main pattern pieces plus the ear and appears, at first glance, to be a jointed bear. He is an Overtime bear because he can be a throw pillow or autograph bear as well as a regular Teddy Bear.*

115

SITTING BEAR

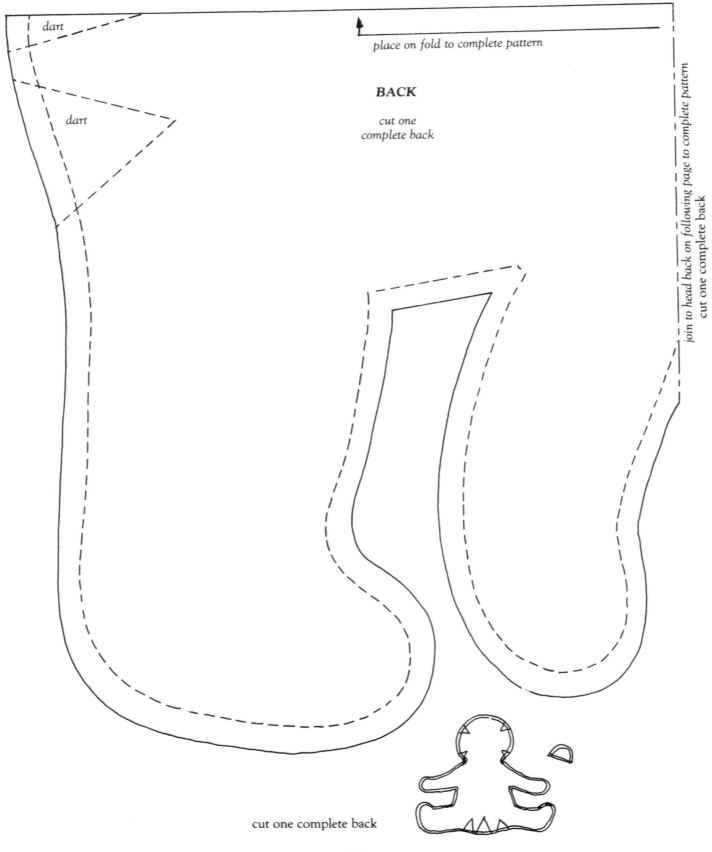

dart

dart

place on fold to complete pattern

BACK

*cut one
complete back*

join to head back on following page to complete pattern
cut one complete back

cut one complete back

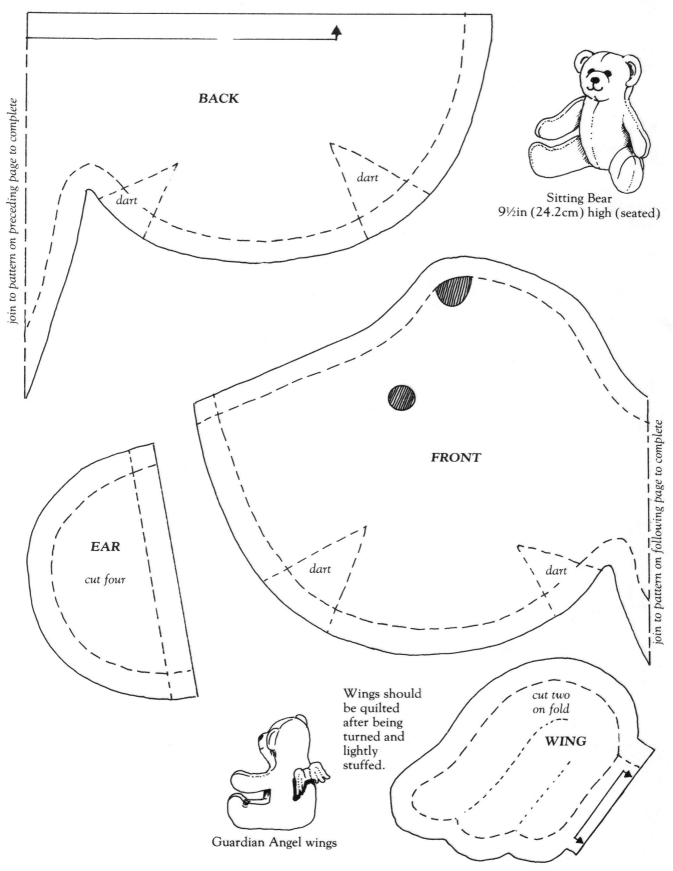

SITTING BEAR

BACK

join to pattern on preceding page to complete

dart

dart

Sitting Bear
9½in (24.2cm) high (seated)

FRONT

dart

dart

join to pattern on following page to complete

EAR

cut four

Wings should
be quilted
after being
turned and
lightly
stuffed.

Guardian Angel wings

*cut two
on fold*

WING

SITTING BEAR

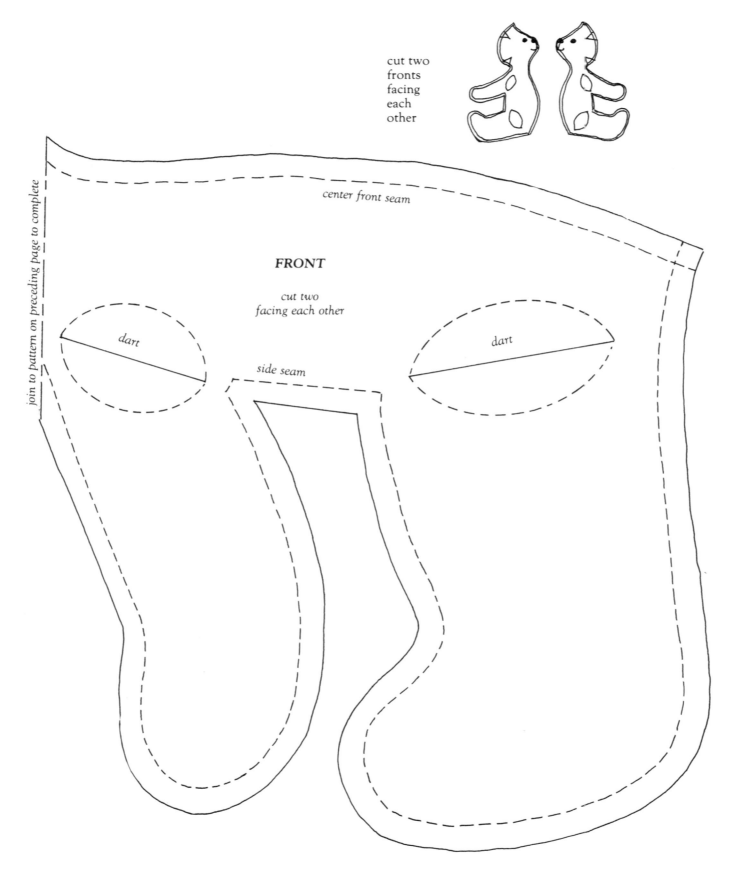

cut two
fronts
facing
each
other

center front seam

FRONT

*cut two
facing each other*

join to pattern on preceding page to complete

dart

dart

side seam

SITTING BEAR'S CLOTHES

All of Cubby's clothes fit Sitting Bear as do Buddy's sleepers. Not only does he wear clothes well, but he is much easier to dress than one would suspect. He is shown in *Illustration 73* wearing Cubby's overalls, dark red ski sweater and stocking cap.

Scarf, Hat and Mitten Set

Cut the scarf of knit cloth about 21 to 24in (53.3 to 61cm) long by about 4½in (11.5cm) wide. Hem the sides and ends, or if you prefer, add fringe as in *Color Illustration 15*.

Cut the cap about 11in (27.9cm) by 6in (15.2cm), fold in half and then sew the ends together, making a tube. Try it on your bear to see if it fits; then hem one end of the tube. Gather the other end and add your yarn pompon or tassle.

For mittens, cut two rectangles 5in (12.7cm) by 3½in (8.9cm) each. Hem one of the long sides of each one; then fold each in half with the hem to the outside. Next, sew down the side and across the bottom of each, rounding the corners as you go. Turn it inside out and presto — you have a pair of bear mittens!

If you give Sitting Bear as a baby gift wearing the scarf, hat and mittens, it would be a good idea to *sew them onto him, securely*. The scarf is long enough and the mittens small enough to possibly be of potential danger to an infant. You might also embroider the eyes just to be on the safe side.

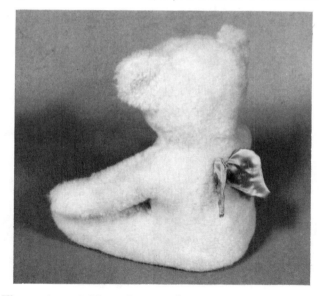

Illustration 75. He can be a guardian angel bear, and sit in a crib corner to watch over baby. Here, he shows his little quilted satin wings. What a unique and sweet gift for a new baby!

BEA BEAR

This little Teddy Bear can be a bean bag, he can be a bath sponge or he can be a baby rattle — that is why he is called Bea Bear. He can be made in two different sizes. The pattern includes both a back and front piece for each bear so actually there are *four pieces* superimposed on the one pattern.

Illustration 76. Bea Bear can be made in two sizes and perform a number of overtime jobs by being bean bags, bath sponges, baby rattles or just plain ole bears. They can be made of modern fabrics in bright colors and make fun baby gifts.

Trace the front. Next, trace the back and then cut it on the fold of your paper so you have a complete back piece, as shown.

Bea can do things that other, more expensive bears should not do like going for a swim or flying through the air like a missile.

Bean Bag Bea can be filled with either beans or rice, uncooked, of course. The stitching at his shoulders, ears, and hips will keep the filling distributed properly.

Bath Bea should be made of terry cloth and filled with shredded sponge, foam rubber, cut up nylon panty hose or cut up nylon net. Make lots of them — they can sit around the edge of your bathtub all day looking bright and cheerful, swim in a swimming pool or even go to the beach with you.

Rattle Bea should be made of a baby-safe fabric since an infant will inevitably teethe on him. A small, inexpensive baby rattle can be purchased to put inside his tummy. It probably will have a handle to be cut off. A homemade rattle can be fashioned from a small plastic pill bottle with a child-proof cap and a little Christmas bell or two dried beans. Put the bell or beans in the bottle, fasten the cap and bury it safely inside the torso stuffing. *Make sure everything is sewn securely so the bottle is safely inside.* As a further safety measure, embroider the eyes instead of using buttons.

He can even be a sachet bear if you make him of a sheer fabric and fill him with potpourri. He can live in a linen or lingerie drawer or hang in your closet.

BEA BEAR'S CLOTHES

All the Bea Bears really need in the way of clothing is a ribbon bow at the neck. If you prefer to make clothes for them, use Classic 9in (22.9cm) Benjamin's patterns for the larger one, making adjustments chiefly in the arm and leg length. For the smaller bear, use the clothes for Tiny Teddy Papa or Petite Père of the Miniature Bears. Bea's arms and legs are a bit fatter and shorter so small adjustments will be needed in your patterns.

119

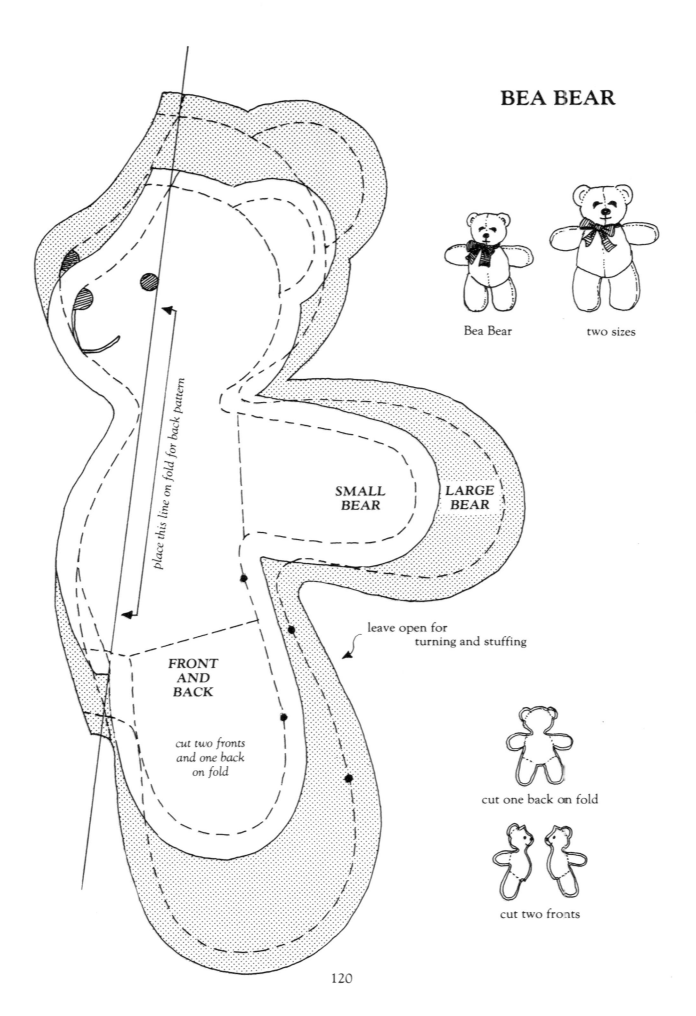

BEA BEAR

Bea Bear   two sizes

place this line on fold for back pattern

SMALL BEAR   LARGE BEAR

leave open for turning and stuffing

FRONT
AND
BACK

*cut two fronts
and one back
on fold*

cut one back on fold

cut two fronts

120

Chapter 10
MINIATURE BEARS

These littlest bears can sit on the palm of your hand, ride in your pocket and go anywhere with you. *There are rumors that lots of people secretly carry miniature Teddy Bears around with them.*

They are designed to fit two different scales of doll houses or miniature rooms. And, you can even sew a safety pin to one's back and wear him as a lapel pin. They are so versatile and so much fun, you will think of other ways to enjoy them.

For a really SPECIAL project why not make a bear family to represent your own or someone else's family. Children (of all ages) love to point out "themselves" to guests and name each member of the family. Such tiny bears cost practically nothing but are capable of bringing a great deal of joy into people's lives!

They may be sewn on the machine or if you like, be made entirely by hand. For hand-sewing, use a backstitch which is as strong as machine stitching. They are so tiny, they do not take up much room in a sewing basket so you can cut out several bears at a time, pin the pieces together for each and put them in a plastic bag with needle and matching thread. They are always ready to be basted and/or sewn when you have a little time to spare.

Use very short pile fur cloth of a light weight, velvet, velveteen, suede-type cloth, sweat shirt fleece, corduroy, terry cloth, fleece coating, fleece lining, cotton flannel, wool flannel or felt.

Furry fabrics can be picked with a large needle or pin at the seams to free the pile fibers caught in the seam to disguise them.

When shopping, always check for suitable fabrics and purchase small amounts of any you think might be the correct weight and color for miniatures. If you accumulate a collection of cloth, it can provide marvelous creative entertainment some wintry or rainy day.

For the classiest miniature Teddy Bears of all, purchase just 1/2yd (45.7cm) each of 100% camel's hair, cashmere or mohair cloth. You cannot imagine a softer, more elegant Teddy than one made of cashmere! As a gift, it can cause an absolute sensation.

SEWING MINIATURES

Small inaccuracies on large bears are hardly noticed but on miniatures a fraction of an inch can make a large imperfection. It takes one only a little more time to make *two patterns* but your time will be well spent. Trace the patterns, as directed, on typing paper; then rubber cement them to a heavy sturdy paper or light-weight cardboard and cut them out *carefully and accurately*. They will last through

dozens of little bears — and take notice — miniature bears are like the famous potato chips that advertise, "You can't eat just one;" you are sure to want to make lots of them!

Illustration 77. *The non-jointed Tiny Teddy Family consists of Papa, 7¼in (18.5cm) tall; Mama, 6in (15.2cm); Bubba or Sissy, 4½in (11.5cm); and Baby, 3¼in (8.3cm). They can live in a doll house or enhance your Christmas tree. They like to go places with you in your pocket and bring you good luck.*

TINY TEDDY FAMILY

Although simply constructed from only two pattern pieces, these tiny non-jointed bears are designed so they appear much more complicated. They range in size from about 3in (7.6cm) to 7in (17.8cm) and take practically no time at all to make.

For Christmas tree ornaments just tie bright ribbons around their necks, make hat and muffler sets or completely dress them. Just take a needle and dark thread, go in and then out of the back of the head in one large stitch, leave the threads about 4 or 5in (10.2 or 12.7cm) long at each end and tie them in a knot. That is all there is to it — it is so simple you can put the hanging thread in, use the bears on your tree and then pull the threads out after the holidays. This way you can enjoy your Tiny Teddies all year round.

CONSTRUCTING TINY TEDDIES

1. Trace patterns for the back and front pieces with seam allowances — the dark areas or cutting line. Do not go

TINY PAPA

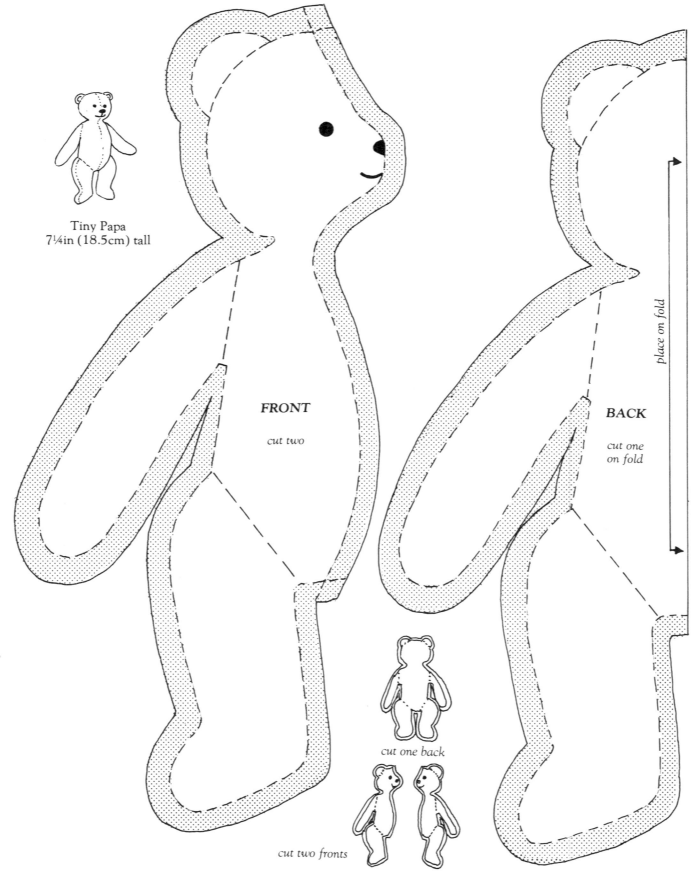

Tiny Papa
7¼in (18.5cm) tall

FRONT

cut two

BACK

*cut one
on fold*

place on fold

cut one back

cut two fronts

TINY PAPA'S CLOTHES

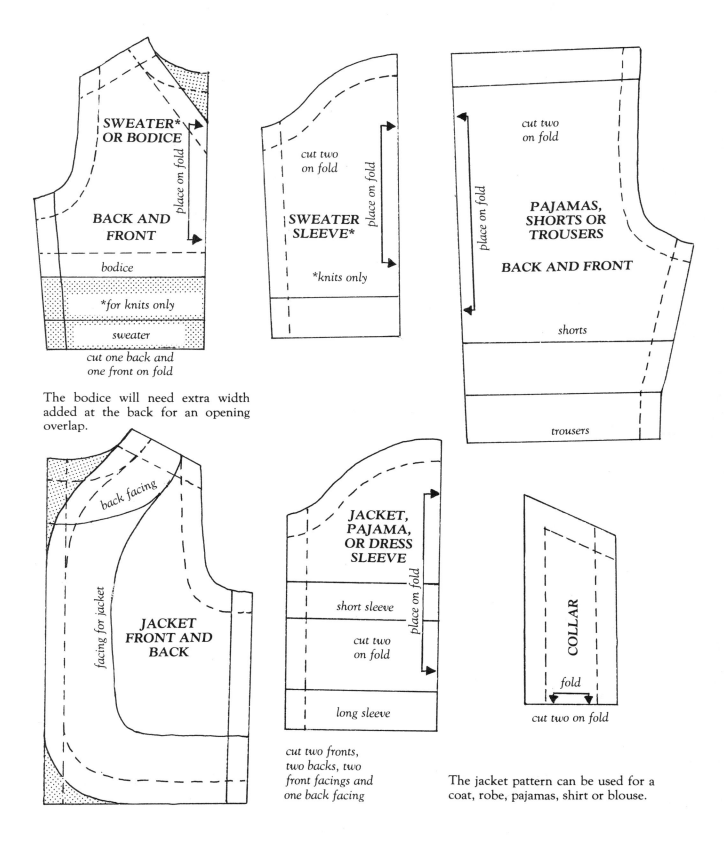

SWEATER* OR BODICE

BACK AND FRONT

place on fold

bodice

*for knits only

sweater

cut one back and one front on fold

The bodice will need extra width added at the back for an opening overlap.

SWEATER SLEEVE*

cut two on fold

place on fold

*knits only

PAJAMAS, SHORTS OR TROUSERS

BACK AND FRONT

cut two on fold

place on fold

shorts

trousers

back facing

facing for jacket

JACKET FRONT AND BACK

JACKET, PAJAMA, OR DRESS SLEEVE

short sleeve

cut two on fold

place on fold

long sleeve

cut two fronts, two backs, two front facings and one back facing

COLLAR

fold

cut two on fold

The jacket pattern can be used for a coat, robe, pajamas, shirt or blouse.

123

TINY MAMA

Tiny Mama
6in (15.2cm) tall

FRONT

*cut two
facing
each other*

BACK

cut one

cut one back and two fronts

TINY MAMA'S CLOTHES

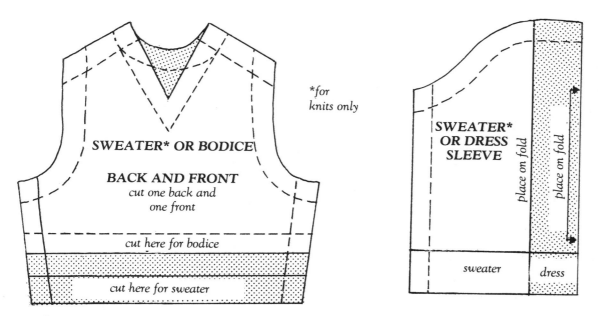

SWEATER* OR BODICE

BACK AND FRONT
*cut one back and
one front*

cut here for bodice

cut here for sweater

*for
knits only*

SWEATER*
OR DRESS
SLEEVE

place on fold

place on fold

sweater   *dress*

Add width
to sweater
sleeve for
dress. For
a full
gathered
sleeve, add
still more
width.

When making the bodice you will need to make either a front or back opening.
Add extra width at the opening for the overlap.

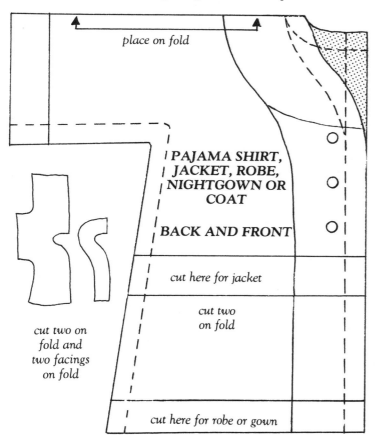

place on fold

PAJAMA SHIRT,
JACKET, ROBE,
NIGHTGOWN OR
COAT

BACK AND FRONT

cut here for jacket

*cut two
on fold*

cut here for robe or gown

*cut two on
fold and
two facings
on fold*

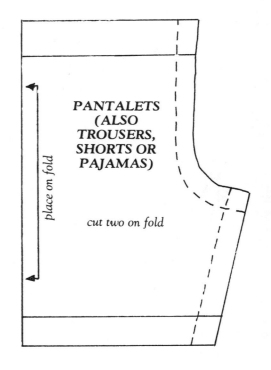

PANTALETS
(ALSO
TROUSERS,
SHORTS OR
PAJAMAS)

place on fold

cut two on fold

TINY SISSY OR BUBBA

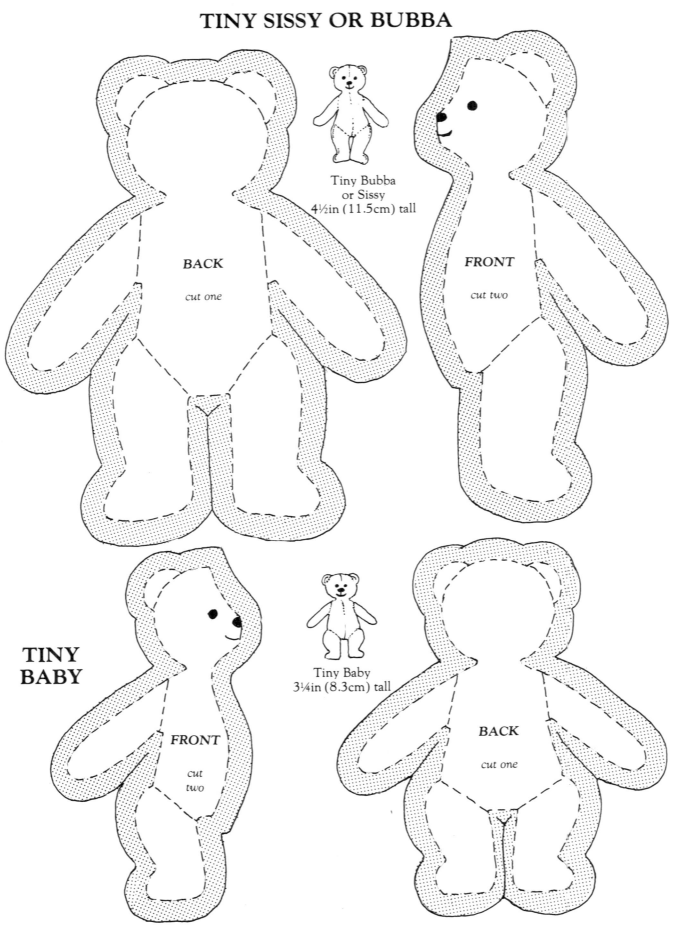

Tiny Bubba
or Sissy
4½in (11.5cm) tall

BACK

cut one

FRONT

cut two

TINY BABY

Tiny Baby
3¼in (8.3cm) tall

FRONT

cut two

BACK

cut one

126

TINY SISSY'S OR BUBBA'S CLOTHES

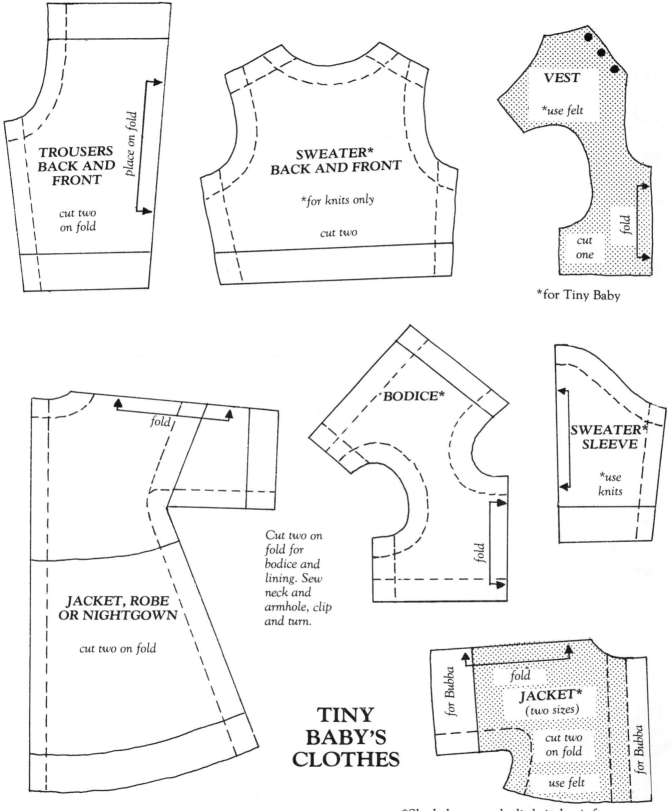

TROUSERS BACK AND FRONT

cut two on fold

place on fold

SWEATER* BACK AND FRONT

*for knits only

cut two

VEST

*use felt

fold

cut one

*for Tiny Baby

JACKET, ROBE OR NIGHTGOWN

fold

cut two on fold

BODICE*

Cut two on fold for bodice and lining. Sew neck and armhole, clip and turn.

fold

SWEATER* SLEEVE

*use knits

TINY BABY'S CLOTHES

for Bubba

fold

JACKET* (two sizes)

cut two on fold

use felt

for Bubba

*Shaded area on the little jacket is for Baby as is the shaded vest above.

127

up between the legs or under the arms when you draw them. *Illustration 78*, left.

2. Trace patterns again *without seam allowances* on the light area or stitching line this time. *Illustration 78*, right.

3. Draw around the larger pattern onto the *back* side of your fabric. This will be your *cutting line*. *Illustration 79*, top.

4. Next, place the smaller pattern *inside* the larger drawn area and draw around it. This will be the line you *sew* on. *Illustration 79*, bottom.

5. Cut out your bear following the larger outside lines.

6. BASTE before machine sewing, making your basting stitches directly on the inside or stitching lines. Begin with the center front seam.

7. Sew the two front pieces together from the top of the head to the crotch. When sewing miniatures, always use a small stitch on your machine.

8. Sew the front to the back by starting at the top of the head and going down the side, around the arm and leg, to the center of the crotch. Repeat on the other side. Be sure to leave an opening on one side of the torso or leg for turning and stuffing.

9. Clip all corners and curves, and between the legs and underarms. (When making the tiniest bear, you may wish to trim your seams to about 1/8in (0.31cm) to facilitate turning.)

10. Turn right side out by using a small dowel or stick to push with. A kelly forceps from a medical supply store is a great help in turning miniature bears.

11. After turning, *before stuffing*, sew or pin across the ears where they join the head as indicated on the patterns. Do not stuff the ears at all.

12. Stuff head firmly.

13. Stuff hands and feet and then the arms and legs up to about 1/2in (1.3cm) below the stitching line at shoulders and hips. Stitch as indicated or place a safety pin on the stitching lines. Leaving space at the shoulders and hips will allow your bear to sit and move his arms. It makes him flexible for dressing, too.

14. Stuff torso firmly.

15. Close the opening with a whip stitch.

16. Remove pins and sew across ears, shoulders and hips.

17. Embroider face. It is fun to use two black headed silk pins for *temporary* eyes. Embroider the nose and mouth and then move the eyes around in different positions till you get just the right facial expression. Remove one pin and embroider an eye in its place; then do the other. Embroider the eyes by doing a satin stitch with black thread over and over in several different directions to make it round over like a bead. Large French knots can be used as can tiny black beads.

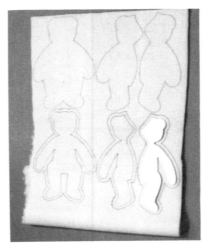

Illustration 79. *First, draw the large back pattern, then draw two large fronts facing each other as shown at top. Next, center the smaller patterns inside the larger drawn outlines and draw around them for your stitching lines as shown at bottom. This method will make sewing miniatures both easier and more accurate. Accuracy is imperative on such small bears.*

TINY TEDDY CLOTHES

Each little bear has enough patterns for clothes to provide him with a whole wardrobe. Most of their little garments are interchangeable with those of Ma Petitie Famille. See *Color Illustration 17* (in sleigh) and inset on front cover.

Illustration 80. *Two Tiny Teddies stand among a collection of small scale striped knit fabrics used for charming little caps and mufflers. Cap pompons are small chenille balls from cotton ball fringe.*

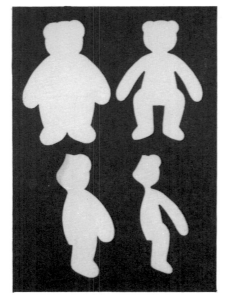

Illustration 78. *Miniature Teddy Bears should be constructed by the double-pattern method, drawing around one for the cutting line and the other for the stitching line. Since Tiny Teddy patterns have two pieces, you will, of course, have four pieces by this method.*

PETITE PÈRE

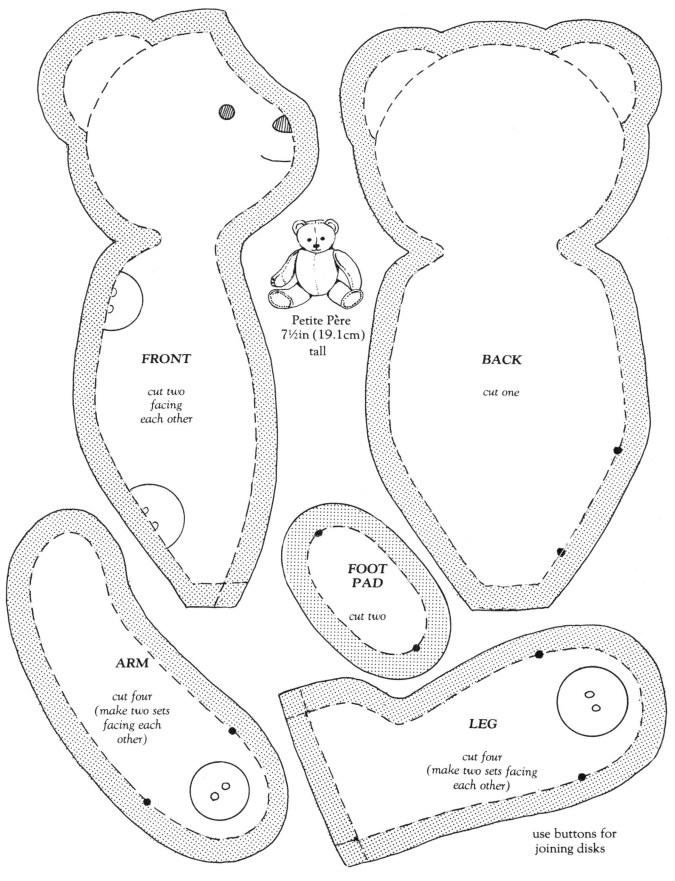

FRONT

cut two facing each other

BACK

cut one

Petite Père
7½in (19.1cm)
tall

FOOT PAD

cut two

ARM

cut four (make two sets facing each other)

LEG

cut four (make two sets facing each other)

use buttons for joining disks

PETITE PÈRE'S CLOTHES

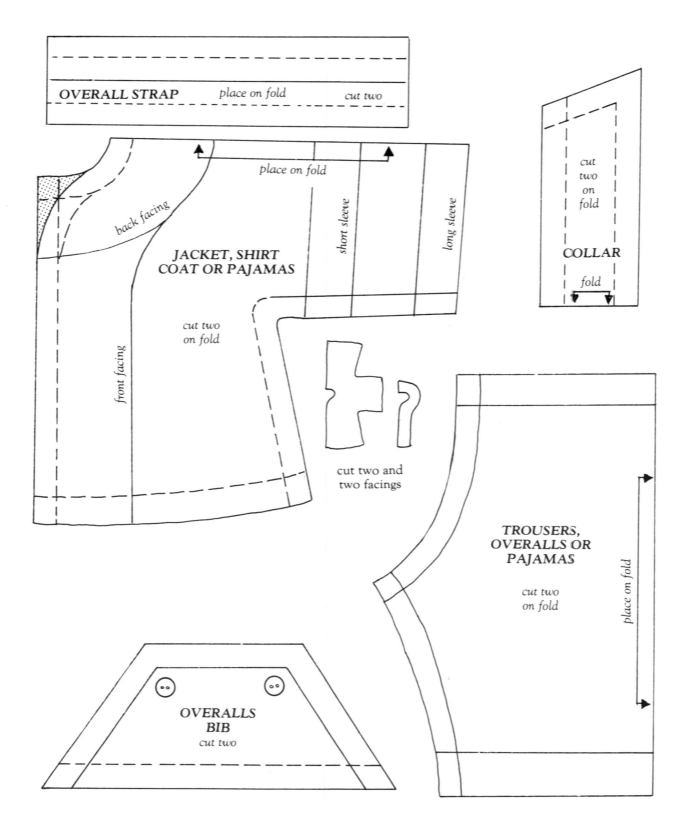

OVERALL STRAP *place on fold* *cut two*

back facing

JACKET, SHIRT COAT OR PAJAMAS

place on fold

short sleeve

long sleeve

front facing

cut two on fold

cut two and two facings

COLLAR

cut two on fold

fold

TROUSERS, OVERALLS OR PAJAMAS

cut two on fold

place on fold

OVERALLS BIB

cut two

PETITE MÈRE

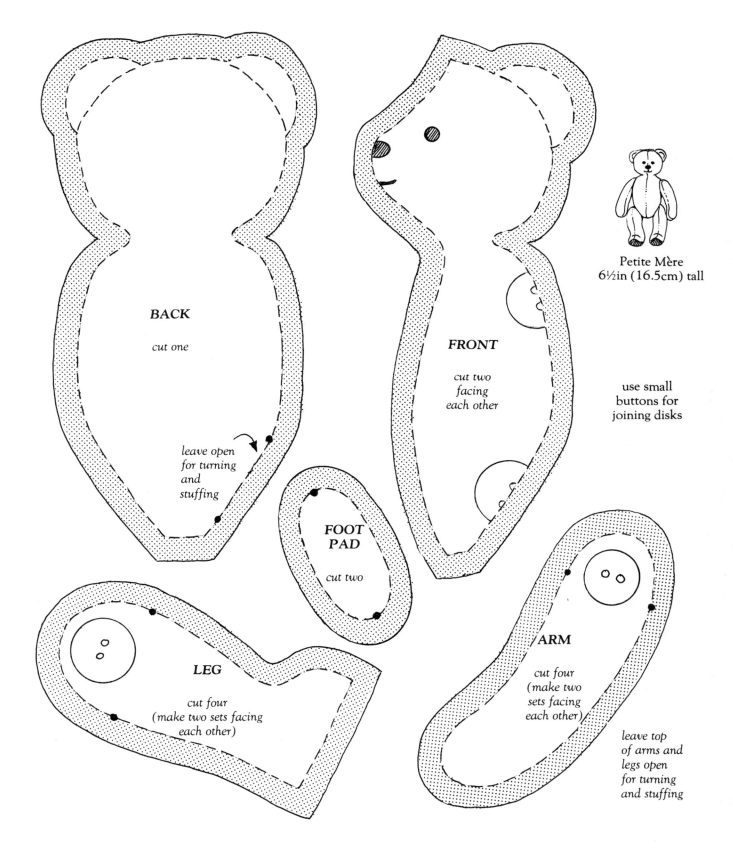

BACK

cut one

*leave open
for turning
and
stuffing*

FRONT

*cut two
facing
each other*

Petite Mère
6½in (16.5cm) tall

use small
buttons for
joining disks

**FOOT
PAD**

cut two

LEG

*cut four
(make two sets facing
each other)*

ARM

*cut four
(make two
sets facing
each other)*

*leave top
of arms and
legs open
for turning
and stuffing*

PETITE MÈRE'S CLOTHES

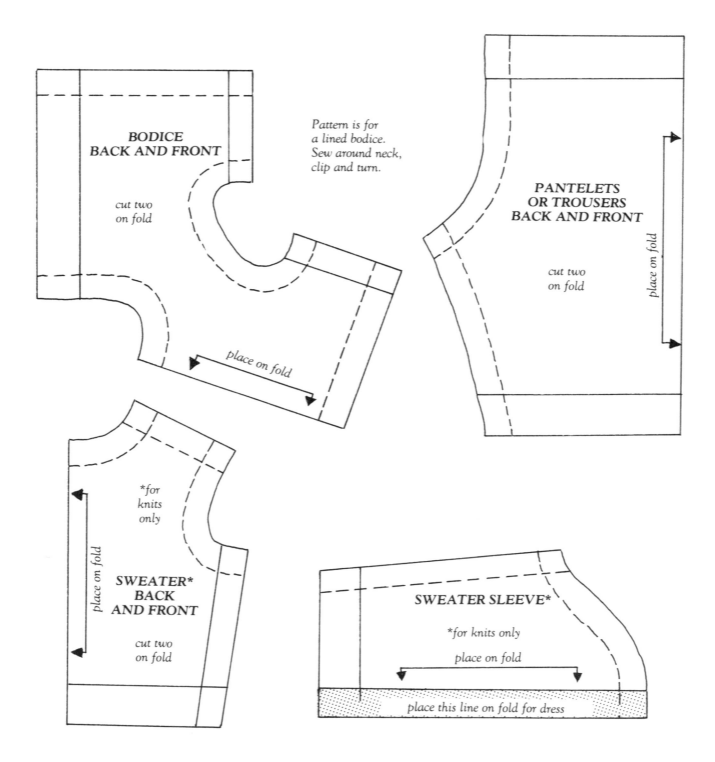

**BODICE
BACK AND FRONT**

*cut two
on fold*

*Pattern is for
a lined bodice.
Sew around neck,
clip and turn.*

place on fold

**PANTELETS
OR TROUSERS
BACK AND FRONT**

*cut two
on fold*

place on fold

*for
knits
only*

place on fold

**SWEATER*
BACK
AND FRONT**

*cut two
on fold*

SWEATER SLEEVE*

for knits only

place on fold

place this line on fold for dress

PETITE BABETTE OR PHILIPPE

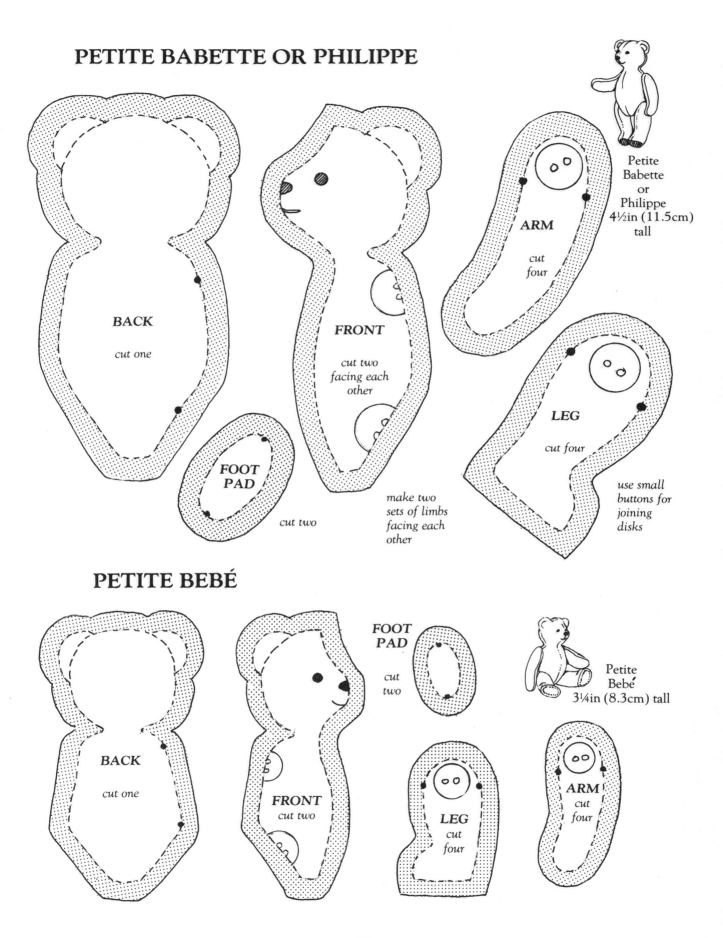

BACK

cut one

FRONT

*cut two
facing each
other*

**FOOT
PAD**

cut two

*make two
sets of limbs
facing each
other*

ARM

*cut
four*

LEG

cut four

*use small
buttons for
joining
disks*

Petite
Babette
or
Philippe
4½in (11.5cm)
tall

PETITE BEBÉ

BACK

cut one

FRONT

cut two

**FOOT
PAD**

*cut
two*

LEG

*cut
four*

ARM

*cut
four*

Petite
Bebé
3¼in (8.3cm) tall

133

PETITE BABETTE'S OR PHILIPPE'S CLOTHES

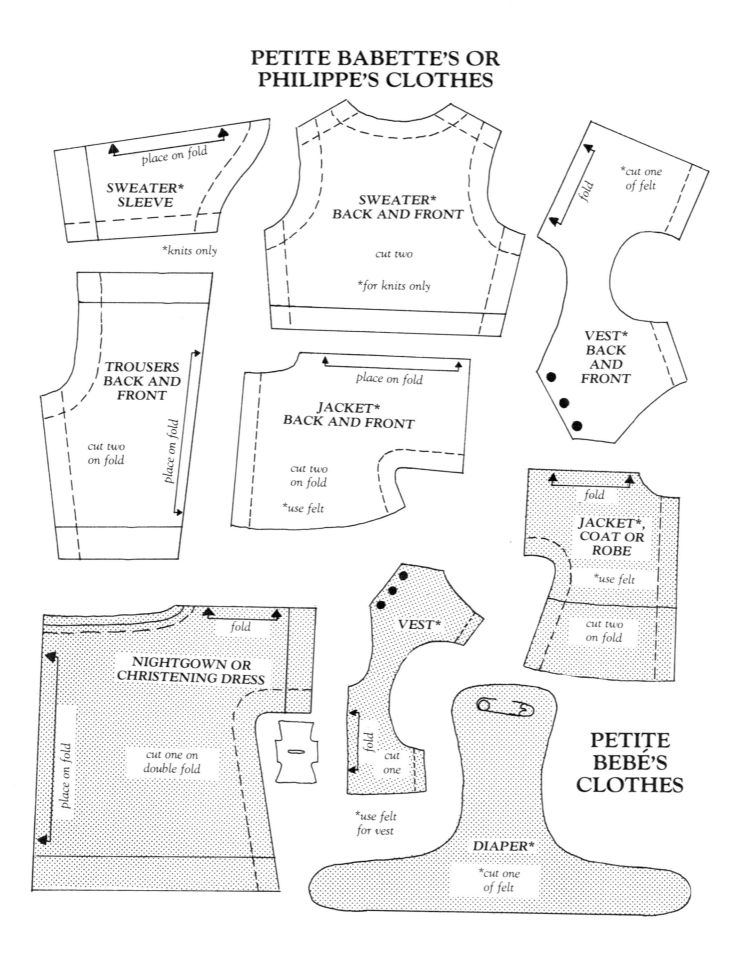

place on fold

SWEATER*
SLEEVE

*knits only

SWEATER*
BACK AND FRONT

cut two

*for knits only

*cut one
of felt

fold

VEST*
BACK
AND
FRONT

TROUSERS
BACK AND
FRONT

cut two
on fold

place on fold

place on fold

JACKET*
BACK AND FRONT

cut two
on fold

*use felt

fold

JACKET*,
COAT OR
ROBE

*use felt

cut two
on fold

NIGHTGOWN OR
CHRISTENING DRESS

cut one on
double fold

place on fold

VEST*

fold

cut
one

*use felt
for vest

PETITE
BEBÉ'S
CLOTHES

DIAPER*

*cut one
of felt

MA PETITE FAMILLE

These jointed bears, made with care, can rival the finest, most expensive commercially-made miniatures. Scaled for two different sizes of doll houses or miniature rooms, they range from 3¼in (8.3cm) to 7½in (19.1cm) in height.

All four members of the family are designed for the larger 2in (5.1cm) to 1ft (30.5cm) doll house or Barbie scale. For the smaller traditional 1in (2.5cm) to 1ft (30.5cm) scale doll houses, use only the two smaller bears with the 4½in (11.5cm) pattern for adults and the 3¼in (8.3cm) for children as in *Illustration 82.*

If you are a miniature enthusiast, you will already know that not many little Teddy Bears are really well proportioned or properly scaled for doll houses. Although these bears require more time and effort than the non-jointed Tiny Teddies, they can be made in far less time than the large jointed bears.

They wear clothes well and each one has enough basic patterns for a variety of garments. Most of their clothes are interchangeable with those of the Tiny Teddy Family. See *Color Illustrations 16* and *17* and Table of Contents page.

CONSTRUCTING JOINTED MINIATURE BEARS

Follow the *first six steps* in the directions for constructing Tiny Teddies concerning tracing double patterns, drawing them onto cloth, cutting out your bear and basting it together.

Although their torso and head is somewhat simplified, their arms and legs are joined to the body in the same manner as the large Classic Bears in Chapter 6. Follow the directions for "Assembling Your Jointed Bear."

Instead of disks, just use old buttons from your button box. It's a good way to use up some of those buttons you have been saving for years. The smallest bears need buttons in the limbs only, not inside the body.

One or two cords are sufficient for such small bears. The secret of good joints is in stuffing the body firmly and then squeezing it as you pull your cords and tie them.

If you have a large enough needle, like those used for upholstering, you do not have to lay the cords in during stuffing. Instead, just push the needle with a double cord through the bear's body using the dots as guides.

Place part of a toothpick over the center of each button, especially old ones, to prevent breaking the center. After tying the cords, place a bit of glue on the knot and toothpick to prevent its ever slipping out of place.

Illustration 81. *Ma Petite Famille are miniature, jointed, doll house-size Teddy Bears. The family consists of Père, 7½in (19.1cm) tall; Mère, 6½in (16.5cm); Philippe or Babette, 4½in (11.5cm); and, Bebé, 3¼in (8.3cm). They can all live in a Barbie-sized dollhouse or, just the two smaller ones, in a traditional 1in (2.5cm) to 1ft (30.5cm) scale doll house.*

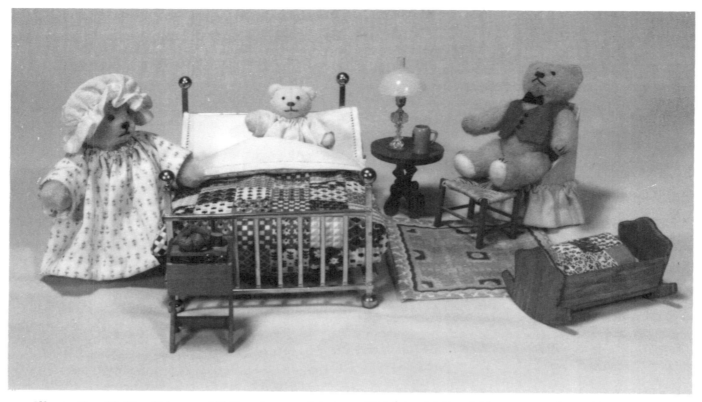

Illustration 82. *Here Babette and Philippe become adult size and Bebé, the child (or children), in a traditional 1in (2.5cm) to 1ft (30.5cm) scale dollhouse. You can make lots of miniature bears to live in your miniature rooms, doll houses or display cabinets for a fraction of the cost of commercially-made miniatures.*

Illustration 83. *Here is Père and Mère's wedding picture with Bebé as a flower girl or ring bearer. Père wears his brown checked suit and pocket watch while Mère looks radiant in her white lace bridal gown and veil. They are small enough to stand on a wedding cake!*

Chapter 11
CIRCUS BEARS

In ancient Rome, and even earlier in Egypt, the circus was a favorite form of entertainment. During the Middle Ages there were no more large circuses, just small traveling acts of jugglers, troubadours and trained animals. The trained bear was a popular animal act throughout Western Europe.

In early America, trained animal acts usually consisted of monkeys or bears, the monkeys brought here by sailors and the bears being caught as cubs by trappers. These trained animals were usually part of medicine shows. The acts would consist of a man "wrestling" a muzzled bear or a bear walking on his hind legs and turning around or "dancing."

In the late 19th century, the great traveling circus of P.T. Barnum and James A. Bailey always had German or Russian bears as part of the show. It was, however, not until the early 20th century that audiences realized for the first time just how enchanting these bears could be. For the first time, bears were taught to wear clothes, roller skate, ride bicycles, walk tight ropes, walk on stilts and even play musical instruments. The famous Pallenberg Family's "Wonder Bears" were billed as "Bruins that do things like humans." And, indeed, they did have an incredible human-like quality. It was as if Seymour Eaton's Teddy G and Teddy B of a few years earlier had come to life! One wonders, upon seeing the old circus posters, if the Pallenbergs did not get the idea for their act from Mr. Eaton's books.

The bears in this chapter were proportioned to be more like real bruins than Teddy Bears although no matter how seriously one tries to make them realistic, they still have a Teddy Bear quality.

Barnum's clown suit was inspired by both an old circus poster and the 1906 book by Seymour Eaton, *The Roosevelt Bears, Their Travels and Adventures. Color Illustration 18* shows several Barnums in clown suits and neck ruffs.

CONSTRUCTING THE CIRCUS BEAR BARNUM

Follow the directions for "Assembling Your Jointed Bear" in Chapter 6 with the exception of step number 5 which concerns sewing on the head. Barnum has a combined torso and head.

BARNUM'S CLOTHES

Because of space, Barnum's clown suit pattern had to be broken and overlapped. Complete as directed. It can also be used for pajamas or trousers and shirt if you reduce the size by taking away width at the underarm and side seam.

By using a straight line at the center front and back instead of the curved trousers line, you can adapt the pattern for a night shirt, full nightgown or bathrobe. Seymour Eaton's 1905 book, *The Adventures of the Traveling Bears*, has an illustration of Teddy B and Teddy G on the cover wearing nightshirts while in a pullman train car.

Illustration 84. Barnum has more realistic, adult bear proportions than the other bears. He is designed after circus bears who perform while standing on their hind legs and act quite human-like.

Illustration 85. Barnum, dressed in a commercially-made "Snoopy" suit, looks as though he stepped from the pages of one of Seymour Eaton's The Roosevelt Bears *books published from 1906 to 1908.*

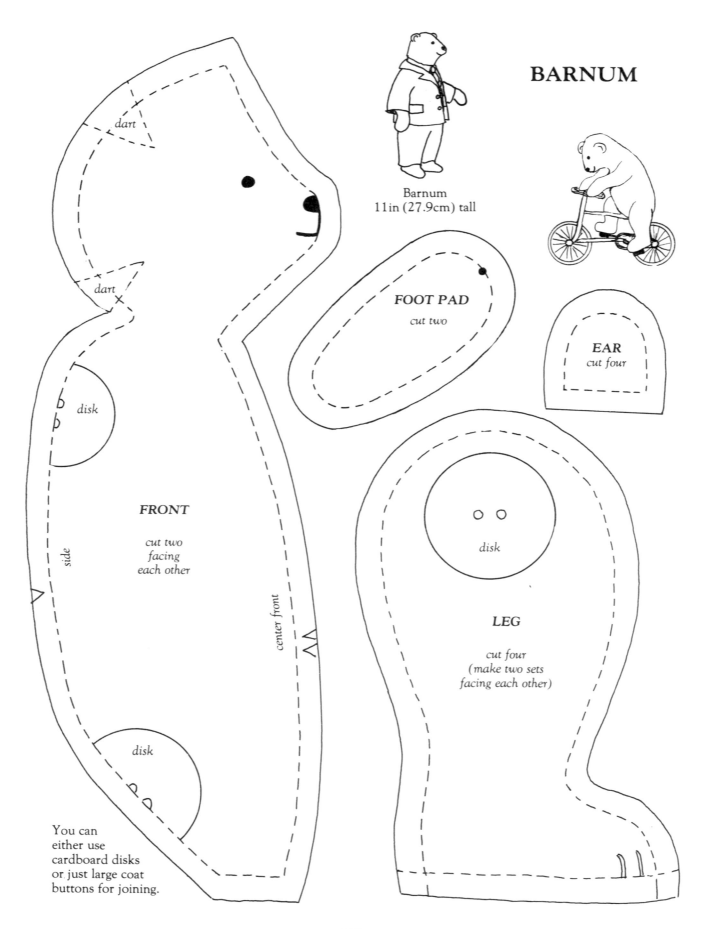

BARNUM

Barnum
11in (27.9cm) tall

dart

dart

×

disk

FRONT

side

*cut two
facing
each other*

center front

disk

You can
either use
cardboard disks
or just large coat
buttons for joining.

FOOT PAD

cut two

EAR

cut four

disk

LEG

*cut four
(make two sets
facing each other)*

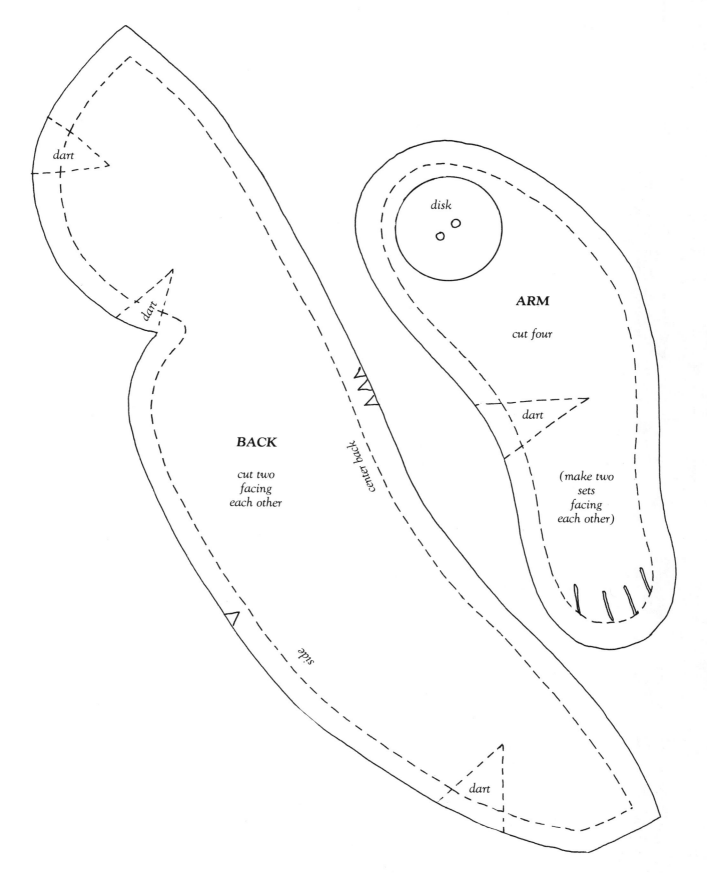

dart

dart

BACK

cut two
facing
each other

center back

side

dart

disk

ARM

cut four

dart

(make two
sets
facing
each other)

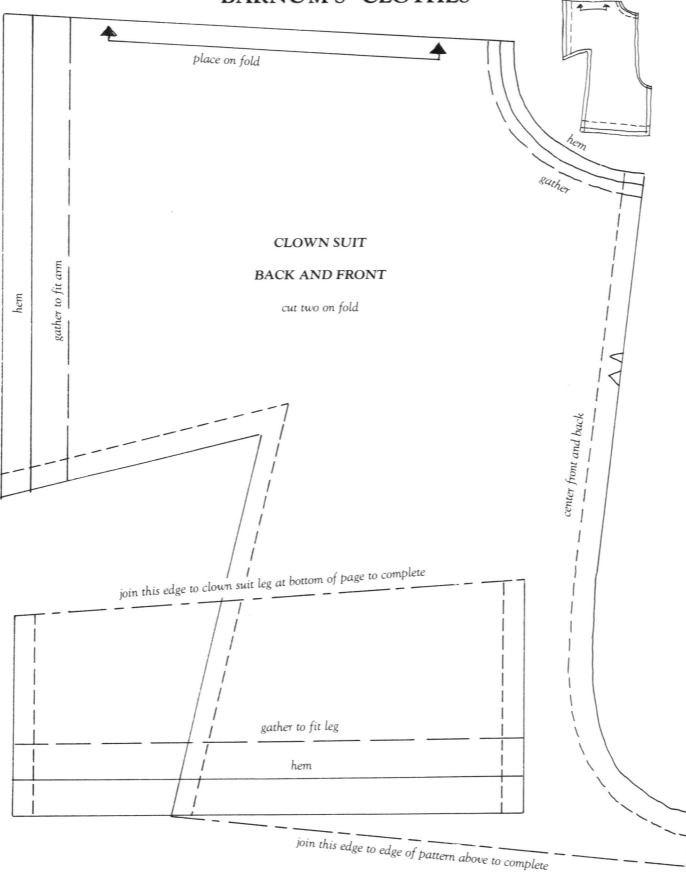

place on fold

hem

gather

CLOWN SUIT

BACK AND FRONT

cut two on fold

hem

gather to fit arm

center front and back

join this edge to clown suit leg at bottom of page to complete

gather to fit leg

hem

join this edge to edge of pattern above to complete

Illustration 86. A three-quarter view....

DANIEL B., THE WILD BRUIN

A real live bear in a real forest was the inspiration for this toy bear who walks on all fours. I had already spent hours of research studying photographs of bears in books and still more at the Cumberland Museum which has three stuffed adult bears and one little cub on display when I received an invitation last spring to spend a few days in the Smokey Mountains with a nephew and his family.

It was curious that of all the bears I have ever seen in the Smokies, one I came upon during my stay was the largest I have ever seen in the wild. Our encounter was much too brief as I hurriedly snapped the camera and tried to observe him as thoroughly as possible from my car window.

He had appeared suddenly from out of the woods, walked down a bank, walked along the roadside for a time, turned toward the car, stopped and then observed me! After a time he turned and walked back along the road, back up the bank and returned to the forest in the same spot from where he had emerged. I last saw him in the woods as he stopped and looked back at us for several seconds, then turned and ambled deeper into the darkness of the forest.

This bear was special to me and I shall never forget how he showed me a front view, both sides and a rear view. What's more, because of the bank I saw him slightly from above and below as well! I designed Daniel as soon as I returned home!

Daniel, whom everyone calls "Danny," is soft and huggable and he can wear pullover sweaters, cardigans, hats and scarves if you like him dressed. In *Color Illustration 19* he wears a simple satin and metallic ruff around his neck. He will become a pull toy if mounted on a little wheeled base with a string pull or he can wear a cat or puppy collar and leash and be a toy trained bear.

Illustration 87. and a side view.

Illustration 88. Daniel, a wild or bruin-type bear who stands on all fours, is named in honor of Daniel Boone who met many a bear during his years in the forest. This front view shows his friendly face — not at all ferocious.

141

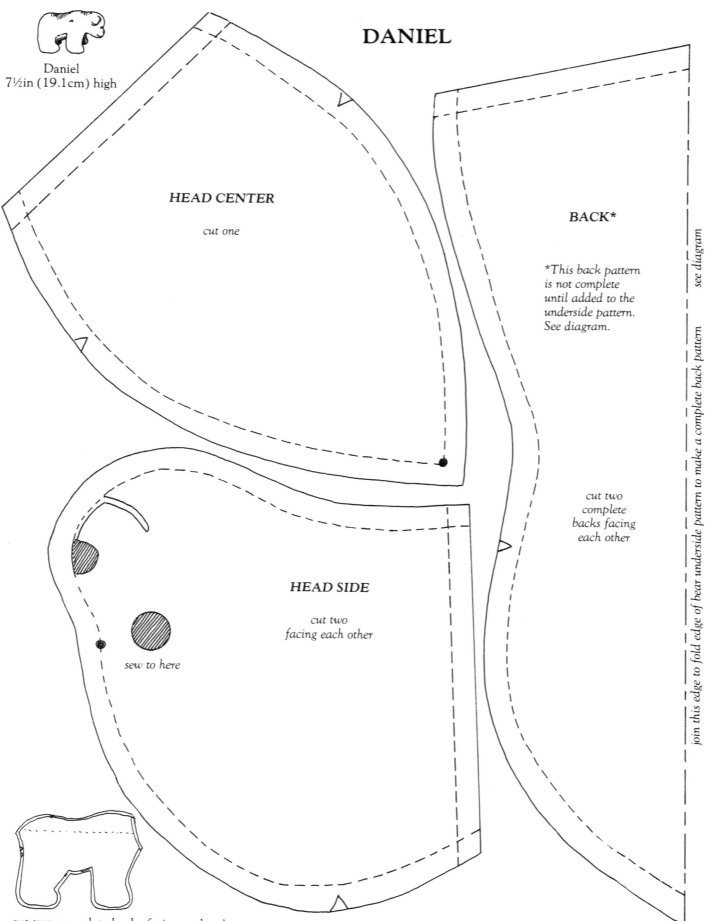

Daniel
7½in (19.1cm) high

DANIEL

HEAD CENTER

cut one

BACK*

*This back pattern is not complete until added to the underside pattern. See diagram.

cut two complete backs facing each other

join this edge to fold edge of bear underside pattern to make a complete back pattern   see diagram

HEAD SIDE

cut two facing each other

sew to here

cut two complete backs facing each other

DANIEL

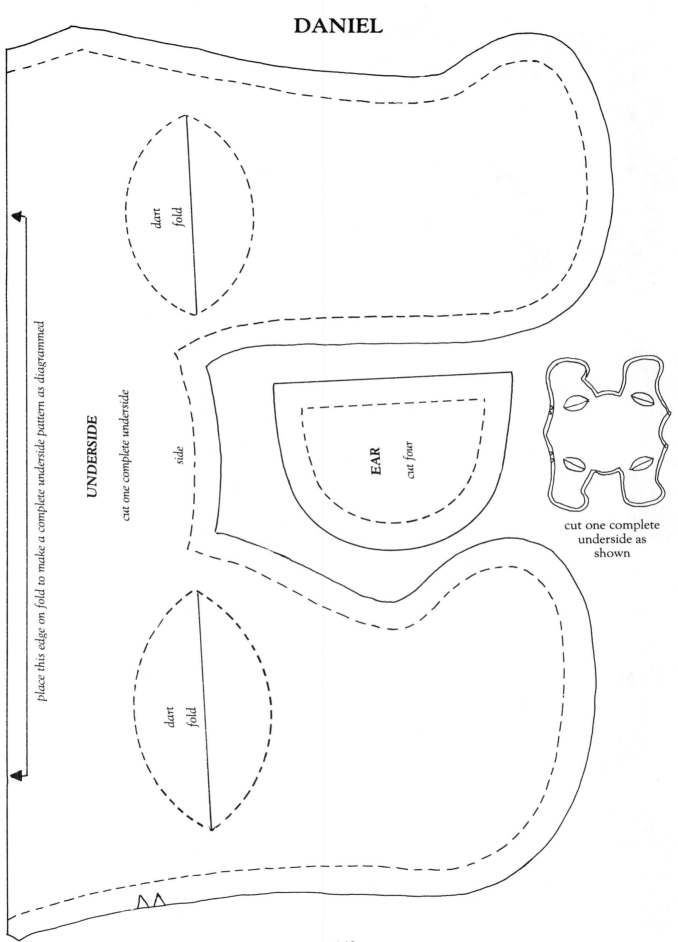

place this edge on fold to make a complete underside pattern as diagrammed

UNDERSIDE

cut one complete underside

dart
fold

side

EAR

cut four

dart
fold

cut one complete
underside as
shown

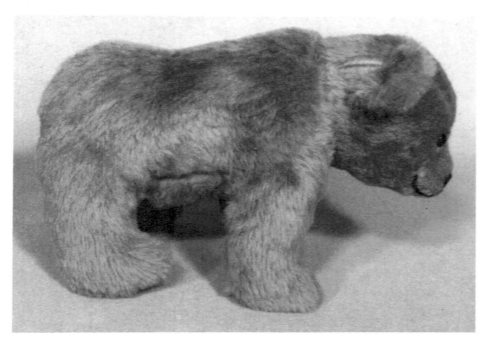

Illustration 89. *He was designed from real live bears and looks natural coming....*

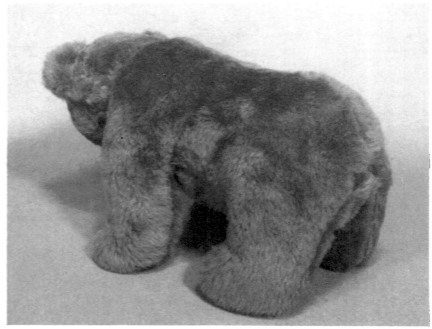

Illustration 90. *or going.*

CONSTRUCTING DANIEL

1. The underside pattern should be traced on the fold of your paper so when you cut it out, you will have the complete pattern as shown.
2. The back is the same underside pattern with a rump and back hump pattern added to it to complete it as shown.
3. After tracing and cutting all the pattern pieces, draw around them onto the back side of fur cloth as directed and cut out.
4. Baste, then sew the two back pieces together along the back seam from the neck opening to the point at the back end.
5. Baste, then sew darts on the underside pieces as indicated.
6. Baste, then sew the back to the underside starting at the center rump, going around the back leg, along the tummy, and around the front to the neck opening. Repeat, going around the other side.
7. Baste and sew head pieces together by going from the neck front, up to the dot on the forehead. Next, baste and sew in head center by starting at the dot and going toward the back of the neck on one side, then the other side.
8. Clip, turn and stuff head.
9. Stuff body *firmly*, pushing and molding the bear into shape as you go since his legs will tend to spread out when you first stuff him.
10. Pin his head to the body in several different positions till you get an attitude you like. Sew head to body, *securely* by hand, using a large needle and several strands of matching thread.
11. Sew on ears.
12. Embroider face and sew on eyes.

Chapter 12
HANIMALS™

Just what is a hanimal? It is a hand puppet-soft toy animal. It is a puppet — yet more than a puppet; it is a soft toy animal, yet more than a toy animal.

What is it about this hanimal that makes him both puppet and Teddy Bear? A secret, unique back panel incorporated during assembly gives him his "double life." Unlike puppets, hanimals never go limp and lifeless. Their full, soft bodies remain life-like and huggable, even after the puppeteer's hand has been removed.

[I originated the idea in 1974 when I created my trademarked Puppedoll™ for my book *Dolls, Puppedolls, and Teddy Bears.* Both my Puppedolls and Hanimals have performed on many television shows throughout the United States. Both have since been widely imitated. My puppets have performed on the TODAY show as well as on Dinah Shore's "Dinah's Place." I also wrote a book on puppetry for children, *Be a Puppeteer!* (McGraw-Hill, 1970) in which I taught the reader to use the puppet creatively. It was this work with puppets plus my love of Teddy Bears that eventually led to the Hanimal.]

Hanimals are not intended to replace the puppet for there is no substitute for the empty body of a well-designed hand puppet during a performance. Children, on the other hand, expect more of a puppet than a mere puppet is capable of giving. Young children are often frustrated with an unresponsive puppet that just hangs limply when they try to love him.

The hanimal can be a clever performer when he has a creative manipulator but he can also be just a soft Teddy Bear who does not have to *do* anything. Children can dress and undress him and sleep with him. They can manipulate him when they feel like making him "come alive." The puppet-puppeteer relationship is an "all or nothing" kind of relationship. In contrast, the owner-hanimal-puppeteer experience is a true give-and-take relationship.

Hanimals need a coat, sweaters, scarves and caps and all kinds of clothes because they love to travel with their owners. They can wave at people, throw kisses, rub their eyes or noses, clap their hands, shake their heads, go to sleep in your arms and look at people over your shoulder. You can "teach" your hanimal to do more and more things as you become more and more experienced at manipulating him.

CONSTRUCTING THE HANIMAL

The Hanimal and Hanimal Baby patterns are the same with a straight leg for Hanimal or a curved leg for Baby. The pattern is designed to fit an adult hand snugly and still be small enough for a child's hand to work it.

Use a *very soft fur cloth* that is not too thick. Softness is an important factor in making hanimals move expressively.

1. The Hanimal back pattern had to be "broken" at the head because of page space but you should trace it so that it is all one piece as shown. Also, place your pattern on the fold so when you cut it out, you will have a complete back as shown.

2. Draw onto the back side of fur cloth and cut two fronts, one complete back, one complete back panel and four of either the Hanimal or Hanimal Baby legs. You should have two sets facing each other.

3. Baste and sew the two fronts together from the crotch to the top of the head. Sew the arm darts. (If your fur cloth is thick, you may want to leave them unsewn until later.)

4. Baste the temporary tuck at the center of the back panel *but do not sew it.* The basting will be removed later to make room for your hand. Step 1.

5. Sew the back seat darts. Baste the back panel to the back with fur sides on *both* pieces *facing up* and treat them as one from here on. Step 2.

6. Lay the back piece down with the fur side up. Place the front on top of it with the fur side down. Step 3.

7. Begin basting at the head center top and stitch around the ear, neck, all the way around the arm, then down to the corner at the hip. Repeat down the other side. Next, baste across the crotch. Baste legs together.

8. Clip all curves and corners and turn right side out using a dowel or sharpened pencil to help push the hands through. Remember the back and back panel are *treated as one piece.* Remove the basting from the temporary tuck in the back panel.

9. Sew across ears as indicated on patterns. (The ears should have no stuffing.)

10. Pack the head well at the top, cheeks and nose but leave the neck loosely packed.

11. Stuff paws and lower arms *lightly,* leaving a good deal of space at the upper arms. Place large safety pins across where the arms join the body.

12. Stuff the chest and shoulder area quite *lightly, just barely filling out the shape* but pack the lower body a bit more firmly, filling out the rump.

13. At this point you should test the hanimal. Remove the pins from the shoulders and put your hand inside the back panel. Hold the lower edge of the panel as you would a glove and work your index and second finger into the head, your third and fourth fingers in one arm and your thumb in the other arm. Force them well into the head and arms. When you move your fingers, the bear should move his head and arms easily.

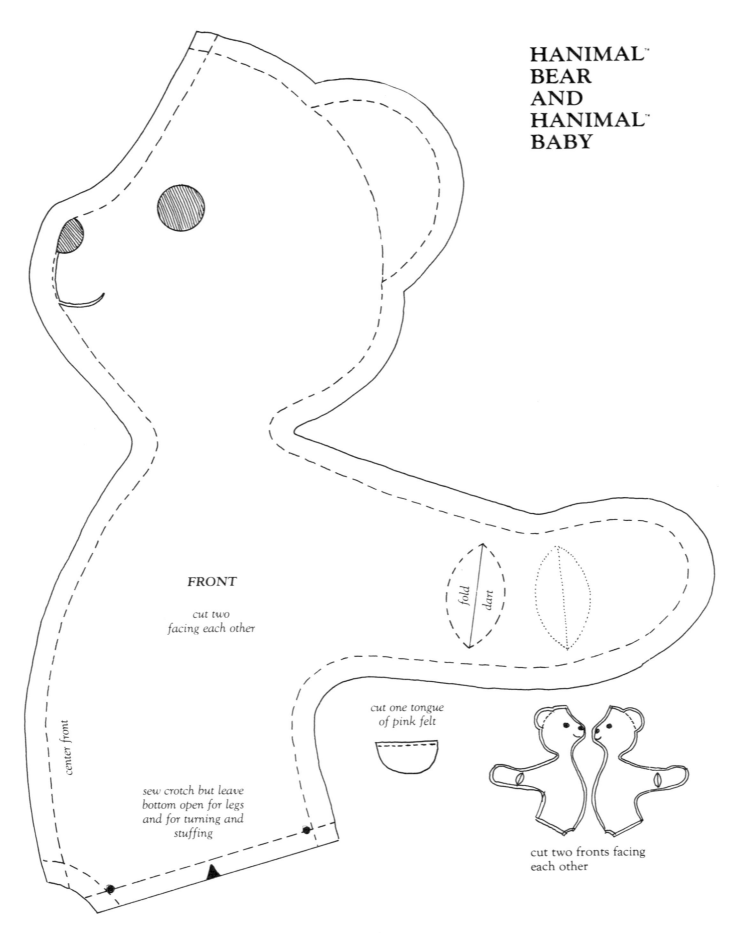

**HANIMAL™
BEAR
AND
HANIMAL™
BABY**

FRONT

*cut two
facing each other*

fold

dart

center front

*cut one tongue
of pink felt*

*sew crotch but leave
bottom open for legs
and for turning and
stuffing*

*cut two fronts facing
each other*

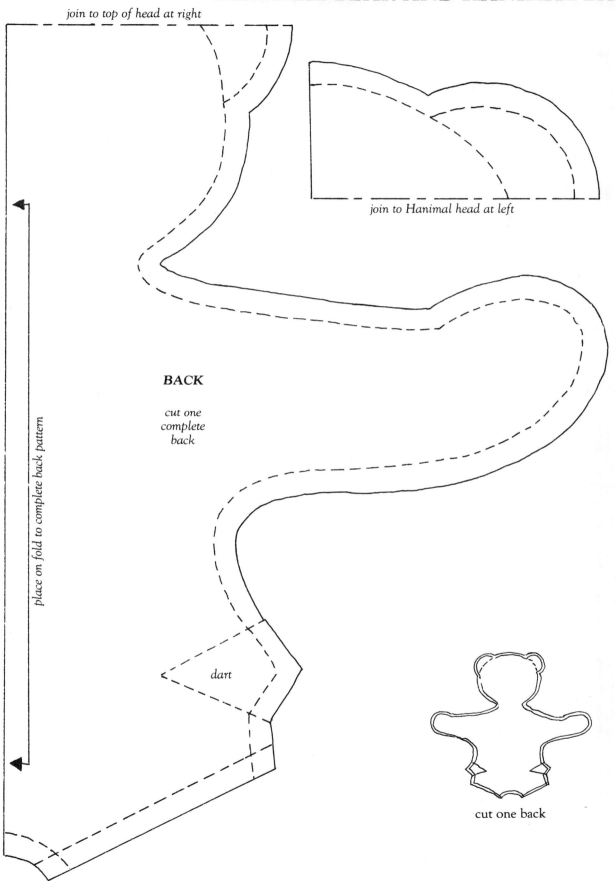

join to top of head at right

join to Hanimal head at left

place on fold to complete back pattern

BACK

cut one
complete
back

dart

cut one back

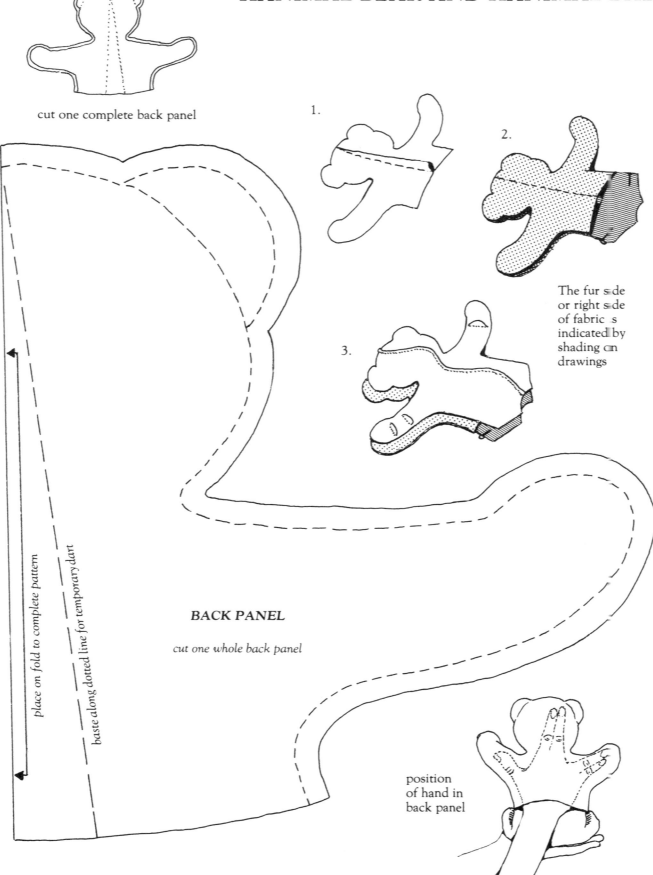

HANIMAL BEAR AND HANIMAL BABY

cut one complete back panel

1.

2.

The fur side or right side of fabric is indicated by shading on drawings

3.

place on fold to complete pattern

baste along dotted line for temporary dart

BACK PANEL

cut one whole back panel

position of hand in back panel

148

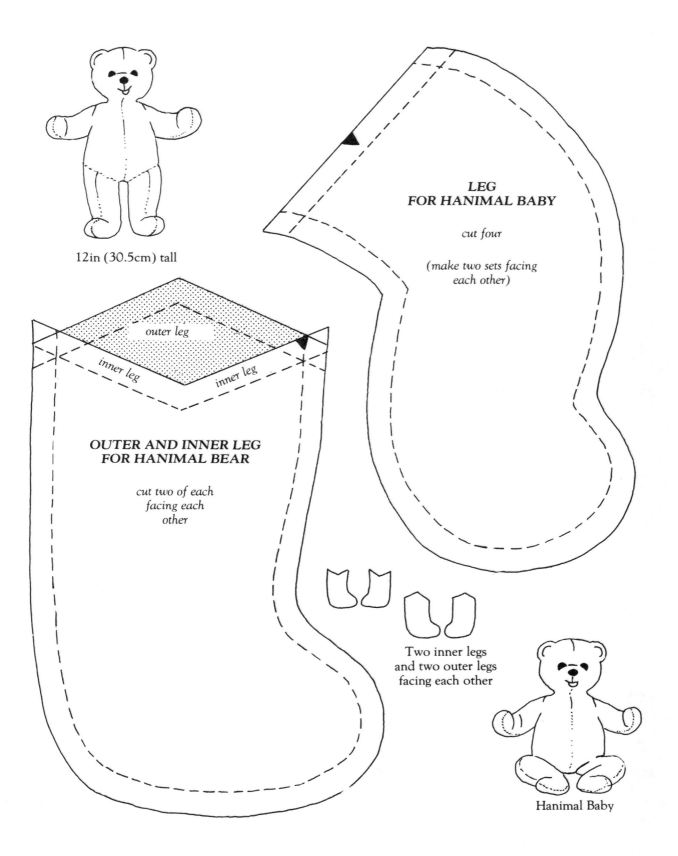

12in (30.5cm) tall

**LEG
FOR HANIMAL BABY**

cut four

*(make two sets facing
each other)*

outer leg

inner leg   inner leg

**OUTER AND INNER LEG
FOR HANIMAL BEAR**

*cut two of each
facing each
other*

Two inner legs
and two outer legs
facing each other

Hanimal Baby

If you did not sew the arm darts earlier, the arms will not yet curve around properly but you should be able to tell if the Hanimal is flexible. If you packed him too firmly he will feel stiff. The secret is in stuffing his neck, chest, shoulders and upper arms just enough to give him form but not enough to make him stiff.

14. Sew the legs into the leg openings by hand with a large needle and several layers of thread. There should be enough space at the upper legs to allow the legs to bend and swing easily. Baby Hanimal does not walk yet but Hanimal bear can be made to swing his legs alternately so you can "walk" him.

15. Stitch the arm darts by hand from the outside. If you want more curve, you can sew *two* darts in one or both arms to bring them around toward the front. With the arms curved and the body properly stuffed, your Hanimal should be able to bring his paws around to his mouth or eyes. Baby Hanimal especially, should be able to "suck" his little paw and rub his sleepy eyes.

16. Embroider the face and sew on a little pink tongue. See "Your Bear's Face" in Chapter 2 for directions. Hanimals can be plain bears if the back panel is omitted during construction.

Illustration 91. *Hanimal Bear loves to wear Sitting Bear's cap, muffler and mittens set. He has the same body as Hanimal Baby but his legs are straight.*

HANIMAL˙ AND HANIMAL˙ BABY'S CLOTHES

Most of Cubby's clothes will fit the Hanimals as will Buddy's sleepers with some adjustments. See "Sleepers" in "Making Your Own Patterns," Chapter 5 for directions. The back opening and elasticized waist drop seat enable you to manipulate him right through his clothes. Just unfasten the lower button on the back when you want him to be a puppet as in *Illustration 92.*

Hanimal clown suits can be made from Barnum's clown suit pattern as in *Color Illustration 20.* Make them open in back so your hand can go into the panel without having to remove them when you manipulate him.

The Buddy sleeper shirt pattern also makes a little knit diaper shirt to be worn with a diaper, or turned so it opens in front, it becomes a baby sacque. You can be creative and make a diaper with ruffles on the seat and a matching shirt or dress. Make the diaper 8in (20.3cm) by 8in (20.3cm) of white cotton flannel or felt as in *Illustrations 93* and *94.*

See "Nightgowns" in Chapter 5, "Making Your Patterns" for instructions for a nightgown for 12in (30.5cm) and 13in (33cm) bears. Once you make your nightgown pattern, it can also be used for an angel robe or even a baby bunting.

For a little coat to wear on outings just lengthen Cubby's Rough Rider Jacket. Make a little knit cap and mittens to go with it from the instructions for Sitting Bear's scarf, cap and mitten set in Chapter 9.

The clown suit pattern for Barnum the Circus Bear can also become a snow suit or one-piece sleepers.

MANIPULATING THE HANIMAL

To work your Hanimal you must, of course, put your hand into his back panel. Think of it as putting on a glove. Hold the panel as you would the back of your glove as you slip your other hand into it as described in construction Steps 13, 14 and 15. Pull on the panel as you work your hand into place with your thumb in one arm, your index finger and second finger into the head and your third finger and pinky into the other arm. *Wiggle your fingers and get them well into Hanimal's body, head and arms.* Only the index finger can go into the head with the other three fingers in the arm if it is more comfortable for you that way.

He can sit on your other hand, on your lap, the arm of a chair or most any surface as you manipulate him. He loves to be cradled in your arms as in *Illustration 96* while you work him, or look over your shoulder as in *Illustration 95.* You can learn to make him move his head to say "no" or "yes" or lay his head on your shoulder. Remember, he is only as alive as you make him. The more you practice, the more you will be able to express through him and the more joy he will be able to give to you and your friends.

References for Further Study of the History of Teddy Bears

A *Collector's History of the Teddy Bear* by Patricia N. Schoonmaker. Hobby House Press, Inc., Cumberland, Maryland, 1981.

Teddy Bear and friends®. A bi-monthly magazine published for Teddy Bear fans who want to keep up with the latest on their furry friends. Hobby House Press, Inc., Cumberland, Maryland.

The Teddy Bear Book by Peter Bull. House of Nisbet Ltd., Winscombe, England, 1969.

Illustration 92. Baby Hanimal being manipulated through his little drop seat sleepers. Ones hand goes into a back panel on the bear to make him become a hand-puppet-toy animal. He is sitting on the puppeteer's other hand covered by his very own security blanket.

Illustration 93. Baby Hanimal (front view) showing his large eyes and little pink tongue. He can do many things and seems startlingly alive. He loves to perform anytime you want him to.

Illustration 94. Wearing only his little diaper, Baby sleepily rubs his eye.

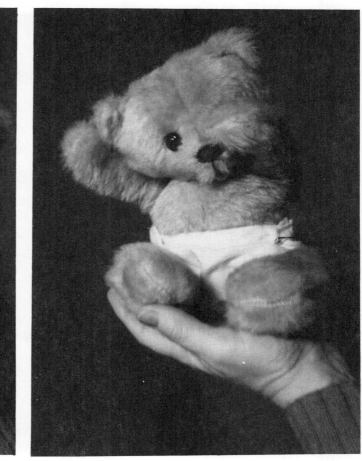

 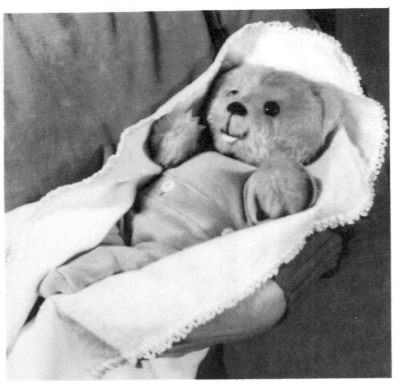

Illustration 95. *Manipulate him at your shoulder and delight everyone around.*

Illustration 96. *Cuddle him in your arms and people will be amazed at how "real" he is.*

Illustration 97. *A bunch o' bear friends! A few friends and relatives brought their own Teddy Bears over to the Worrell studio so readers could see some of the individual interpretations possible. Front row left to right: Basic of white fleece by Judy Smith, dressed in daughter Allison's baby dress; tan ultra suede Tiny Mama, also by Judy Smith; white fleece Tiny Mama in argyle sweater and cap by Allison Smith, age 13; Benjamin by Anne Rogers; Buddy in red pajamas by Elizabeth Worrell; and a beige fleece Tiny Mama by Frances Bayer. Back row left to right: Green wool flannel Basic with appliqued shamrock by Judy Martin for her mother, Lorraine Brown, whose birthday is on St. Patrick's day; caramel fur cloth Basic made by Margie Redditt and owned by Paula Smartt; and another wool flannel Basic owned by Kathy Jones and made by Judy Martin, dressed in a large "Snoopy" business suit.*